973.922 K35g

Goldzwig, Steven R.

In a perilous hour

MAY 2001

DATE DUE

	MAY 1 9 2005		
	JAN 0 2 2008		

DEMCO 38-297

ENTERED FEB 1 2 1996

"In a Perilous Hour"

Address to the Nation on the Nuclear Test Ban Treaty, July 26, 1963. (Courtesy John F. Kennedy Library, Columbia Point, MA)

"IN A PERILOUS HOUR"

The Public Address of John F. Kennedy

Steven R. Goldzwig
and
George N. Dionisopoulos

Foreword by Halford R. Ryan

Great American Orators, Number 22
Bernard K. Duffy and Halford R. Ryan, Series Advisers

Greenwood Press
Westport, Connecticut • London

```
973.922 K35g

Goldzwig, Steven R.

In a perilous hour
```

Library of Congress Cataloging-in-Publication Data

Goldzwig, Steven R.
  "In a perilous hour" : the public address of John F.
Kennedy / Steven R. Goldzwig and George N. Dionisopoulos ; foreword
by Halford R. Ryan.
      p. cm.—(Great American orators, ISSN 0898-8277 ; no. 22)
    Includes bibliographical references and index
    ISBN 0–313–27770–2 (alk. paper)
    1. Kennedy, John F. (John Fitzgerald), 1917–1963—Oratory.
2. Political oratory—United States. 3. United States—Politics and
government—1961–1963. I. Dionisopoulos, George N. II. Title.
III. Series.
E842.1G65   1995
973.922′092—dc20   95–2095

British Library Cataloguing in Publication Data is available.

Copyright © 1995 by Steven R. Goldzwig and George N. Dionisopoulos

All rights reserved. No portion of this book may be
reproduced, by any process or technique, without the
express written consent of the publisher.

Library of Congress Catalog Card Number: 95–2095
ISBN: 0–313–27770–2
ISSN: 0898-8277

First published in 1995

Greenwood Press, 88 Post Road West, Westport, CT 06881
An imprint of Greenwood Publishing Group, Inc.

Printed in the United States of America

The paper used in this book complics with the
Permanent Paper Standard issued by the National
Information Standards Organization (Z39.48–1984).

10 9 8 7 6 5 4 3 2 1

Copyright Acknowledgments

The authors and publisher gratefully thank the following for allowing use of their material in this volume:

Selected excerpts from *Kennedy* by Theodore C. Sorensen, Copyright © 1965 by Theodore C. Sorensen, Copyright renewed 1993 by Theodore C. Sorensen. Reprinted by permission of HarperCollins Publishers, Inc. (U.S.) and Hodder Headline PLC, London (U.K.).

Excerpts from *A Thousand Days* by Arthur M. Schlesinger, Jr., Copyright © 1965 by Arthur M. Schlesinger, Jr. Reprinted by permission of Houghton Mifflin Co. All rights reserved.

Excerpts from *Parting the Waters* by Taylor Branch, Copyright © 1988 by Taylor Branch. Reprinted by permission of Simon & Schuster, Inc.

Selected excerpts from *The Crisis Years: Kennedy & Khrushchev, 1960–1963* by Michael R. Beschloss, Copyright © 1991 by Michael R. Beschloss. Reprinted by permission of HarperCollins Publishers, Inc. Also, Copyright 1992 by Michael Beschloss, by permission of International Creative Management, Inc.

Excerpts from *JFK: The Presidency of John F. Kennedy* by Herbert S. Parmet, Copyright © 1983. Reprinted by permission of The Dial Press.

Contents

Series Foreword by Bernard K. Duffy and Halford R. Ryan — ix

Foreword by Halford R. Ryan — xi

Preface — xiii

Acknowledgments — xv

PART I: CRITICAL ANALYSIS

1. John F. Kennedy: A Rhetorical Introduction — 3
2. A New Beginning — 21
3. Kennedy and Civil Rights — 55
4. President Kennedy's Foreign Policy Discourse: A Rhetoric of Romantic Pragmatism — 91
5. Conclusion — 139

PART II: COLLECTED SPEECHES

Speech to the Greater Houston Ministerial Association, September 12, 1960 — 151

Inaugural Address, January 20, 1961 — 155

Address Before the American Society of Newspaper Editors,
April 20, 1961   159

Radio and Television Report to the American People on the
Berlin Crisis, July 25, 1961   163

Radio and Television Report to the American People on the
Soviet Buildup in Cuba, October 22, 1962   171

Radio and Television Report to the American People on
Civil Rights, June 11, 1963   177

Commencement Address at American University,
June 10, 1963   181

Radio and Television Address to the American People on the
Nuclear Test Ban Treaty, July 26, 1963   189

Selected Chronology of Major Presidential Speeches and Remarks   195

Selected Bibliography   199

Index   215

Series Foreword

The idea for a series of books on great American orators grew out of the recognition that there is a paucity of book-length studies on individual orators and their speeches. Apart from a few notable exceptions, the study of American public address has been pursued in scores of articles published in professional journals. As helpful as these studies have been, none has or can provide a complete analysis of a speaker's rhetoric. Book-length studies, such as those in this series, will help fill the void that has existed in the study of American public address and its related disciplines of politics and history, theology and sociology, communication and law. In a book, the critic can explicate a broader range of a speaker's persuasive discourse than reasonably could be treated in an article. The comprehensive research and sustained reflection that books require will undoubtedly yield many original and enduring insights concerning the nation's most important voices.

Public address has been a fertile ground for scholarly investigation. No matter how insightful their intellectual forebears, each generation of scholars must reexamine its universe of discourse, while expanding the compass of its researches and redefining its purpose and methods. To avoid intellectual torpor new scholars cannot be content simply to see through the eyes of those who have come before them. We hope that this series of books will stimulate important new understandings of the nature of persuasive discourse and provide opportunities for scholarship in the history and criticism of American public address.

This series examines the role of rhetoric in the United States. American speakers shaped the destiny of the colonies, the young republic, and the mature nation. During each stage of the intellectual, political, and religious development of the United States, great orators, standing at the rostrum, on the stump, and in the pulpit, used words and gestures to influence their audiences. Usually striving for the noble, sometimes achieving the base, they urged their fellow citizens toward a more perfect Union. The books in this series chronicle and explain the accomplishments of representative American leaders as orators.

A series of book-length studies on American persuaders honors the role men and women have played in U.S. history. Previously, if one desired to assess the impact of a speaker or a speech upon history, the path was, at best, not well marked and, at worst, littered with obstacles. To be sure, one might turn to biographies and general histories to learn about an orator, but for the public address scholar these sources often prove unhelpful. Rhetorical topics, such as speech invention, style, delivery, organizational strategies, and persuasive effect, are often treated in passing, if mentioned at all. Authoritative speech texts are often difficult to locate, and the problem of textual accuracy is frequently encountered. This is especially true for those figures who spoke one or two hundred years ago or for those whose persuasive role, though significant, was secondary to other leading lights of the age.

Each book in this series is organized to meet the needs of scholars and students of the history and criticism of public address. Part I is a critical analysis of the orator and his or her speeches. Within the format of a case study, one may expect considerable latitude. For instance, in a given chapter an author might explicate a single speech or a group of related speeches, or examine orations that comprise a genre of rhetoric such as forensic speaking. But the critic's focus remains on the rhetorical considerations of speaker, speech, occasion, and effect. Part II contains the texts of important addresses that are discussed in the critical analysis that precedes it. To the extent possible, each author has endeavored to collect authoritative speech texts, which have often been found through original research in collections of primary source material. In a few instances, because of the extreme length of a speech, texts have been edited, but the authors have been careful to delete material that is least important to the speech, and these deletions have been held to a minimum.

In each book there is a chronology of major speeches that serves more purposes than may be apparent at first. Pragmatically, it typically lists all of the orator's known speeches and addresses. Places and dates of the speeches are also listed, although this is information that is sometimes difficult to determine precisely. But in a wider sense, the chronology attests to the scope of rhetoric in the United States. Certainly in quantity if not always in quality, Americans are historically talkers and listeners.

Because of the disparate nature of the speakers examined in this series, there is some latitude in the nature of the bibliographical materials that have been included in each book. But in every instance, authors have carefully described original historical materials and collections and gathered critical studies, biographies and autobiographies, and a variety of secondary sources that bear on the speaker and the oratory. By combining in each book bibliographical materials, speech texts, and critical chapters, this series notes that text and research sources are interwoven in the act of rhetorical criticism.

May the books in this series serve to memorialize the nation's greatest orators.

Bernard K. Duffy
Halford R. Ryan

Foreword

The potency of Professors Steven Goldzwig's and George Dionisopoulos's book on John F. Kennedy's presidential rhetoric is their research. By examining original materials in the Kennedy Library and augmenting their findings with an impressive and exhaustive bibliography of books and articles, which encompasses the disciplines of history, political science, the rhetorical presidency, and speech criticism, Goldzwig and Dionisopoulos have composed a highly readable yet integrated nexus of Kennedy and his rhetoric and his administration.

Those who naturally expect an exegesis of the Kennedy canon of speeches—the Houston Ministerial address, the Inaugural Address, and the Cuban Missile Crisis address—will not be disappointed, for these persuasive communications figure prominently in this book. Yet, that famous triad of speeches barely represents the run of JFK's rhetoric. Accordingly, Goldzwig and Dionisopoulos explicate JFK's lesser known, but nonetheless important communications, such as the civil rights speeches, address on the Berlin crisis, and the American University address. Thus, the authors have mastered the difficult task of balancing breadth with depth in illuminating President Kennedy's rhetoric.

Halford R. Ryan

Preface

This book is being prepared for publication at an interesting intersection of history, politics, and popular culture. More than thirty years after his assassination, John F. Kennedy continues to garner attention. With the recent death of his wife Jacqueline Kennedy Onassis, pundits declared the passing of Camelot and heralded the end of a political epoch. But the Kennedy era refuses to bow to such declarations, just as the confluences and legacies of the Kennedy presidency refuse to go their way in quiet rest. What Kennedy did and said, and left unsaid, in leading the nation through a brief, self-described "perilous hour," remains important. For good or evil, the political life and rhetorical events recorded here in these pages still reverberate in hearts and minds, in policies and procedures, in war and peace. John Kennedy was fond of drawing lessons from history. It is hoped that the reader will do likewise with this effort.

ACKNOWLEDGMENTS

Any book-length project usually incurs indebtedness to others. This book is no exception. We would particularly like to thank the Bradley Institute for Democracy and Public Values, Marquette University, and the Graduate School, San Diego State University for making significant parts of the research possible. We also received generous assistance from the College of Communication Research Committee, Marquette University.

We are especially indebted to the staff of the Kennedy Library whose helpfulness and patience proved invaluable during two long hot summers. We are most grateful to William Johnson, Maura Porter and Michael Desmond.

In addition, a number of graduate and undergraduate research assistants have lent their considerable talents to the cause. We received excellent and timely contributions from Edward Lemke and Jennifer Kwasney. We wish to express a special note of thanks to Lori Kornely for her careful shepherding of the speech texts and the final manuscript. K. C. Walsh provided vital assistance in the final production of this book. We also wish to extend our gratitude to Matthew Payne for his contributions in assembling the index.

We would like to thank Halford Ryan, our series editor, and Mim Vasan at Greenwood Press for their unrelenting patience on and encouragement of a project that seemed too-long postponed for all parties. We are also indebted to Penny Sippel for copyediting and production assistance. Finally, we express our gratitude to all the scholars who have lent their considerable talents to the Kennedy literature. Without them our pathway would have been much obscured, if not obstructed. In particular we would like to thank Theodore C. Sorensen for allowing us to quote him copiously throughout, Michael R. Beschloss for helping us better understand the "crisis years" in foreign policy, and Theodore Otto Windt for his impeccable, groundbreaking scholarship and for his helpful comments on an earlier version of our chapter on civil rights. Obviously, any imperfections in this work remain singularly our own.

I
CRITICAL ANALYSIS

1

JOHN F. KENNEDY: A RHETORICAL INTRODUCTION

John F. Kennedy was the youngest man and the only Catholic ever elected to the U.S. presidency. He would serve as the 35th president approximately "a thousand days," but in that brief period his evocative words would engage and energize the nation—imbuing its citizens with the feeling that anything was possible if they applied themselves in a collective, selfless effort on behalf of change. Kennedy's rhetoric summoned each citizen to face the opportunity and challenge of the new decade. It was to be "a time of quite extraordinary transformation of national values and purposes—a transformation so far-reaching as to make the America of the sixties a considerably different society from the America of the fifties." By focusing our inquiry on some of the public rhetoric of John F. Kennedy we offer herein a partial, but nonetheless important, insight into how such a transformation was initiated, if not realized. The symbolism of the Kennedy era—with its images of wealth, youth, vigor, idealism, pragmatism, and steely determination—was a product of both words and deeds.[1]

RATIONALE FOR OUR STUDY

The need for another book about John F. Kennedy would, at first glance, seem questionable. The literature on Kennedy is immense. Historians, political biographers, even psychologists have repeatedly plumbed both the image and the substance of the man and his administration. Admirers and detractors, friends and adversaries, revisionists and revivalists, have taken him on and lathered his memory with praise, blame, awe, and pity. Yet the interest in him continues unabated.

The national fascination with John F. Kennedy is partially due to the fact that because his life was taken so violently and so suddenly his youthful charm still haunts the national psyche. There is something about the idealism of the era that was personified in the man, and something in the man that no amount of titillating revelations of poor health, sexual excess, and arcane tabloid discussions of assassination plots can erase. And despite our growing knowledge of his presidency, opinion is deeply divided concerning its successes and failures.

Our interest in Kennedy is born of professional occupation and personal preoccupation. As baby boomers we feel personally connected to his presidency. Eisenhower is like a grandfatherly face in the distant recesses of memory. Kennedy however, was our president, and fulfilled our first tentative longings of trying to figure out what it meant to grow up to be thinking, feeling responsible citizens in a political society. When death visited the young leader we shared the feeling that somehow a new age had come and gone with his passage, and things would never be quite the same.

Our professional responsibilities have come with adulthood and some knowledge of our particular discipline. While Kennedy has been lauded as a great speaker, we know of no published book-length critical study of his public address. This book is an attempt to repair this oversight—and it is only a beginning. Indeed, we believe that Kennedy's public address provides rich material for those interested in a better understanding of how public policy arguments shape both the direction and nature of presidential decision making and policy implementation. We premise that belief on several compelling rationales.

First, we agree with James David Barber that rhetoric formed the very core of John Kennedy's political style. Believing that the fundamental problem of a democracy was how to overcome its inherent inertia and arouse it to action, Kennedy's rhetoric was chiefly concerned with what Alexander Welsh called "the problem of collective energy"—the need to excite "the commitment, the responsibility, the obligation of the individual," by summoning the American people "to a sense of their national mission." Thus, Kennedy's rhetoric focused on arousing his fellow citizens to rise to the opportunities and challenges he defined for them.[2]

Second, and related to the above, our focus on the public address of John F. Kennedy stems in no small part from the importance he himself attached to it. Rejecting a restricted concept of the presidency, Kennedy viewed the Oval Office as "the vital center of action in our whole scheme of government," demanding a leader who would "place himself in the very thick of the fight," exercising "the fullest powers of his office." As such, he believed that presidential leadership included rhetorical influence on national opinion. The amount of special energy and effort that Kennedy invested in his public address bears witness to the fact that he was "sensitive to words"—to their power to influence through symbolic inducement. Indeed, whatever political success Kennedy had was in no small part attributable to his ability to communicate, to touch sympathetic chords within both national and international communities. Kennedy's rhetoric, then, also provides us an opportunity to probe the roots of the extension of executive power in a modern democracy.[3]

Third, the importance of Kennedy's rhetoric goes beyond its role in communicating his world view to others; it also helped him to shape and clarify aspects of that world view for himself. As he observed in *The Strategy of Peace*— a 1960 campaign book comprised of his Senate speeches concerning foreign policy—"The statements contained in this volume represent my own attempt to make plain to myself and to others my thoughts on the leading questions of foreign policy that have borne down so hard on all of us." Kennedy was interested in communicating a cohesive foreign policy that was different from that of the Eisenhower administration while simultaneously reassuring domestic audiences and allies that previous U.S. commitments would be honored.[4]

Fourth, Kennedy's personal commitment to his rhetoric aided his political career, and helped establish his "reputation as a speaker of uncommon ability." While not all or even the majority of his presidential addresses would sustain that reputation, it is true that a few of them were of a caliber to lift "Kennedy to a place of eminence among twentieth-century orators. Today his speeches appear in numerous texts and resource books as models of persuasive discourse and vivid style."[5]

Fifth, by inquiring into the dramaturgy of linguistic strategies associated with Kennedy's symbolic inducement, we hope not only to provide additional understanding of presidential discourse as a manifestation of presidential power, but also to extend scholarship in the areas of presidential leadership style, political issue management, and the concept of a rhetorical presidency.[6]

Sixth, we feel that much of President Kennedy's rhetoric concerned events that have proved to be "watersheds" in the American experience for over three decades. Other presidents had addressed concerns regarding civil rights and relations with the Soviet Union. However, Kennedy's three years in the White House witnessed some of the more dramatic incidents in those arenas, and his public address helped define them for Americans. The rhetorical strategies employed by Kennedy helped "set the themes used or abused by subsequent administrations." Thus, we hope that our analysis of Kennedy's public rhetoric also will provide additional insights into some of the important political outcomes and consequences that have shaped our collective lives and memories in the last half of the twentieth century.[7]

THEORETICAL GROUNDING AND METHODOLOGICAL ASSUMPTIONS

Our effort here is grounded primarily in the belief that political reality is a rhetorical construction. That is, "political rhetoric creates the arena . . . within which political thought and action take place." The events that make up the flux of the political environment do not per se "carry an inherent meaning with them," and thus have no political significance until rhetorically framed in such a way as to provide salience. Political public argument, then, describes, labels, and frames those events endowing them with meaning—"making that leap from event to meaning." As Murray Edelman writes, the "terms in which we name or speak of anything do more than designate it; they place it in a class of objects, thereby suggest with what it is to be judged and compared, and define the perspective from which it will be viewed and evaluated."[8]

As political actors offer competing definitions, contemporary American politics becomes filled with a variety of rhetorical interpretations. Of those actors competing to define the nature of political reality, "none is more powerful than the president of the United States" in establishing "the terms of discourse." While not unchallenged, the ethos of the office combines with ready access to the media to accord the president significant advantages over those who would offer competing rhetoric. Indeed, the president is foremost among American politicians as the "chief inventor and broker of the symbols of American politics."[9]

As the "primary source of symbols about public issues," much of the president's power rests on the ability to construct the political world symbolically in ways that mobilize public opinion in support of preferred presidential actions, for a president "can move events only if he can first persuade." It is thus important to keep in mind that the president's rhetorical construction of political reality is more than merely educational, it is strategic—seeking to construct the political environment in such a way that the faithful are rallied behind the president. Addressing this point, Theodore Windt observed: "Politics is not an academic seminar. A president is not a distinguished professor occupying an endowed chair of American government. And the primary purpose of presidential rhetoric is not to educate, but to assist in governing."[10]

One of the most forceful elements of presidential public address is the power of definition—the ability to define the issues and thus set the agenda facing the American people. We will focus on definition primarily as the ability to label and thus contextualize political behavior and events. As Doris A. Graber observed, "the facts and concepts which have been selected for political attention are usually placed into some kind of verbal context which affects their meaning and hence their impact. The chance to set this context for an audience—to define the situation verbally by imaginatively combining and recombining the data of politics—permits the politician to encourage others to view the world from his [or her] perspective and act accordingly."[11]

We agree with David Zarefsky that "language plays a central role in the formation of social policy by shaping the context with which people think about the social world." And while context "does not absolutely determine response, . . . it contains presumptions. A presumption is a person's predisposition to think or act in a certain way in the absence of compelling reasons to the contrary. The burden of proof is on the advocate who would disrupt or overturn presumption. Consequently, the president's goal is to place ambiguous situations into a context such that the presumed response is congenial to his purpose." By setting the "terms through which to perceive and around which to organize responses," definition goes a long way toward determining the range of proper reactions on the part of those who accept the definition. Thus, to "choose a definition is to plead a cause." [12]

As will become evident, with Kennedy, both the definition and the context of a political situation were often associated rhetorically with "crisis." It is true that this linguistic designation or marker was often little more than an "inflated description for making hard decisions." But strategically it served Kennedy's goal of "arousing the democracy to action." As Theodore White pointed out, Kennedy was elected to preside over a nation "to which no crisis was clear" but in which many citizens seemed to feel a collective sense of unease. In the campaign Kennedy was "able to persuade enough Americans that their vague concerns were justified enough to require a change in leadership that might arrest those trends carrying America irresistibly to less noble ends than those for which men [and women] believed their fathers had come to this country." Kennedy believed that too many Americans neither recognized the true extent of the dangers in the world nor realized the fragility of peace and prosperity. Thus, his rhetoric focused upon "informing the nation of its true condition and arousing it from its slumbers. That would not happen without . . . broadcast[ing] the facts and ring[ing] the alarm." Sounding that alarm was a dominant part of Kennedy's rhetorical legacy.[13]

In trying to appreciate how Kennedy defined his rhetorical demands and responded to them, we will center our investigation upon the substantive, stylistic, and situational constraints associated with his presidency. We will isolate some of the sources of his ideas, the means by which he gave them flight, and the internal and external political limitations attached to his discursive attempts. By so doing, we hope to touch upon both generic and eclectic aspects of presidential discursive governance.[14]

KENNEDY'S EVOLUTION AS A PUBLIC SPEAKER

There was very little in Kennedy's early political career to suggest that he would leave a rich rhetorical legacy. Elected to Congress in 1946 in a rather lackluster campaign, he was not widely perceived as a gifted orator during his tenure in the House. In fact, his fellow Democrats were more likely to remember him as the "29-year-old Congressman who looked nineteen and appeared for House debates in khaki pants with his shirt-tail out" than for memorable or distinctive oratory. Elected to the Senate in 1952, he gave some "carefully researched, widely publicized and officially ignored" speeches. He was known as one of the heaviest borrowers of materials from the Library of Congress and a great deal of staff research went into his Senate speeches. But he was "conspicuous not for achievements of legislation or leadership but for youth, good looks, wealth, and the aura he exuded of being bound for higher places." [15]

That aura first began glowing brightly on a national level during the 1956 Democratic convention in Chicago. In a last-minute decision Adlai Stevenson's advisers asked Kennedy—who had come to the convention "with ambition and friends and little else"—to deliver a pre-written nomination speech for Stevenson. Accepting the offer to nominate Stevenson, Kennedy "characteristically rejected" the draft that had been prepared by Stevenson's staff. Instead, Kennedy and Theodore Sorensen "labored till dawn" writing a new speech that would provide Kennedy his first major national prominence.[16]

Kennedy was so well received by the convention "that he and his advisors decided to attempt to win the vice-presidential nomination the next day." Although he lost a close vote to Estes Kefauver, the attention Kennedy received during the 1956 Democratic convention made him "a national figure with national possibilities." It is probably fair to say with little exaggeration that his drive for the presidency in 1960 actually began with the events at the Democratic convention in Chicago in 1956.[17]

In the aftermath of Stevenson's defeat by Eisenhower, Kennedy announced to a few close associates his intention to seek the Democratic nomination for president in 1960. According to Alonzo L. Hamby, Kennedy realized that if he was to establish himself as a serious presidential contender he would need to be perceived as "more than an attractive personality and a popular politician." But as a veteran of several campaigns, he knew that the projection of those characteristics established a crucial beginning. In 1957, the Kennedy staff began the efforts to make him a household name. Several articles articulating his political views were published "under the Kennedy signature" in popular magazines and serious journals. Simultaneously, he began a vigorous speaking campaign around the country as well as on the floor of the Senate, and by 1958 "was becoming a leading spokesman of a new Democratic foreign policy." Although it is generally conceded that Kennedy's delivery improved dramatically during the 1960 election, critics are less charitable concerning his 1957 and 1958 efforts. Donald F. Barnes, who later became a presidential interpreter at the Department of State, observed Kennedy during this period and reflected, "he spoke fast, sometimes in extremely rapid bursts; he has been clocked at well over two hundred words a minute in short bursts." This, of course, affected intelligibility. Frederick G. Dutton, who later became special assistant to the president and assistant secretary of state for congressional relations, remembers Kennedy during late 1957 and/or early 1958 as "a terribly inadequate orator at that time. He raced through his script; no dramatic emphasis or anything like that. . . . [H]e disappointed just about everybody in terms of his speech." ABC news commentator Edward Morgan said that Kennedy's delivery at the 1958 Jackson-Jefferson Day celebration "was about like a high school orator who was unaccustomed to the audience, and he certainly didn't get them with him."[18]

Kennedy was, by all accounts, a voracious reader and could retain a good deal of what he read to aid his efforts at rhetorical invention. When "time permitted and the occasion challenged him," Kennedy was capable of writing an excellent speech. "Here he selected his own topic and emphasis, gathered much of his supporting material, then organized and expressed the ideas in handwritten manuscripts." But the demands on his time after 1957 were such that he wrote fewer and fewer of his speeches. Instead there developed around Kennedy a "system" for producing the public addresses he would deliver as candidate and president.[19]

Integral to this system was his desire to "draw upon the brains of others." Kennedy had learned early "in his career as a senator . . . that a large group of advisors could submit ideas, propose outlines and suggest revisions." As the demand for speeches increased that group of advisers expanded, eventually including, among others, university professors (primarily from Harvard or the Massachusetts Institute of Technology), syndicated columnists, cabinet members, the White House staff, ambassadors, as well as ex-presidents and their associates. The actual writing of final drafts often was done by two men, Theodore Sorensen and, to a lesser extent, Richard Goodwin.[20]

Richard Goodwin was a 1958 graduate of Harvard Law School who had served briefly as a clerk for Supreme Court Justice Felix Frankfurter. Goodwin joined Kennedy's Senate staff in 1959. Schlesinger remarked that Goodwin—who was viewed by some as driving, impatient, and arrogant—was a man of "uncommon intelligence, perception and charm," with an "immense facility, both literary and intellectual." Schlesinger labeled Goodwin "the archetypal New Frontiersman," and observed that Kennedy liked his "speed, wit, imagination and passion." [21]

The staff member most associated with and responsible for cohesion in Kennedy's rhetoric, however, was the man who had written most of his speeches since the Senate days, Theodore Sorensen. Sorensen was from Nebraska, and, after graduating first in his class at the University of Nebraska Law School, had gone to Washington to work for the Federal Security Agency. After a series of brief interviews he formally joined the senator's staff in 1953. Described as "[s]elf-sufficient, taut and purposeful," Sorensen was—as were most members of the immediate staff—completely devoted to Kennedy. Their relationship was such that Sorensen was often referred to as Kennedy's "alter ego," and in 1961, the *New York Times Magazine* observed that when "Jack is wounded, Ted bleeds." Although Sorensen jealously guarded their professional relationship and seemed, at times, resentful of "interlopers," socially the two men fraternized little. During the White House years, Sorensen was special counsel to the president—and served the Kennedy administration in several capacities. However, he was considered by people on staff to be "the speechwriter" for Kennedy, and that is the chief role that interests us here.[22]

Sorensen's function was more akin to being a "speech collaborator"—a term he himself fashioned as a description of his relationship to Kennedy. In essence, he considered himself a junior partner in the Kennedy-Sorensen team of speech construction. Those who observed the team in action agreed that Kennedy was very involved in the development of what became the final product and "remained the master of the process." Well-read and articulate, Sorensen provided "the glory of words," and was gifted at writing in a style that seemed to suit Kennedy. In fact, Schlesinger observed that by 1961 Kennedy's and Sorensen's "styles had fused into one." As Sorensen observed, "The very fact that I was involved in his other activities and decisions and constantly present to hear his public and private utterances, made it increasingly easy for me to fulfill the speech-writing role." Others who tried to write for Kennedy would often find that their drafts went unused because they were not in the "Kennedy style." For example, when Goodwin moved to the State Department Schlesinger found himself "increasingly involved in speech drafting." But Kennedy found Schlesinger's efforts "too Stevensonian," in style, "by which he meant too complicated in syntax and fancy in language." [23]

When facing the prospect of an upcoming speech, it was not uncommon for different members of the staff to be asked to contribute ideas concerning the issue involved. Often these people were "unaware that others were working on the same project." Kennedy would listen to staff input and then get together with the main speechwriter—usually Sorensen—to sketch out his own thoughts on the topic. Kennedy's contributions to the drafts often "went beyond a generalized statement describing the major emphasis or thrust of the arguments. Often it included a request for a compelling introduction, a list of suggested main points, and the approximate length of the speech." It also often contained requests for specific information to be included in the speech such as "an appropriate quotation from F.D.R." or "relevant Biblical citations." [24]

Research for the speech might take several forms. For example Dr. Robert Turner—who served as a speechwriter in both the Truman and Kennedy administrations—noted that Sorensen would "have a conference with other people on the White House staff . . . and staff people from other agencies. Sometimes we'd have twenty people in the room talking over the problem of what the speech or message was to be about. That might be a three or four hour meeting; it might be continued the next day. We'd go over all the angles of the issue." [25]

Besides the conferences, speechwriters would routinely examine Kennedy's previous speeches concerning the assigned topic. Thus shaped and constrained by the president's prior discourse, the ideas of the staff experts, and the relevant new research, a speechwriter would undertake a first draft. If the writer was Sorensen, he would usually write his drafts in pen on yellow legal paper. That draft would be examined by other members of the speech preparation "task force," who would work together under the leadership of the main writer to refine the speech until it was felt they could present it to Kennedy.[26]

Kennedy—who would "never blindly accept or blandly deliver a text he had not seen and edited"—would rarely be completely satisfied with the first draft he saw. He would rework it, sometimes exhaustively, changing specific words or phrases, writing suggestions in the margins, and raising ideas and points that needed clarification. As Sorensen wrote, Kennedy "always, upon receiving my draft, altered, deleted or added phrases, paragraphs or pages. Some drafts he rejected entirely." According to Sorensen, "the more time he had to edit and rewrite, the better the speech would be." [27]

Many of Kennedy's very important speeches went through several drafts before he would see them, and a number of revisions after that. Even after a speech text had received "final approval," it was often reworked right up until the moment of delivery, with Kennedy deleting a troublesome passage in favor of one that was deemed more felicitous, or, in some cases, disregarding the prepared text entirely. [28]

Kennedy's intimate involvement in the construction of his speeches indicates that he was personally invested in his rhetoric. The amount of time and effort he devoted to ensuring the quality of the final draft suggests strongly that he "understood the power of words. He did not use them slackly; he used them self-consciously" toward his purpose. They were "regarded as tools of precision, to be chosen and applied with a craftsman's care to whatever the situation required." We agree with Golden's assessment that students "of public address can feel confident that a Kennedy speech contains both Kennedy's ideas and his language." [29]

According to Sorensen, neither he nor Kennedy was aware at the time of many of the stylistic devices that critics later claimed marked this style. They were really the by-products of an audience-centered approach mandating that the "test of a text was not how it appeared to the eye but how it sounded to the ear." Writing a speech for the listening audience meant that their "chief criterion was always audience comprehension and comfort, and this meant: (1) short speeches, short clauses and short words wherever possible; (2) a series of points or propositions in numbered or logical sequence, wherever appropriate; and (3) the construction of sentences, phrases and paragraphs in such a manner as to simplify, clarify and emphasize." Thus, alliteration, for example, was used "not solely for reasons of rhetoric but to reinforce the audience's recollection of his reasoning." The use of parallel construction and contrasts stemmed from Kennedy's "emphasis on a course of reason—rejecting the extremes of either side." Speeches were between twenty and thirty minutes in length and were "too short and too crowded with facts to permit any excess of generalities and sentimentalities." [30]

This style, when appropriate, also was marked at times by an intellectual tone and a sense of humor that became hallmarks of the Kennedy persona. The intellectuality of the rhetoric was in large measure attributable to Sorensen, who could "always find exactly the right classical reference to bring a major point into critical focus." Kennedy's speeches, at least those after Sorensen joined the staff, are marked by the extensive, didactic use of historical analogies, literary references, and quotations. The speeches were crafted to construct Kennedy's persona as a well-read, eloquently literate man of reason, possessing the detached sagacity of the seasoned historian—basing his calculations on the "facts" contained in the relevant historical lesson. One recent historical biographer claims that the "wit, sophistication, and literary prowess" in Kennedy's speeches were conspicuously absent prior to the time Sorensen came on board. Stylistically, "Kennedy's image owed much to the wisdom and words of Ted Sorensen." [31]

Although there is scant humor in the speeches examined in this book, humor was an important part of Kennedy's public speaking persona. He believed that "topical, tasteful, pertinent, pointed humor at the beginning of his remarks" was "a major means of establishing audience rapport," and would work "diligently for the right opening witticism, or take as much pride the next day in some spontaneous barb he had flung, as he would on the more substantive paragraphs in his text." That humor is best found in Kennedy's witty repartee with reporters at press conferences and in extemporaneous remarks before various groups and organizations.[32]

Kennedy's 1960 campaign speeches also "were encrusted with gems of humor. The humor was topical, tasteful, and relevant. It was pointed, irreverent, and original, and it was generally subtle and self-belittling, a reflection of Kennedy's personality and private wit." There were at least three sources for Kennedy's humor. The first was the humor file kept by Sorensen, where humorous anecdotes and stories would be stored and condensed on a "typewritten 'humor list' of one-line reminders" Kennedy often carried. The second was from the work of advance persons who would "precede . . . Kennedy on the stump, scour the local scene," and provide him with "the relevant local humor that established an immediate rapport between JFK and his audiences." His best humor, however, was spontaneous, and as his confidence increased during the campaign, so did his "spur-of-the-moment gibes." [33]

As others have noted, some speeches were important enough that Kennedy did not stray from the carefully prepared text. Most notably these were televised speeches to the nation concerning "crises" or speeches in which "every word had been carefully chosen for its impact both on the nation and on foreign governments." On other occasions, however, Kennedy would often deviate substantially from his prepared text. His mood, the reaction of the listening audience, and his constant efforts at revising his speech texts prompted him to speak extemporaneously "on the vast majority of occasions, deviating sometimes slightly with his own interjections and interpretations, more often substantially and sometimes completely." [34]

Kennedy read a great deal during his rather sickly childhood and his "childhood consolation had become an adult compulsion." He read constantly, at about 1,200 words a minute, and had an excellent ability in recalling "the felicitous statement" or the quotation "which distilled the essence of an argument." Kennedy's general reading "provided him with the historical perspective that extemporaneous speaking situations required," giving him "an understanding of the broad issues to be discussed in an extemporaneous address and furnish[ing] him with models of eloquence demonstrating a leader's ability to handle difficult ideas during moments of crisis." The well-honed reading skills he developed in childhood would serve him well when he began to write. For example, he turned his master's thesis into *Why England Slept* and later penned the Pulitzer Prize-winning *Profiles in Courage*. There is little question that these books were written like his speeches—with collaborators.[35]

As his confidence grew during the 1960 campaign he departed from his prepared texts more frequently, and his reputation grew as "a gifted extemporaneous speaker." Kennedy's abilities in this mode of presentation had the advantage of allowing him "to establish a vital relationship with his audience." Indeed, even the head speechwriter noted that Kennedy's "spontaneous remarks were consistently more effective than his prepared texts because they were delivered with more conviction and vitality." [36]

His spontaneous departures from his prepared texts might have facilitated his relationship with the audience, but it did cause at least some concern for two groups of people. The first was his speechwriters. As one election reporter wrote in October 1960, the Kennedy election team included a gifted group of speechwriters headed by "his close friend and advisor, Theodore Sorensen." This group had "collaborate[d] with Kennedy" to produce "prepared speech texts for every stop" along the campaign trail. "They ha[d] long since resigned themselves to seeing their daily masterpieces flutter to the ground as Kennedy discard[ed] them and [took] off on his own line of thought. This happen[ed] about 97 percent of the time." [37]

The other group concerned over Kennedy's extemporaneous departures from the prepared speeches were reporters, who dubbed him a "text deviate." On the campaign trail the problem was addressed by having a stenographer take down the speech as delivered. Then, within about fifteen minutes, that stenographic record would be typed and available for reporters to use when filing their stories. The White House press corps also was confounded by Kennedy's deviations from his text. Reporters often quoted in print or on the air from White House-supplied speeches, only to find out later that Kennedy disregarded the previously distributed text. Pierre Salinger informed Kennedy that the audience would "pick up the morning paper, read quotes you never said and decide that the reporter was either too drunk to take notes or didn't show up for the speech. Unless you stick to the text, the reporters won't file until after you're through speaking and you'll miss most of their editions." Kennedy's only concession on this matter was to "stand by every word in the text, whether I read it or not," and to examine the advance AP and UPI stories to make sure he would actually say the things attributed to him in the lead to the story.[38]

During the 1960 election Kennedy was described as "somewhat of a paradoxical figure" to the American electorate:

> To a nation winding up eight comfortable years under the leadership of one of the most popular Presidents in U.S. history, he brings a message of anxiety and discontent. To a nation strong enough to flex its power from Lebanon on one side of the world to Formosa Strait on the other, he preaches a warning of declining prestige. To a country that has marched down the middle of the road behind Dwight Eisenhower to the highest level of shared prosperity of any nation in history, he campaigns with Depression fervor for welfare-state reform.

There certainly was nothing substantive in his campaign rhetoric that could account adequately for the reaction he engendered among supporters. Kennedy's delivery provided assurance even as he talked "of grave trouble to come"; projecting a sense of "mystery, sex appeal, to-the-manner-born confidence" that audiences viewed as leadership, as he "urged without preaching, inspired without condescending"—to get the country "moving again." [39]

Sorensen described Kennedy as speaking "crisply, earnestly, with his chin thrust upward and forward. The chopping right hand with which he emphasized his points was his only gesture." This is far from the unanimous opinion of those who commented on his delivery style. Negative reaction to his campaign speaking usually focused on his tone and speaking rate. White said that he spoke "from the platform in a high, resonant, almost melancholy tone of voice," but was, in private, "one of the more gifted conversationalists of politics." In a *Saturday Review* article concerning *The Strategy of Peace*, Blair Clark said that Kennedy sounded "a little like an earnest young professor of social sciences, in a hurry to get to the next class but anxious to communicate as much of his knowledge as he can to a class that has a right to know. And the audiences lend attentive ears even as he rattles off statistics on steel production in India and calorie consumption in Africa." [40]

When Kennedy remembered "to speak without breaking the speed limits or straining his vocal chords," he employed a "conversational tone which [wa]s at once engaging and persuasive." In December 1959, approximately one month before Senator Kennedy would make the official announcement of his candidacy for the presidency, he wrote University of Missouri speech professor Loren Reid: "I have never had any formal training in public speaking or debating except that which has come from a career in politics. Currently I average approximately 50 Senate speeches and 100 speeches off the Senate floor per year." Kennedy's confidence and his reputation as a public speaker grew as the campaign progressed and continued to grow during his all-too-brief term as president.[41]

Kennedy's presidential discursive messages were sometimes complex and ambiguous. At various times, Kennedy's public rhetoric called upon Americans to reflect upon their best qualities: vision, mission, character, and competence. He gave voice to human rights by expressing the idea that religion should not be a determining factor in American politics or that a citizen's skin color should not bar access to the American Dream. In a rhetorical style "more suited [to the] Stalinist era than [to] the 196[0s]," Kennedy exacerbated Cold War tensions by describing a world fraught with danger and polarized by fifteen years of East-West conflict. Yet he also would argue, most profoundly, for an end to conflict and for peaceful coexistence among humankind. His public rhetoric during 1961 and 1962 seemed to stress competition, but by 1963 a common theme also was found in cooperation. As the president sought to rally the nation behind his policies, he embodied and expressed idealistic values and pragmatic plans of action that contained implicit and explicit cues concerning his visions of and dreams for the American people. At times, he extended that vision and was a proponent of that dream to the other nations of the world.[42]

ORGANIZATION OF THIS BOOK

We seek in this analysis to mine some of John F. Kennedy's public visions and dreams through an examination of three distinct areas. Each is designed to help us probe further into the mystique of his public address.

Chapter 2 examines Kennedy's efforts to address the "religious issue" during the 1960 election and closes with an examination of the sources, rhetorical strategies, and outcomes of the first speech of his presidency, the Inaugural Address.

Chapter 3 explores Kennedy's public discourse in response to the struggle for civil rights. Unrest associated with civil rights presented Kennedy with the greatest firestorm he would encounter in domestic politics. Kennedy's civil rights rhetoric during his tenure in office suggests an evolution from arguments grounded in law to arguments grounded in morality. For Kennedy this would be a long, torturous transition. We focus here on two televised speeches as touchstones of his civil rights rhetoric—his speech of September 30, 1962, concerning the events at the University of Mississippi, and his speech of June 11, 1963, defining the civil rights struggle as a moral issue.

In Chapter 4, we focus on Kennedy's public rhetoric concerning the relationship between the United States and the Soviet Union. We examine major foreign policy addresses including: a speech responding to the Bay of Pigs fiasco delivered on April 20, 1961, to the American Society of Newspaper Editors; the Berlin Crisis address delivered on national television on July 25, 1961; the October 22, 1962 speech concerning the American response to Soviet emplacement of nuclear weapons in Cuba; the eloquent plea for detente at American University on June 10, 1963; and, finally, the announcement of a Limited Test Ban Treaty between the United States, the U.S.S.R., and the U.K., broadcast on July 26, 1963. These speeches reflect a period in which the threat of war competed with dreams of peace, and the nation and the world stood horrified and enthralled. We suggest that Kennedy concerned himself in the first two years with a defense of freedom at the expense of peace. In 1963, Kennedy set about designing a self-reflexive campaign for peace.

In laying claim to these three areas we do not profess to be exhaustive. We acknowledge that we are painting with some rather large brushstrokes and that there are many aspects of Kennedy's rhetoric that are left unexplored here, including the famous Kennedy wit and his facility for extemporaneous address. But we feel that the speeches and press conference remarks that we have selected will help us represent some of the more interesting aspects of the rhetorical legacy of John F. Kennedy. Our judgments regarding that legacy appear in Chapter 5.

Finally, we believe that the discourse recorded in these pages is an essential part of rhetorical history. For example, Kennedy's attempt in Houston to counter religious bigotry and his eloquent Inaugural Address both offer significant public definitions of our national character. Furthermore, his public address concerning civil rights represented a nation that had encountered its dark underside and a question of moral conscience—both law and morality were on trial—all in one sweepingly encompassing stroke of historical intersection.[43]

The president's foreign policy discourse reflects a critical period in our history and stands, for good or evil, as an embodiment of the tradition and legacy of post-World War II U.S. foreign policy. The idealism and pragmatism in these speeches, with their bellicosity and their eloquent appeals for conciliation, are redolent of the divided mind of Cold War America.

The ideas, values, and political, social, and economic interests of the time are interwoven into the speech texts and, for that reason alone, these public statements deserve our sustained attention. The historical-critical method driving our study thus engages a portrait of a people as well as that of a president. By taking on the tasks of the historian, political scientist, and critic, we hope to add to existing bodies of knowledge and understanding through sustained reflection on presidential public discourse. In the process, we encounter a transitional president in a transitional time who was trying desperately to cope with crises that were both self-inflicted and externally imposed—and thereby we encounter a leader ensconced in governance and history. It is a place we also hope the reader will find him or herself. For, in our view, a focus on words, as significant human action in and upon the political environment, is both a humane and human enterprise. Herein, both the wealth and the poverty of the polis is laid bare. Herein, we encounter both virtue and vice. Ultimately, such a venture helps explain us to ourselves. The past, after all, is merely prologue—and the mirror the past provides reflects our common future.

NOTES

1. Following the assassination of William McKinley, former vice-president Theodore Roosevelt, at age 42, took his place in history as the youngest president ever

inaugurated. At his inauguration, John F. Kennedy was 43. The quotation is drawn from Arthur M. Schlesinger, Jr., *A Thousand Days: John F. Kennedy in the White House* (Boston: Houghton Mifflin, 1965), 714.

2. James David Barber, *Presidential Character: Predicting Performance in the White House*, 3rd ed. (Englewood Cliffs, N.J.: Prentice-Hall, 1985), 268; Henry Fairlie, *The Kennedy Promise: The Politics of Expectation* (Garden City, N.Y.: Doubleday, 1973), 87-88; Theodore Otto Windt, Jr., *Presidents and Protesters: Political Rhetoric in the 1960s* (Tuscaloosa and London: University of Alabama Press, 1990), 17-87.

3. Theodore H. White, *The Making of the President, 1960* (New York: Atheneum, 1962), 367; Schlesinger, *A Thousand Days*, 120; "Political Notes: Fight Talk," *Time*, January 25, 1960, p. 20; John D. Morris, "Kennedy Pledges Firm Presidency," *New York Times*, January 15, 1960, A1; Hugh Sidey, *John F. Kennedy, President* (New York: Atheneum, 1964), 83; Senator William Benton Oral History, Interviewed by Newton Minow, JFK Library; Joseph P. Berry, *John F. Kennedy and the Media: The First Television President* (Lanham, Md.: University Press of America, 1987).

4. Senator John F. Kennedy, *The Strategy of Peace*, edited by Allan Nevins (New York: Harper & Row, 1960), 3. Fairlie noted the importance of the reflexive nature of Kennedy's rhetoric by suggesting that the campaign addresses revealed "the way in which he was making himself the kind of President he would be." Fairlie, *The Kennedy Promise*, 38.

5. Windt, *Presidents and Protesters*, 22; James L. Golden, "John F. Kennedy and the 'Ghosts,'" *Quarterly Journal of Speech* 52 (1966): 348.

6. Theodore Windt notes in the Introduction to the Third Edition of *Presidential Rhetoric: 1961 to the Present* that the study of presidential rhetoric "is a study of how Presidents gain, maintain, or lose support of the public. It is not a study in literary or rhetorical style. It is not an academic study of rhetorical techniques intended to refine rhetorical theory. It is a study of power, of the fundamental power in a democracy: public opinion and public support." (Dubuque, Iowa: Kendall/Hunt Publishing, 1983), 2. For an early article on the rhetorical presidency see James W. Ceaser, Glen E. Thurow, Jeffrey Tulis, and Joseph M. Bessette, "The Rise of the Rhetorical Presidency," *Presidential Studies Quarterly*, 11 (1981): 158-171. A full discussion of the rhetorical presidency can be found in Jeffrey Tulis, *The Rhetorical Presidency* (Princeton, N.J.: Princeton University Press, 1987). For our purposes, a rhetorical presidency is one that leads through the evocation "of a common purpose and a spirit of idealism." Its function is to gain the support of the public as well as the Congress. The president usually relies on the mass media, and the electronic media in particular, to take his message directly to the people. Thus, the president is required to address multiple audiences in his symbolic attempts to influence the American public. We will argue that this was Kennedy's quintessential stance—and is reflected especially in the televised addresses analyzed in this book. See, e.g., David Zarefsky, *President Johnson's War on Poverty: Rhetoric and History* (University: University of Alabama Press, 1986), 7-8.

7. Theodore Windt, "Presidential Rhetoric: Definition of a Discipline of Study," in *Essays in Presidential Rhetoric*, 3rd ed., ed. Theodore Windt and Beth Ingold (Dubuque, Iowa: Kendall/Hunt Publishing, 1992), xxix. Windt noted elsewhere that Kennedy's presidential rhetoric was echoed by "a generation of presidents." Windt, *Presidents and Protesters*, 18.

8. Windt, *Presidents and Protesters*, 3; Windt, "Presidential Rhetoric: Definition of

a Discipline of Study," xxxvi; Murray Edelman, *The Symbolic Uses of Politics* (Urbana: University of Illinois Press, 1964), 131.

9. Windt, *Presidents and Protesters*, 3; Zarefsky, *President Johnson's War on Poverty*, 8-9.

10. Zarefsky, *President Johnson's War on Poverty*, 6-7; White, *The Making*, 370; Windt, *Presidents and Protesters*, 3.

11. Doris A. Graber, *Verbal Behavior and Politics* (Urbana: University of Illinois Press, 1976), 48. Windt called this aspect of presidential public address "the most potent argument in a president's arsenal," and argued that a concern for the "political definitions that presidents assign to events, policies, and people" should be "[t]he starting point for any study of presidential rhetoric." See Theodore Windt, "Presidential Rhetoric: An Update, 1992," in *Essays in Presidential Rhetoric,* 3rd ed., ed. Theodore Windt and Beth Ingold, lv; Windt, *Presidents and Protesters*, 4.

12. Zarefsky, *President Johnson's War on Poverty*, xi, 11, 8; Hermann G. Stelzner, "Ford's War on Inflation: A Metaphor That Did Not Cross," *Communication Monographs* 44 (1977): 291.

13. Theodore Windt, "The President and Speeches on International Crisis: Repeating the Rhetorical Past," *Speaker and Gavel* 2 (1973): 6-14. Reprinted in Theodore Windt and Beth Ingold eds., *Essays in Presidential Rhetoric*, 3rd. ed. (Dubuque, Iowa: Kendall/Hunt Publishing, 1992), 92; White, *The Making*, 378; Barber, *Presidential Character*, 266.

14. We draw the terms "substantive," "stylistic," and "situational" from Karlyn Kohrs Campbell and Kathleen Hall Jamieson, "Form and Genre in Rhetorical Criticism: An Introduction," in *Form and Genre: Shaping Rhetorical Action*, ed. Karlyn Kohrs Campbell and Kathleen Hall Jamieson (Falls Church, Va.: Speech Communication Association, 1978), 9-32. Some of Kennedy's speeches would establish and/or fulfill a generic pattern; others would not. But all of the elements listed are aspects we will take cognizance of in our application. We do not mean to imply that ours is a generic study; our focus here is on a particular president with a particular set of rhetorical concerns. Nonetheless, our method will be informed by these key elements.

15. Barber, *Presidential Character*, 255; Theodore Sorensen, *Kennedy* (New York: Harper & Row, 1965), 65; "Democrats: The Reverberating Issue," *Time*, July 18, 1960, 10.

16. Schlesinger, *A Thousand Days*, 8.

17. Robert N. Bostrom, "'I Give You a Man'—Kennedy's Speech For Adlai Stevenson," *Speech Monographs* 35 (1968): 129.

18. Alonzo L. Hamby, *Liberalism and Its Challenges*: *F.D.R. to Bush* 2nd. ed. (New York: Oxford University Press, 1992), 194; James N. Giglio, *The Presidency of John F. Kennedy* (Lawrence: University Press of Kansas, 1991), 15; Donald F. Barnes Oral History, Interviewed by John Plank, JFK Library; Frederick G. Dutton Oral History, Interviewed by Charles T. Morrissey, JFK Library; Edward P. Morgan Oral History, Interviewed by William McHugh, JFK Library.

19. Golden, "Ghosts," 353.

20. Sorensen, *Kennedy*, 66; Golden, "Ghosts," 349.

21. Schlesinger, *A Thousand Days*, 193.

22. Schlesinger, *A Thousand Days*, 208; Golden, "Ghosts," 349; Lois J. Einhorn, "The Ghosts Talk: Personal Interviews with Three Former Speechwriters,"

Communication Quarterly 36 (1988): 98.

23. Fairlie, *The Kennedy Promise*, 39; Pierre Salinger, *With Kennedy* (Garden City, N.Y.: Doubleday, 1966), 66; Schlesinger, *A Thousand Days*, 690; and see Sorensen, *Kennedy*, 60.

24. Berry, *Media*, 83. For an example of this process see Schlesinger, *A Thousand Days*, 615-616; Golden, "Ghosts," 351.

25. Einhorn, "The Ghosts Talk," 98.

26. This routine of examining Kennedy's previous speeches suggests the staff's recognition of the reflexive nature of Kennedy's rhetoric—the power of words to both form and limit those who have spoken them. The president's public address bound him "to a view of politics of which there had been little hint in his earlier career, and from which he could not as President escape." See Fairlie, *The Kennedy Promise*, 38. As Windt observed, the rhetorical record of presidents becomes a two-edge sword, as they "are both liberated and imprisoned by language." Windt, *Presidents and Protesters*, 4.

27. Sorensen, *Kennedy*, 60.

28. Golden, "Ghosts," 352.

29. Fairlie, *The Kennedy Promise*, 39; Sorensen, *Kennedy*, 61; Golden, "Ghosts," 357.

30. Sorensen, *Kennedy*, 60-61.

31. Golden, "Ghosts," 349; Thomas C. Reeves, *A Question of Character: A Life of John F. Kennedy* (New York: The Free Press, 1991), 118.

32. Sorensen, *Kennedy*, 63.

33. Gerald Gardner, *The Mocking of the President: A History of Campaign Humor from Ike to Bush* (New York: Harper and Row, 1989), 204-205; Sorensen, *Kennedy*, 63-64.

34. Salinger, *With Kennedy*, 67; Sorensen, *Kennedy*, 177.

35. Schlesinger, *A Thousand Days*, 104-105; Golden, "Ghosts," 350-351. Kennedy's penchant for using collaborators has generated continuing controversy over his credentials to authorship. According to Thomas C. Reeves, Arthur Krock assisted Kennedy on *Why England Slept* and Sorensen and Georgetown historian Jules David were chief contributors, along with other minor assistants, in the development of *Profiles in Courage*. See Reeves, *Character*, esp. 49 and 127-128.

36. Golden, "Ghosts," 357; Sorensen, *Kennedy*, 177.

37. Beverly Smith, "Campaigning with Kennedy," *Saturday Evening Post*, October 29, 1960, 80.

38. Salinger, *With Kennedy*, 67.

39. "Democrats: Candidate in Orbit," *Time*, November 7, 1960, 26; Barber, *Presidential Character*, 273.

40. Sorensen, *Kennedy*, 180; White, *The Making*, 54; Blair Clark, "Book in the News: *The Strategy of Peace*," *Saturday Review*, May 28, 1960, 19.

41. Smith, "Campaigning," 80; Letter from Senator John F. Kennedy to Professor Loren Reid, December 3, 1959, Theodore C. Sorensen Papers, Campaign Files, 1959-1960, Speeches, Box 25, JFK Library.

42. Barber, *Presidential Character*, 275.

43. Rhetorical history "takes rhetoric as its subject matter and perspective," and as such, concerns itself with the role of persuasion in the history of ideas, events, politics, and society. Using the methods of historiography and criticism, we plumb the past to

find a greater clarity and, hopefully, a unique purchase on the future. See Martin J. Medhurst, Robert L. Ivie, Philip Wander, and Robert L. Scott, *Cold War Rhetoric: Strategy, Metaphor, and Ideology* (Westport, Conn.: Greenwood Press, 1990), 8.

2

A NEW BEGINNING

In this chapter we examine John F. Kennedy's campaign discourse, primarily through an analysis of his speech to the Houston Ministerial Association and the Inaugural Address. The former has been labeled the most dramatic and pivotal speech of the campaign. We consider the latter speech to be the last and best representative of Kennedy's campaign for the presidency as well as setting key themes for the new administration. Both speeches provide representative anecdotes for national rituals associated with U.S. presidential campaigns where the processes of peaceful change in governance signal a new beginning.[1]

CONFRONTING THE RELIGIOUS ISSUE IN HOUSTON

As others have indicated, the "religious issue"—at least as it applies to Catholics in this country—was probably dismissed more by President Kennedy's behavior in office than by anything he said during the campaign. But Kennedy's Catholicism made the presidential election of 1960 "the most unusual and absorbing White House race in the nation's history."[2]

Kennedy addressed the issue publicly many times during his quest for the White House—in a *Look* magazine article in March 1959, during the West Virginia primary, at the Al Smith Memorial Dinner in New York less than a month before election day, and in response to the hundreds of questions asked of him during the campaign. But we are concerned here with his speech of September 12, 1960, addressing a meeting of the Greater Houston Ministerial Association. Our analysis of this effort is dependent upon an understanding of the nature of the religious issue during the campaign.[3]

Religion as an Issue in 1960

Kennedy's staff considered his Catholicism to be the biggest obstacle in his quest for the presidency, and concern for it dictated strategy for a great many campaign decisions. For example, the strategy of entering primaries was, in part, to prove to the leaders of his party—many of whom were Catholics themselves—that Kennedy's religion was not the problem to voters that it was perceived to be. Decisions concerning which primaries to enter, the selection of a vice-presidential running mate, and even the naming of a new chair of the Democratic party were, to some extent, affected by concerns regarding Kennedy's Catholicism.

As an issue, Kennedy's Catholicism was described as "as elusive and indestructible as quicksilver." One Kennedy campaign staff member stated that it was like "a fire in a coal mine . . . suppressed at one point only to go on smoldering far underground and out of reach." Although many voters found the "intrusion of religion into national politics [to be] distasteful and embarrassing," polls indicated that it was "being talked about in practically all states, and in some almost to the exclusion of every other political topic." Difficult to define or track, religion had become a "great imponderable" element in the campaign, confounding "pollsters, the politicians, and the pundits." It soon provided an "ominous counterpoint to the main theme of the Presidential campaign."[4]

In 1960, public dialogue regarding the religious issue revolved around two main concerns. Probably the most important was a belief that the tenets of Catholicism did not allow practicing Catholics to accept the principle of separation of church and state as embodied in the First Amendment to the Constitution. Patricia Barrett maintained that this belief underscored a perception that the threat to the liberties of non-Catholics was "proportionate to the political power which Catholics achieve, since they are conscience-bound to implement the 'established church' doctrine whenever this becomes possible." The other aspect of the religious issue was the "divided loyalty" argument, a belief that all American Catholics—presumably including a Catholic president—would have a dual allegiance to both an "infallible" Pope and to the United States. The "divided loyalty" argument implied that the political decisions of a Catholic president would be influenced, or maybe even controlled, by the hierarchy of the church. This concern may have been magnified when one considered that the Catholic hierarchy had taken specific stands on several political issues, some of which would come before the next president.[5]

Much of the public dialogue was marked by an unmistakable patina of unyielding prejudice against Catholics and Roman Catholicism. Some of those who were the most vocal, and commanded significant media attention, did not even make an effort to deny their bigotry. However, a great deal of the concern over how Kennedy's religion might affect his conduct as president was being expressed more out of genuine fear than prejudice. As Sorensen stated, Kennedy "knew that Catholics were under suspicion by Americans of goodwill as well as by bigots." He privately felt that it was "unfair that none of the other Presidential contenders in either party" were asked the same kinds of questions about their religious beliefs. But he also realized that "their churches, rightly or wrongly, had less often been accused of accepting foreign control or seeking public funds and influence." There was a profound realization within the Kennedy camp that the religious issue would have to be addressed if his candidacy was to remain viable throughout the campaign.[6]

Although both Hubert Humphrey and John F. Kennedy tried to minimize the religious issue in the primary, the media accentuated it as a focal point. Thus, when media analyses of Kennedy's victory in Wisconsin explained it in terms of the religious factor—labeling the four districts he lost as "Protestant"—and pointed out that his margin of popular votes was provided in the "Catholic areas," the Kennedy forces realized that the results of the Wisconsin primary "would be read . . . wherever [people] read politics as a Catholic-Protestant split."[7]

In predominantly Protestant West Virginia, which evidenced distrust of a Catholic candidate, the Kennedy campaign adopted a basic rhetorical strategy for handling the religious issue from which they did not deviate for the duration of the campaign. First, the candidate indicated that he would not be dismissing out-of-hand public concerns regarding his Catholicism. He would acknowledge that it was a genuine factor for some people, and that he did not consider all such concerns to be the product of bigotry or prejudice. As such, he would continue to "answer not only all the reasonable questions but many unreasonable questions as well. He knew he could not afford to be defensive, angry, impatient or silent, no matter how many times he heard the same insulting, foolish or discriminatory questions."[8]

Of equal importance, Kennedy would address the issue publicly as often as necessary, proffering his definition of its only legitimate aspect—his independence of ecclesiastical pressure—proclaiming over and over that the Catholic hierarchy had no influence over him when it came to the weighty matters of American politics. He thus acknowledged the trepidation many felt, but would define the issue in such a way that legitimated only those concerns regarding the candidate—not the candidate's religion. In other words, he would only defend himself, not Catholic actions, doctrine, or history. If successful, this strategy of delimiting the legitimate parameters of the issue would minimize its negative effects by reframing it against more transcendent concerns of tolerance, fair play, and even the very Constitution his candidacy was purportedly undermining. This allowed Kennedy to highlight the bigotry of those who would oppose his candidacy solely on religious grounds.

Kennedy's decisive victory in West Virginia did not bury the religious issue; rather, it was kept from becoming the issue during the remainder of the primary season. The complexities of religion would surface again during the general election, which began with an undercurrent concerning the issue of Kennedy's Catholicism. In a memorandum dated August 15, 1960, Theodore Sorensen would observe: "Senator Kennedy will win in November unless defeated by the religious issue. This makes neutralization of this issue the key to the election."

24   *"In a Perilous Hour"*

On September 7, President Eisenhower assured reporters that he did not "believe in voicing prejudice," felt none, and was sure that "Nixon feels exactly the same. . . . Mr. Nixon and I agreed long ago that one thing we would never raise is the religious issue in this campaign." However, Eisenhower's hope that religion "could be laid on the shelf and forgotten until after the election is over," was to go unfulfilled. On that same day, two Protestant organizations released public statements that were to bring religion into dramatic new focus during the election.[9]

Protestant Statements

The first statement was released by Protestants and Other Americans United for Separation of Church and State (POAU). This statement called for "calm analysis and sober speech about the religious issue in the current political campaign," and labeled as "trash" "literature expressing religious bigotry and scandal." However, the POAU continued, it was impossible to "avoid recognition of the fact that one church in the United States, the largest church operating on American soil, officially supports a world-wide policy of partial union of church and state wherever it has the power to enforce such a policy." The statement lamented that American Catholic bishops had "specifically rejected the Supreme Court's interpretation of the separation of church and state," and had committed themselves "to an interpretation of the Constitution which would permit full tax support for sectarian schools." The statement praised "the candidate of the Roman Catholic faith" for his position that federal aid to parochial schools was unconstitutional, but was "skeptical about his equivocal words on birth control," and "concerned, too, about his silence in regard to the official boycott of public schools contained in the canon law of his church."[10]

After citing repression against Protestants by the current governments in Spain and Columbia, the POAU statement questioned the effect the "election of a Roman Catholic as President" would have on "governments which practice such suppression with the knowledge and cooperation of the Vatican." The POAU regretted "the evasive journalism which . . . has declined to face its responsibility" concerning a forthright and mature examination of the religious issue. "Some editors do not even recognize the elementary fact that one church in the United States has for centuries pursued a policy of partial union of church and state, and that the adoption of such a policy in this country would be a calamity of the first magnitude. When a candidate belongs to an organization which champions such a policy, it is not bigotry or prejudice to examine his credentials with the utmost care and frankness, and to ask how far his commitment goes."

The final paragraph in the POAU statement commended the patriotism of American Roman Catholics, acknowledged "that there are other issues in this campaign beside the church-state issue," and cautioned that it was "the duty of the voters to choose the man they consider best fitted to meet all the exacting demands of the office." However, the first sentence of this paragraph asked members "to decide for themselves, on the basis of all the evidence, whether the election of a Roman Catholic would promote or hinder the historic American principle of church-state separation."

As dramatic as the POAU statement was, it did not command the lion's share of media attention when it was released. On that same day the newly formed National Conference of Citizens for Religious Freedom—a group consisting of 150 conservative clergy and laity representing 37 "primarily fundamentalist or evangelical Protestant church groups"—also released their statement. The conference became known in the media as the "Peale Group" because one of its leaders and spokespersons was the well-known author Norman Vincent Peale. Undoubtedly his popularity was partially responsible for the large amount of media attention paid to the group's press release. Indeed, the New York Times coverage of the two statements featured a picture of Peale, with the caption "Sees a faith issue." Other leaders of the conference included Daniel Poling, editor of the *Christian Herald*; Billy Graham's father-in-law, Nelson Bell, editor of *Christianity Today*; and Harold J. Ockenga, a former president of the National Association of Evangelicals.[11]

According to "eavesdropping" reporters who attended the conference's closed meeting at the Mayflower Hotel in Washington D.C., Peale presided during a series of statements by leaders of the National Conference. Bell drew similarities between the methods of "the Roman church" and those of Communist governments; and Ockenga said that Kennedy and Khrushchev were both "captive[s] of a system." Peale was quoted as saying "Our American culture is at stake. I won't say it won't survive, but it won't be what it was." Following the closed meeting, Poling and Ockenga met with reporters and released a pre-written 2,000-word "manifesto that more than any other statement thus far in the campaign served to make religion the most emotional issue of the 1960 election."[12]

The National Conference statement began by observing that "the religious issue remains a major factor in the current political campaign" despite "efforts to ignore or to stifle it." The statement declared the issue "should be handled with utmost discretion," and "discussed only in a spirit of truth, tolerance and fairness" without "hate mongering, bigotry, prejudice or unfounded charges." After proclaiming a belief in religious freedom and acknowledging that Catholics can "be just as honest, patriotic and public spirited" as members of other faiths," the statement specified "the key question": "[W]hether it is in the best interest of our society for any church organization to attempt to exercise control over its members in political and civic affairs. While the current Roman Catholic contender for the Presidency states specifically that he would not be so influenced, his church insists that he is duty-bound to admit to its direction. This unresolved conflict leaves doubt in the minds of millions of our citizens."

The statement then detailed points of concern regarding Kennedy's Catholicism. First, the Roman Catholic Church was "a political as well as a religious organization . . . maintain[ing] diplomatic relations with the Governments of forty-two countries." It was thus "inconceivable that a Roman Catholic President would not be under extreme pressure by the hierarchy of his church" concerning such matters as "representation to the Vatican." Second, the Catholic Church had "specifically repudiated" the principle "that every man shall be free to follow the dictates of his conscience in religious matters." Furthermore, pronouncements by the Catholic church—including "the belief that Protestant faiths are heretical and counterfeit and that they have no theoretical right to exist"—were binding upon "every Roman Catholic, including the Democratic nominee . . . as well as upon all members of this church." Third, in countries where it had predominated, the Catholic church had denied "equal rights for all of other faiths." Fourth, the Catholic church had "repeatedly attempted to break down the wall of separation of church and state," and the signatories were "not altogether reassure[d]" by the realization that "many American Catholics would disagree with the policies of their church." Was it "reasonable to assume that a Roman Catholic President would be able to withstand altogether the determined efforts of the hierarchy of his church to gain further funds and favors for its schools and institutions, and otherwise breach the wall of separation of church and state?"[13]

Finally, the statement observed that because canon law prohibited a Catholic from participating in interfaith meetings or worshipping in a Protestant church, a Catholic president would "be gravely handicapped in offering to the American people and to the world an example of the religious liberty our people cherish."[14]

The formal statement ended with the declaration that the reason "there is a 'religious issue' in the present political campaign is not the fault of any candidate. It is created by the nature of the Roman Catholic Church which is, in a very real sense, both a church and also a temporal state."

These two statements produced an almost immediate negative reaction, much of it by more liberal Protestant spokespersons such as Reinhold Neibuhr and James Pike, and most of it focused on Norman Vincent Peale, who left the country after telling the media that he had only attended one meeting and had been "duped." But the statements served to breathe a new vitality into the religious issue. They were not written by uneducated hate mongers, and were, indeed, treated by much of the media as representative of the reasonable and legitimate concerns regarding Kennedy's Catholicism. This mediated attention renewed the urgency of addressing religion yet again.

Kennedy was campaigning in California when the statements were released. According to several accounts his staff was divided concerning how to proceed. Many of his closest advisers counseled to do nothing and hope that the issue would not continue to command attention, but Kennedy himself reluctantly made the decision to face the issue directly.

We, however, would agree with Stelzner's observation that this reluctance "is not easily explained." In fact, it seems as though the decision to face the issue where he did and in the way he did was actually predicated on sound political intelligence-gathering. In late August, the Kennedy campaign had received a report by the Simulatics Corporation suggesting that any votes Kennedy would lose over the religious issue had already been lost. Further, it was suggested that meeting the issue "head-on" might gain him support. As the report noted:

> The net worst has been done. If the campaign becomes embittered, he will lose a few more reluctant Protestant votes to Nixon, but will gain Catholic and minority group votes. Bitter anti-Catholicism in the campaign would bring about a reaction against prejudice and for Kennedy from Catholics and others who would resent overt prejudice.... On balance he would not lose further from forthright and persistent attention to the religious issue and could gain.[15]

Thus armed, the Kennedy camp was "always looking for the right forum in which to confront the [religious] issue." The opportunity was provided by an invitation from the Greater Houston Ministerial Association. The candidate was called on to deliver an address "defending the right of a Catholic to be president of the United States."[16]

After being informed of the candidate's decision to speak to the association, a worried Sam Rayburn told Kennedy that the Houston Ministerial Association would be a hostile audience of "mostly Republicans." "These are not ministers. These are politicians who are going around in robes and saying they're ministers, but they're nothing but politicians. They hate your guts and they're going to tear you to pieces, and you shouldn't have done it." Aide Kenneth O'Donnell also was against going to Houston and told the candidate, "I think it would be a mistake. If you have to meet the religious issue, Houston is not the place to do it."[17]

But as David Halberstam observed, this decision was an example of Kennedy's "great new skill in televised politics: deliberately allowing someone else to rig something against you that is, in fact, rigged for you. Their ambush of you becomes instead your ambush of them." The publicly mediated image of the Catholic candidate defending the principle of religious freedom to a well-known group of those rallied against him probably conveyed a visual message as substantial as anything Kennedy actually said at the meeting. Coverage of the meeting frequently used words like "inquisition," and remarked how the candidate was going "into the lion's den" to "face the religious issue head-on." Thus, the press told the story in a way that emphasized the lone hero bravely facing down one of the darker aspects of American sociopolitical heritage. The *Houston Chronicle* made this point succinctly: "There is something in the sight of an American having to defend his religious beliefs that repels Americans."[18]

SPEECH TO THE GREATER HOUSTON MINISTERIAL ASSOCIATION

The meeting with the ministers was to be televised throughout Texas and was taped by Kennedy's aides for possible future use in the campaign. Kennedy was to be introduced precisely at 9:00 P.M. and then give his speech, followed by a question and answer period between the candidate and the assembled ministers. The bulk of our critical focus here is on the prepared part of his presentation, which was written by Sorensen and drew upon the candidate's "previous statements on religion to the [American Society of Newspaper Editors], to the convention, to press conferences," as well as a 1959 *Look* magazine piece. When completed, the text of his opening remarks was reviewed by campaign staff and a former writer with *Commonweal* magazine.[19]

The candidate spent September 12 barnstorming across Texas, with stops in El Paso, Lubbock, San Antonio, and an earlier speech at Houston's Sam Houston Coliseum. By 8:30 P.M., the pink and green carpeted ballroom of Houston's Rice Hotel was filled with about 300 members of the Greater Houston Ministerial Association and another 300 guests and members of the press from New York and Washington. Wearing a dark suit—but brown shoes because his black shoes were left on the plane by aide Dave Powers—Kennedy entered the ballroom just before 9:00 P.M. and took his place on the speaker's platform. After an uneasy period of silence, the Reverend Herbert Meza offered the opening prayer and told the audience to remember who they were and who they served. Then Kennedy, a tad nervous before striding to the lectern and sensing the "tension and hostility" in the room, was introduced and began a confident but somber address.[20]

From the beginning, Kennedy constructed the reformative framework along which his speech would proceed. After thanking the association for its "generous invitation to speak my views," Kennedy stated that although discussion of the "so-called religious issue" was "necessarily and properly" the purpose of their meeting that evening, the overall significance of the issue was minimal compared to the more important issues facing the electorate. Itemized by Kennedy, these included spreading Communist influence "until it now festers ninety miles off the coast of Florida"; a loss of respect for American power; the devastating effects of poverty on children, the elderly, and farmers; "an America with too many slums, with too few schools, and too late to the moon and outer space." According to the candidate, these were the decisive issues of the campaign "for war and hunger and ignorance and despair know no religious barriers."

Kennedy's laundry-listing of these issues was almost devoid of any meaningful detail. But it did serve to contextualize the events that were about to transpire. The candidates and the electorate were prevented from addressing these important issues because they had been obscured—"perhaps deliberately, in some quarters less responsible than this"—by an overriding concern for Kennedy's religion. Given this situation, Kennedy said, it was "apparently necessary for me to state once again—not what kind of church I believe in, for that should be important only to me—but what kind of America I believe in."

In his opening Kennedy deftly and subtly placed the immediate audience—and through them those that would make his religion an issue—on the defensive. Kennedy's allowance that there were "some quarters less responsible than this," only addressed how deliberate the Protestant ministers were in obscuring the "real issues in this campaign." As presented in the speech, whether deliberate or not, the pronounced focus on Kennedy's religion harmed the country by sublimating the concerns that should have been foregrounded in the campaign.

This strategy of placing the audience on the defensive was furthered by Kennedy's statement that his beliefs about his church should only be important to him. From the perspective of his audience, these beliefs were the very reason he was invited to speak. Thus, early on, Kennedy constructed a situation in which he was purportedly precluded by his audience from discussing the real issues of the election, and he maintained he would not discuss his religious beliefs because, like most Americans, he considered them a private matter. So it was "apparently necessary" to state "once again" his beliefs concerning the one subject he could and would discuss: "what kind of America I believe in." There was an exasperated tone to this section of his remarks, conveying the sense that he had done this many times before, but evidently such statements were ignored by those he addressed at the Rice Hotel. His introduction delimited the parameters of concern which could be discussed legitimately and thus redefined the religious question—from a concern regarding his Catholicism to a concern for the role of religion in political America and a definition of our national character.

His presentation of "the kind of America I believe in" was contained in three statements. The first was a belief "in an America where the separation of church and state is absolute." This stated ideal was undoubtedly a principle uniting Kennedy with his immediate audience. But his operationalization of this ideal neatly juxtaposed the concerns of the immediate audience with concerns about the immediate audience. As presented, Kennedy's ideal America defined a place "where no Catholic prelate would tell the President [should he be Catholic] how to act, and no Protestant minister would tell his parishioners for whom to vote." Equally, it evoked a country where "no church or church school is granted any public funds or political preference—and where no man is denied public office merely because his religion differs from the President who might appoint him or the people who might elect him." Thus, Kennedy's first statement drew the issue of church-state separation in such an absolute way that it would, in essence, preclude the very purpose of the present meeting and the candidate's address. To the wider audience, Kennedy implied that he was actually a stronger proponent of the separation of church and state than his accusers.

Kennedy's second proclamation built upon the first. It expressed a belief "in an America that is officially neither Catholic, Protestant, nor Jewish—where no public official either requests or accepts instructions on public policy from the pope, the National Council of Churches, or any other ecclesiastical source—where no religious body seeks to impose its will directly or indirectly upon the general populace or the public acts of its officials." Here again, Kennedy proclaimed his belief in such a way that his accusers were placed on the defensive. His statement that the principle of separation was absolute would equally prohibit interference from the pope and from the Greater Houston Ministerial Association.

Kennedy supported an absolute separation of church and state by connecting his position to the principle of religious tolerance, and remonstrating against intolerance. He constructed an America "where religious liberty is so indivisible that an act against one church is treated as an act against all," and framed his plea for tolerance by drawing from the shared past of all Americans. While the current "finger of suspicion" was pointed at a Catholic, Kennedy warned, "in other years it has been, and may someday be again, a Jew—or a Quaker—or a Unitarian—or a Baptist." Extending his history lesson, Kennedy adapted his argument directly to his immediate audience, drawing upon one of the Founding Fathers in the process. "It was Virginia's harassment of Baptist preachers, for example, that helped lead to Jefferson's Statute of Religious Freedom. Today I may be the victim—but tomorrow it may be you—until the whole fabric of our harmonious society is ripped at a time of great national peril." As presented by Kennedy, the dangers of intolerance threaten more than religious practice; indeed the threat was to America as a whole. Because he did not make direct accusations, it was left to his audience to determine who was being intolerant of whom and where the real danger lay.

Kennedy's historical description and warnings of peril prepared the audience for his third and final principle; his belief in an America "where religious intolerance will someday end." This "tolerant" America was drawn equally along lines concerning religion ("where every man has the same right to attend the church of his choice"; "where Catholics, Protestants, and Jews . . . will refrain from those attitudes of disdain and division which have so often marred their works in the past, and promote instead the American ideal of brotherhood"), and politics ("where there is no Catholic vote, no anti-Catholic vote, no bloc voting of any kind").

Kennedy's description of the "kind of America in which I believe" was proffered as the basis for his concept of the presidency—"A great office that must neither be humbled by making it the instrument of any one religious group nor tarnished by arbitrarily withholding its occupancy from the members of any one religious group." In this vision, the president's religious views "are his own private affair, neither imposed by him upon the nation nor imposed by the nation upon him as a condition to holding that office."

Kennedy assured the audience that he would "not look with favor" upon any president "working to subvert the First Amendment's guarantees of religious liberty." But his pledge to maintain the Constitution's declaration of religious freedom was juxtaposed against his statement of concern regarding "those who would work to subvert Article VI of the Constitution by requiring a religious test—even by indirection—for public office. If they disagree with that safeguard, they should be out openly working to repeal it." Kennedy's labeling of Article VI as a "safeguard"—instead of merely a "provision"—offered a distinct moral challenge to the public pronouncements of the immediate audience.

This view of America was presented as more than just an election-inspired convenience. This was, indeed, the America "I fought for in the South Pacific, and the kind my brother died for in Europe." Against this backdrop of personal and familial sacrifice, Kennedy converted the concerns many in the audience harbored against him into grounds for self-reflection by declaring that no one had "suggested then that we might have a 'divided loyalty,' that we did 'not believe in liberty,' or that we belonged to a disloyal group that threatened the 'freedoms for which our forefathers died.'"

Having already assumed the role of interpreting the dynamics of the issues concerning the separation of church and state, Kennedy offered a history that reframed much of the argument contained in the statement of the National Conference. He told the audience that this was "the kind of America for which our forefathers did die—when they fled here to escape religious test oaths that denied office to members of less favored churches—when they fought for the Constitution, the Bill of Rights, the Virginia Statute of Religious Freedom— when they fought at the shrine I visited today, the Alamo. For side by side with Bowie and Crockett died Fuentes, and McCafferty and Bailey . . . and Carey— but no one knows whether they were Catholics or not. For there was no religious test there."[21]

Having defined the "American tradition" for his audience, Kennedy asked them to "follow in [it]," by judging him by his record and declared stands on issues, instead of by the often vitriolic anti-Catholic materials "we have all seen that carefully select quotations out of context from the statements of Catholic church leaders, usually in other countries, frequently in other centuries, and always omitting, of course, the statement of the American bishops in 1948 which strongly endorsed church-state separation, and which more nearly reflects the views of almost every American Catholic."

Kennedy declared that since he did not consider any statements by the Catholic church to be "binding upon my public acts," neither should anyone else. Indeed, "contrary to common newspaper usages," he was "not the Catholic candidate for President. I am the Democratic Party's candidate for President who happens also to be a Catholic. I do not speak for my church on public matters — and the Church does not speak for me." Arguing that his public views were independently derived, he refused to apologize to critics of either Catholic or Protestant heritage. All his decisions as president would be made "in accordance with these views, in accordance with what my conscience tells me to be the national interest, and without regard to outside religious pressures or dictates. And no power or threat of punishment could cause me to decide otherwise."

He then moved into what would be one of the most widely repeated sections of this speech. "But if the time should ever come—and I do not concede any conflict to be even remotely possible—when my office would require me to either violate my conscience or violate the national interest, then I would resign the office; and I hope any conscientious public servant would do the same."

Toward the closing, Kennedy reiterated his belief that there were "real issues" in this campaign, and that there was a danger posed by concentration on religion, which he labeled a "non-issue." If he should lose "on the real issues," he would "return to my seat in the Senate, satisfied that I had tried my best and was fairly judged. But if this election is decided on the basis that forty million Americans lost their chance of being President on the day they were baptized, then it is the whole nation that will be the loser, in the eyes of Catholics and non-Catholics around the world."

However, if he were to win the election, he would "devote every effort of mind and spirit to fulfilling the oath of the Presidency," an oath that was "practically identical" to "the oath I have taken for fourteen years in Congress." He then closed his prepared remarks by reciting the Presidential oath of office: "[W]ithout reservation, I can 'solemnly swear that I will faithfully execute the office of President of the United States, and will to the best of my ability, preserve, protect, and defend the Constitution . . . so help me God.'"

Kennedy was greeted with polite applause and "a barrage of questions, none of them wholly friendly," covering "the areas of Protestant concern over Catholic policy." He fielded these questions with an ease borne of having faced them many times before during the campaign. He became a bit testy over repeated questions on the Poling incident: "I have been in Congress 14 years. This took place in 1947. I had been in politics probably two months and was relatively inexperienced. Is this the best that can be done after 14 years? Is this the only incident that can be charged?" The retort received respectable applause from a once hostile group. In closing the question-and-answer session Kennedy seemed quite circumspect—and was even able to add a note of humor into this less structured part of the evening. He began: "I don't want anyone to think because they interrogate me on this important question, that I regard that as unfair questioning or unreasonable or somebody who is concerned about the matter is prejudiced or bigoted. I think this fight for religious freedom is basic in the establishment of the American system, and therefore any candidate for office should submit himself to the questions of any reasonable man." After receiving a round of applause for this statement, Kennedy reiterated a basic theme of the address: "My only objection would be . . . if somebody said: 'regardless of Senator Kennedy's position, regardless of how much evidence he has given that what he says he means, I still would not vote for him because he is a member of that church.' I would consider that unreasonable." Kennedy closed by saying, "I am grateful to you for inviting me tonight." And after a deft pause in comic timing added: "I am sure I have made no converts to my Church." After the laughter subsided, he humbly expressed the hope that his words were of "some value in assisting you to make a careful judgment."[22]

Immediate media reaction to this speech was predominantly positive, highlighting the major elements of Kennedy's message and offering praise for the views expressed by the Democratic candidate. A spokesperson for the Citizens for Religious Freedom was even quoted as saying that the speech was "the most complete, unequivocal and reassuring statement which could be expected of any person in [Kennedy's] position."[23]

Some coverage highlighted the confrontational nature of the meeting in Houston, using labels like "inquisition" to describe the atmosphere. For example, the *New York Times* noted that the speech "constituted an affirmation of [Kennedy's] belief in the separation of church and state" and lauded his effort to "meet the religious issue head on." The same article also noted that one part of Kennedy's speech had "struck at the group of Protestant clergyman, led by the Rev. Dr. Norman Vincent Peale," while another had "bore on a controversy with . . . Dr. Daniel Poling." *Time* observed that when Kennedy had completed his opening remarks, "the ministers applauded politely, then opened fire, often with complex questions."[24]

As David Halberstam pointed out, the confrontational nature of the event made the Kennedy organization's film of the drama a "staple of the campaign." According to a Houston advertising executive, it was "pure gold." "The film had what television loved, real drama, real confrontation, and there he was, a real live war hero, walking into the pit and winning."[25]

Kennedy's speech to the Houston Ministerial Association is often pointed to as one of the most dramatic events in the campaign. Its effect on the religious issue, which continued to command a great deal of media space during the race, can never be assessed. But if, indeed, the Simulatics report was accurate, Kennedy's performance in Houston may have done much to reframe the religious issue away from concerns over his Catholicism toward larger and more profound considerations of tolerance, and therefore may have had an effect on the final vote tally in November 1960.

KENNEDY'S INAUGURAL ADDRESS AS CAPSTONE OF THE 1960 CAMPAIGN

In the United States a presidential inauguration is a last vestige of earlier times when monarchs assumed the throne. In the modern American democracy, the ceremony, pomp and circumstance of ritual investiture is occasioned by the single Constitutional requirement that the president recite the 35-word oath of office. Everything else is extraneous to this demand. In a mass-mediated age, however, the attempt to "ritualize the majority voice" by summoning past virtues, celebrating a present peaceful transition of power, and auguring a common political future has global implications. Thus the linkage of the inaugural address to the oath of office serves as a profound prerequisite and first test of any modern rhetorical presidency.[26]

Inaugural addresses can be seen as both closing and opening statements. They are often efforts to heal any wounds brought on by a long divisive campaign. They attempt to bring closure by evoking unity and commonality through traditional values, which are employed as assurances of continuity. As opening statements, inaugural addresses set the basic themes for and outline the governing principles of the new administration; acknowledge the constraints and limitations of executive office as an expression of the president-elect's "worthiness"; and finally, as forms of epideictic address—ceremonial occasions for praise and blame—reinvigorate the compact between the people and their president by enacting communicative verbal and nonverbal symbols encouraging contemplation of the renewed covenant.[27]

Not many inaugural addresses have been memorable. Sparse in erudition and eloquence and marked by pedestrian goals, most efforts have foundered on the shoals of orotund political pedantry. John F. Kennedy's Inaugural Address was an exception. In trying to find out why, rhetorical scholars have focused, for the most part, on the stylistic devices and the imagery that helped Kennedy achieve eloquence.[28]

We are most interested in how Kennedy saw his task and in the constraints he perceived as impediments to reaching his goals as a speechmaker. Thus our investigation is concerned primarily with John F. Kennedy's use of rhetorical definition as a strategy for encompassing his particular situation. This focus necessitates a discussion of campaign themes and the election results, the role of the mass media in preparing audiences for the inaugural event, and, finally, the specific processes of speech construction that resulted in the final product. After touching on each of these issues, we will analyze the address, report on others' evaluations, and add our own interpretive conclusions.

CAMPAIGN THEMES AND ELECTION RESULTS

Kathleen Hall Jamieson has summarized the dominant concerns of the campaign as religion, experience, and competence. Approximately one month before the first of the "Great Debates," a public opinion report dated August 25, 1960, indicated that Kennedy's "personal image" was "somewhat more favorable" than Nixon's. Voting behavior was said to turn on three issues: "religion, party, and foreign affairs." Religion could be used to the candidate's advantage, party would provide his "greatest source of potential strength," and foreign policy was perceived as his "greatest weakness." Kennedy also was informed that domestic concerns were "cutting very little ice with voters," that he was "not doing well" among African-Americans, and that while at this point he was behind in the polls, a full "23% of the voters [we]re as yet undecided." The religion issue was largely defused at Houston in September. The negatives on foreign policy implicated Kennedy's youth and competence, perhaps a product of a relative lack of effectiveness in fourteen years of service in Congress and a perception early in the campaign that Kennedy might be "soft" on the Communists. Thus, Kennedy's ability to lead was still in question. Such issues affected Kennedy and his speechwriters.[29]

In an untitled report dealing with "the media side of campaigning," Kennedy was advised: "[P]robably the key starting point of a successful campaign is a basic theme that not only fits the needs of the campaign and the candidate, but ties in with the mood of the voting public." It continued: "[Y]ou need to try and think what the campaign is all about (something which many politicians never get around to). Then you have to find a theme to fit that need, a central idea around which you can build a flood of words and ideas that later will be inflicted upon the electorate. In other words, every minister preaches from a text—and every campaign if it is to be successful has to have a theme." Theodore Sorensen, in a "private and confidential" memo for speechwriters and television writers, indicated that the theme of all campaign speeches ought to constitute images of "action," "result," and "purpose," that is, "summoning every segment of our society. . . to restore America's relative strength as a free nation . . . in order to regain our security and leadership in a fast-changing world menaced by communism."[30]

The above directive was in perfect harmony with the sheer activity championed by the liberalism of the time. Kennedy was able to encapsulate his activist theme in his chief campaign slogan: "Let's get this country moving again!" This also provided a direct challenge to the Eisenhower administration, which seemingly had become as listless, tired, and rudderless as the national mood. The country seemed mired in its inability to form a vision, fashion a purpose, and implement a plan for a future that looked increasingly uncertain. Material abundance had led to an unwillingness to sacrifice for others. In short, the country felt itself in a political and moral vacuum. During the campaign, Kennedy had contributed to a *Life* magazine series on the subject of "national purpose," which was entitled "'We Must Climb to the Mountaintop.'" In this essay, Kennedy noted a "current widespread sense of staleness, of frustration," and "the gnawing feeling that we may have lost our way." This was attributed to a national "dynamism" that "wooed us from tough condition" and a decided lack of "leadership" at the highest levels. National renewal, the candidate assured readers, was a constant quest—a process of finding individual "purposefulness" in doing "our moral best" while "striving, risking, choosing, making decisions," and "engaging in a pursuit of happiness that is strenuous, heroic, exciting and exalted." Such a prescription seemed to provide a fitting antidote to the perceived malaise. It also fit extraordinarily well the carefully crafted Kennedy image of personal courage and vigor. The next president seemed to promise that he would add to his considerable duties the dual roles of national educator and moralist.[31]

Kennedy announced his official candidacy for the Democratic presidential nomination on January 2, 1960. He said: "The Presidency is the most powerful office in the Free World. Through its leadership can come a more vital life for our people. In it are centered the hopes of the globe around us for freedom and a more secure life." Toward the end of the announcement he focused on his thematic—and we believe a prophetic—core: "I have developed an image of America as fulfilling a noble and historic role as the defender of freedom in a time of maximum peril—and of the American people as confident, courageous and persevering. It is with this image that I begin this campaign." Adding vitality to the quality of life of "people" at home and abroad through the defense of freedom indeed became a common theme in Kennedy's rhetoric. During the campaign, Archibald Cox would memo the Senator: "When the question is asked: What is the most important issue in the campaign?—reply that the issue is 'people.' This evokes the explanation—or you can volunteer it—that you mean caring about the needs of people—the need for education—for old age assistance—for housing—for an end to discrimination. And abroad it means recognizing the aspirations of people, especially in the new countries." Cox felt that tack would build "enthusiasm."[32]

Meaningful public service on behalf of the "people" would require more effective leadership in the new decade: "The major issue of this campaign is which party offers our nation the imagination, the drive, the boldness and the leadership to meet the challenges of the sixties on which survival depends." In a speech to the Senate sixteen days after he declared his candidacy, Kennedy would characterize the presidency as "a center of moral leadership" as well as political influence. The "new generation of leadership" theme found a wide audience in Kennedy's Democratic Presidential Nomination Acceptance Address, where he outlined the contours of a "New Frontier," which would advance a morally superior political and social world—forsaking "promises" for "challenges." "It sums up not what I intend to offer the American people, but what I intend to ask of them. It appeals to their pride, not their pocketbook—it holds out the promise of more sacrifice instead of more security." A world racked by complex changes of revolutionary magnitude would present "new problems and new opportunities." It was especially incumbent upon the leader to restore the American "will" and "sense of historic purpose." Kennedy enacted his willingness to lead by isolating the challenges of perilous times. In Lincolnesque tones he implored: "We must prove all over again whether this nation—or any nation so conceived—can long endure—whether our society—with its freedom of choice, its breadth of opportunity, its range of alternatives—can compete with the single-minded advance of the Communist system. . . . Have we the nerve and the will?"[33]

The results of the national election left Kennedy in a relatively precarious position. The people's mandate had hardly been decisive. Receiving less than a majority of the popular vote, Kennedy's trump card had been in the electoral college. Sixty-four million people participated in the election, more than ever before. Kennedy received 49.7 to Nixon's 49.6 percent of the popular vote—a margin of 112,881 votes—a meager one-tenth of one percent between them. With an additional 32,500 votes split between Illinois and Texas, Kennedy could have lost the race to Nixon, who would have added these two states to his electoral college column. While Kennedy had predicted he would do well with the Catholic vote, he also made substantial gains with the African-American community. Importantly, however, he lost ground in the Deep South. Regardless of gains and losses, as Theodore White observed, the actual "margin of popular vote [wa]s so thin as to be, in all reality, nonexistent."[34]

MEDIATED EXPECTATIONS CONCERNING THE PRESIDENT-ELECT

Despite the shortcomings of the popular vote, expectations regarding the new president and his administration continued to mount. The mediated images in the 72 days between election and formal installation into office helped set the tone for the inaugural. There was a euphoria in press accounts that celebrated the Kennedy family and their "saga of success." A youthful image was reinforced with stories of the good Irish boy whose wealth, physical prowess, and interesting mix of idealism and realism set the stage for high expectations and anticipation of effective change. Even the Kennedy negatives were transformed in transition coverage. Kennedy's supposed political ruthlessness was now explained as "eagerness always to win . . . [and] fierce competitiveness and desire to achieve his goals." If experience and competence were at issue, Kennedy's new "Idea Men"—the so-called "practical eggheads" slated to run the new administration—would come to the rescue. Audiences were assured that the transition was going well. The president-elect had "recruited an impressive team" with both "balance and depth," conducted "systematic reviews of most of the major problems pressing on the nation," and was already using "the soothing Kennedy magic" to placate feisty and intransigent Congress members. All of this augured a kind of governance based upon "informed political consent."[35]

This is not to say that audiences were not apprised of some very daunting problems. On the home front, the president-elect was about to encounter a menacing conservative coalition in Congress, a recession, a "barely balanced" budget, a devalued dollar, a controversy over farm support programs, opposition to the proposed increase in the minimum wage, and demands that he make good on his promise to unions to "strike down" right-to-work laws. In addition, Kennedy would have to concentrate on rebuilding the infrastructure of

American cities, restoring public housing, increasing health and social security benefits for the elderly, and the growing unrest over civil rights. Abroad, Kennedy would be asked to face a growing Soviet threat, a purported "missile gap," concerns over Cuba, the Congo, and Southeast Asia, as well as deliver on his promise to create a "Peace Corps." He would also be expected to strengthen alliances with and within OAS, NATO, and the UN.[36]

By inauguration time, prior mediated predictions of a "thousand days of action" were being modified. On the domestic front, "Sweeping changes [we]re not to be blasted through Congress." The reason: "Kennedy ha[d] trimmed his legislative sail to suit election returns." The Southern Democratic-Republican bloc was now viewed as a serious obstacle to domestic change. In the foreign policy arena, "the legacy that Mr. Eisenhower passe[d] to Mr. Kennedy [wa]s studded with crises and dilemmas." "[T]he young new President—and the U.S.—[faced] a time of great challenge." The news was sobering. The newly elected president seemed "aged by the imminence of grave responsibility" and his "brashness" was said to have been replaced by "a new seriousness, a palpable sense of the awesomeness of his position."[37]

Still, as press reports on the inaugural preparations were to emphasize, there remained a Dickensian sense of "Great Expectations." Kennedy would attend all five simultaneous inaugural balls, the inaugural concert, and a five-hour-long parade in frigid temperatures. Each of these galas promised to be studded with politicos, literati—even artists and entertainers—all the priests and priestesses of both high and low culture that Washington, New York, and Hollywood could provide. Whether anticipating the highly styled Inaugural Parade along Pennsylvania Avenue or parading the latest in chic coiffures and fashions, the promise of a new savoir-faire and high elegance filled the air with an enthusiasm that had not decorated Washington environs in a singularly long time. In early January, *Time* magazine would capture the tenor of the times: "The mood of expectancy swept through Washington. It lurked in the crowded corridors of the Capitol Building, where returning Congressmen jostled painters touching up Brumidi frescoes. . . . Along Pennsylvania Avenue, workmen rushed new tiers of spectator stands for [the] inaugural parade, and the request for tickets reached blizzard stage." To protect the spectators, workers were found "spraying the trees with a bird repellent" to fend off gifts from Washington's "plague of starlings." The Capitol buildings "gleamed after a scrubdown" and, while there seemed to be "warrens of chaos" almost everywhere in the bustle to make preparations, Americans could take pride in the fact that the Capitol Dome itself had just received "a dazzling, million-dollar facial." The theme of transformation and renewal had been enacted in the material as well as spiritual wellsprings of the nation. It remained to be seen whether or not this cosmetic surgery would last.[38]

CONSTRUCTING THE INAUGURAL SPEECH

In a bloc wire dated December 23, 1960, Theodore Sorensen requested suggestions for the Inaugural Address from Allen Nevins, Douglas Dillon, Arthur Goldberg, David Lloyd, Adlai Stevenson, Joseph Kraft, Dean Rusk, John Kenneth Galbraith, Chester Bowles and Fred Dutton. The wire also had the names [Myer] "Feldman" and [Richard N.] "Goodwin" hand-written in the left margin. There is evidence to suggest that these two also contributed ideas that Sorensen would coordinate with the president-elect to fashion a final reading text.[39]

Stevenson responded with comments limited to foreign affairs. He made eleven major suggestions. Those numbered (9) and (11) were crossed out—apparently the work of some other adviser in the Kennedy camp. The deleted passages included advice to announce to the world that we would "liquidate overseas military bases as fast as progress towards disarmament makes this possible" and "perhaps" provide "a conditioned hint of reexamination of our China policy to advance controlled disarmament and reduce the danger of war in Asia." Suggestions that were not crossed out included the following: (1) "A frank acknowledgement of the changing equilibrium in the world and the grave dangers and difficulties which the West faces for the first time"; (2) "The assertion that our objective is peace" and a desire "to end, not prolong the cold war"; (3) "An unequivocal commitment to disarmament"; (4) "Recognition that the first order of business is to halt the proliferation of nuclear powers and to reduce the ever-growing danger of war by accident"; (5) "An unequivocal commitment to the western defensive alliance to deter aggression and keep the peace"; (6) a call for "world-wide cooperation on the part of industrialized nations toward lifting the living standards of the underprivileged," with the understanding that as long as the Communists wished to "compete" in this arena that the industrialized nations would mount "a multilateral cooperative effort to win the non-military cold war"; (7) "Recognition of a special U.S. responsibility for Latin America"; (8) "A disavowal of the Republican proposal to reduce economic aid and a pledge to increase it . . . provided other industrialized nations do their share (especially Germany)"; (10) Eagerness to reduce tensions in the "hot spot areas (Germany, the Taiwan Strait, the Middle East, Congo, Cuba, Laos)." Finally, Stevenson wrote: "The main thing of course is to create the impression of new, bold, imaginative, purposeful leadership; to de-emphasize the bi-polar power struggle; and to emphasize the affirmative approaches to peace. (In this connection, what about a proposal to put all space exploration under UN control?)" We have quoted at length from this document not only because it seems important to history but also because it establishes some key themes that were indeed taken up in the final version of the inaugural speech.[40]

Piecing together the exact contributions of the other solicited contributors is difficult, at best. A few things can be said with more or less certainty—each of which will highlight the tenuous if not thankless task of crafting a ghosted speech for a chief executive. Douglas Dillon sent his contributions with the understanding from the president-elect that problems having to do with the Treasury Department might receive "more complete treatment in either the State of the Union Message or in a separate message to follow the Inaugural." Allen Nevins would write Sorensen: "Of course Mr. Kennedy can write any one of fifty different addresses, and I do not know on what lines his mind has been running. But here is a suggestion of one particular tone and set of ideas that seems to me practicable. I have given it so much work that I hope you will read it carefully. If it does so much as to point in any useful direction I shall feel immensely pleased." Joseph Kraft remarked, "I did do a draft of the Inaugural at Ted's . . . request, some of which got used, but all of which got transformed." Such is the tortured, byzantine alchemy of professional wordsmithing for a modern presidency.[41]

No less taxing is the chore of tracking down the evolution of key phrases and memorable slogans. The most memorable of the new president's eloquent phrasings relied upon rhetorical antithesis: "[A]sk not what your country can do for you—ask what you can do for your country." Kathleen Hall Jamieson has observed how eloquence is often a process of reworking a phrase so that it becomes both distinctive and memorable. Great presidential orators summon collective memory to effect a contemplative mood. Campbell and Jamieson have noted that the "ask not" phrase may have been a product of Kennedy's prep school days at Choate where headmaster Rev. George St. John reportedly advised: "Ask not what your school can do for you; ask what you can do for your school." Arthur Schlesinger, Jr. maintains seeds for the idea that led to the line can be traced to a quotation from Rousseau, which Kennedy had placed in a looseleaf binder circa 1945: "As soon as any man says of the affairs of the state, What does it matter to me? the state may be given up as lost." Interestingly, while Schlesinger maintains that the line was "clearly Kennedy's own," he also cites "historic analogues." For example, in 1884 Oliver Wendell Holmes delivered a Memorial Day address that included the following words: "It is now the moment when by common consent we pause to become conscious of our national life and to rejoice in it, to recall what our country has done for each of us, and to ask ourselves what we can do for our country in return."[42]

Regardless of origins, the contemporary reworking of the phrase is clear. Kennedy had used weaker forms of the "ask not" line during campaign stops in Anchorage, Detroit, and Washington, D.C., and in the nomination acceptance address. For example, in the Washington, D.C. address, televised on September 20, 1960, Kennedy remarked: "We do not campaign stressing what our country is going to do for us as a people. We stress what we can do for the country, all of us." All of this suggests that the evolution of this memorable phrase was no accident. It was the product of time, reflective nuance, and accretion of experience with audiences. The process mirrored the care with which the entire inaugural was honed. Indeed, as Sorensen has noted, "No Kennedy speech ever underwent so many drafts. Each paragraph was reworded, reworked and reduced."[43]

Finally, we note that John Kenneth Galbraith was said to have contributed the famous antithesis: "Let us never negotiate out of fear, but let us never fear to negotiate." Even specific words became products of others' suggestions. For example, Galbraith also substituted the term "cooperative ventures" for "joint ventures" with allies in an attempt to reinforce new administration themes and avoid sounding "like a mining partnership." In an attempt to transcend "the cliches of the cold war," relying upon the advice of the columnist Walter Lippmann, Kennedy would replace the word "enemy" in the address with the word "adversary," which connoted both the changed circumstance of the generational transfer of power as well as a new philosophical approach to Cold War relations—"competition" rather than "confrontation." Kennedy would "employ" the term "adversary" "for the rest of his life." Taking his cue from an earlier campaign speech, the President himself would insert "a new alliance for progress" in his references to Latin America.[44]

As Sorensen collected the contributions from various sources, he kept in mind the basic campaign themes and the precedents of past inaugurals. In fact, the president-elect had instructed him to read all past inaugural addresses as well as try to account for the effectiveness of Lincoln's Gettysburg Address. He found the latter distinguished by an economy of words that lent the speech eloquence. Under this influence, Sorensen set about condensing two and three syllable words in his drafts to one syllable wherever possible. He reports Kennedy was "dissatisfied with each attempt to outline domestic goals." Moreover, Kennedy wanted to tell his audiences that what he was contemplating for his presidency would not "be finished in a hundred days or a thousand." Kennedy also wanted all the "I" pronouns in the speech changed to "we." Most importantly, he finally told Sorensen, "Let's drop out the domestic stuff altogether. It's too long anyway." Kennedy wanted his inaugural to be brief, which had the effect of distinguishing it from its predecessors in that such brevity had been reserved traditionally for second inaugural addresses.[45]

Despite the generous gifts of ghosts, Sorensen maintains that the "principal architect" of the Inaugural Address was Kennedy himself. Indeed, if anything, over the years Sorensen has become even more adamant about this claim: "John Kennedy was the true author of all of his speeches and writings. They set forth his ideas and ideals, his decisions and policies, his knowledge of history and politics." And while he employed speechwriters and appreciated their efforts, "he alone was responsible for the decision that lay at the heart of every major speech." While it is certainly the case that Kennedy edited and collaborated on his public address, outlining topics, requesting specific materials and, less frequently, serving as his own main speechwriter, even a cursory examination of most of his important prepared speeches reveals the steady, guiding hand of

Theodore Sorensen. However, if the responsibility for one's words resides with the speaker, then there is some argument for saddling Kennedy, just as we do other presidents, with both the "burden and the glory" of words written by a committee of speechwriters.[46]

KENNEDY'S INAUGURAL ADDRESS

The presidency itself was about to experience a "contrast" in "old and new" that had not been equalled since the inaugural of Theodore Roosevelt—who followed seven presidents of military age at the start of the Civil War. Kennedy was the first person elected to the presidency who had been born in the twentieth century. He rightly laid claim on a generational divide between himself and other elder statesmen in the world—Eisenhower, Adenauer, De Gaulle, MacMillan, Mao Tse-tung—each of whom was now past the age of sixty-five. But as a man schooled in the Cold War tradition, he was not unlike his elders in his outlook on foreign policy.[47]

Since foreign policy would take up the bulk of his address, it is necessary to outline the particular concerns Kennedy seemed to have in mind. On January 6, 1961, Nikita Khrushchev delivered a speech at the Kremlin that outlined a worldwide retreat of capitalism and simultaneous revolutionary socialist gains, especially in the Third World. The speech seemed to commit Communists to "wars of national liberation," which would establish dominant Soviet satellites through global struggle. Moreover, Khrushchev proclaimed the Soviets had outdistanced the United States in ICBMs. A condensed version of Khrushchev's speech arrived two days before the inauguration. While Eisenhower seemed unmoved by the characteristic bluster, Kennedy became agitated and alarmed. Both timing and content seemed to pose a direct challenge to the new president.[48]

As Sorensen makes clear and as our reading suggests, the purpose of Kennedy's Inaugural Address was fourfold: (1) to combat lingering campaign perceptions of inexperience, (2) to provide a U.S. answer to the Soviet's "revolutionary" challenge, (3) to speak to a variety of audiences with a clear and compelling voice—including the American public, the "free" and "emerging" nations of the world, and the Soviets who would be asked to choose between "cooperation and confrontation" (or as Kennedy put it—to address "friends and foes" alike), and finally (4) to achieve eloquence.[49]

Kennedy faced formidable odds in weaving the above goals with the generic requirements of the address. Those requirements included healing the wounds of the campaign, giving assurances of continuity, outlining basic themes and principles that would govern the new administration, acknowledging the constraints and limitations of office, and finally, reinvigorating the compact between the people and their government. These generic requirements will provide a framework for our analysis of how Kennedy defined and met his specific goals.[50]

On his way to one of the inaugural galas, Kennedy was perusing the program for the Inaugural Concert held at Constitution Hall. It contained a reprint of Jefferson's First Inaugural. Upon finishing the address, Kennedy would smile wryly and remark to his friend William Walton: "Better than mine." The night before the inauguration, a heavy snow blanketed the Capitol, snarling traffic and heating tempers in an already overloaded city. The next day the ceremonies would begin in cool, 20 degree temperatures. Kennedy characteristically refused to wear a topcoat to deliver his address; this act reinforced his youthful image. (Always a master at political symbols, he had already replaced the traditional obligatory homburgs designated for formal events with the more debonair tophats as a signal of generational change). At the stage area Kennedy would sit through an "interminable invocation" by Richard Cardinal Cushing and a recitation by Robert Frost, who, a bit frightened and unable to see from the glare, fumbled at reading his planned dedication; finally, he stopped—and recited "The Gift Outright"—a poem he had long committed to memory. The elderly poet was yet another symbol that a torch was being passed to the next generation—"tempered by war, disciplined by a hard and bitter peace," and "proud" of their "ancient heritage." Chief Justice Earl Warren administered the somber 35-word oath that would transform the 43-year-old Kennedy from Senator to President.

Kennedy rested his left hand on the podium and—unseen by the assemblage and prying television cameras—kept his right hand in his right pocket. Throughout the speech he would use his famous staccato phrasing and deliver key lines by bringing his right hand up from his pocket to gesture just above the podium—at times using a half circle motion, at others pointing a jutting forefinger toward the crowd. He used the left hand throughout the speech to control the large-type manuscript from which he read. He began with the obligatory: "Vice-President Johnson, Mr. Speaker, Mr. Chief Justice, President Eisenhower, Vice-President Nixon, President Truman, Reverend Clergy, Fellow Citizens . . . ."[51]

Healing and Continuity. Kennedy spent very little time trying to heal any lingering divisiveness stemming from the campaign. "We observe today not a victory of party but a celebration of freedom." Here the antithesis introduced both a transcendent appeal to unity and the key theme: preserving liberty. Continuity was achieved through contemplative observation of the meaning of the events: this after all was a process "symbolizing an end as well as a beginning—signifying renewal as well as change." But this change was not new nor was it to be feared: "I have sworn before you and Almighty God the same solemn oath our forebears prescribed nearly a century and three quarters ago." Moreover, his remembrance included the acknowledgment that "the same revolutionary beliefs for which our forebears fought are still at issue around the globe" and today "we are the heirs of that first revolution." Not only is continuity preserved here but the audience is being prepared for a U.S. definition of the word "revolution," which will be held out as the alternative to the Communist "revolutionary" aspirations and goals.

This revolution, Kennedy observed, would center upon protecting human rights "at home and around the world." Therefore, as in the past, "Let every nation know, whether it wishes us well or ill, that we shall pay any price, bear any burden, meet any hardship, support any friend, oppose any foe to assure the survival and success of liberty." The elegant parallelism also enacted "leadership through strength." "In the long history of the world, only a few generations have been given the role of defending freedom in its hour of maximum danger. I do not shrink from this responsibility—I welcome it." The tough hyperbole invited the audience to measure the commitment of the new man at the helm and was intended to vanquish charges of "softness."

Another sense of continuity was achieved through renewal of commitments: "To those old allies whose cultural and spiritual origins we share, we pledge the loyalty of faithful friends" and "cooperative ventures"; "To that world assembly of sovereign states, the United Nations, our last best hope in an age where the instruments of war have far out-paced the instruments of peace, we renew our pledge of support." Yet along with continuity there would be change.

Governing Principles. The new administration's policies would be advanced through a focus on regional hot spots around the world. Here, Kennedy outlined what appeared to be a fresh approach. The changes to be wrought by his administration were premised upon and promised a different ideology. Our analysis suggests that there was a marked ambivalence in these foreign policy discussions. In seeking to strike a balance between confrontation and conciliation, Kennedy seemed to be overly bellicose. At the time, however, he was interpreted as evenhanded. Many of the issues suggested by Stevenson were incorporated into the speech and this, we believe, actually helped keep the address from being even more warlike.

In addressing newly emergent nations where competition with the Soviets was fierce, Kennedy issued a cautious warning: "To those new states whom we welcome to the ranks of the free, we pledge our word that one form of colonial control shall not have passed away merely to be replaced by a far more iron tyranny. We shall not always expect to find them supporting our view. But we shall always hope to find them strongly supporting their own freedom" by "remember[ing] that, in the past, those who foolishly sought power by riding the back of the tiger ended up inside." The metaphors had been honed over time and their simplicity was striking. The Communist menace was an "iron tyranny" summoning images of Soviet tanks in Hungary in 1956. Emerging nations who would truck with this menace risked their national sovereignty—being "eaten up" by the "tiger"—a metaphor the world community could well understand.

There also was a pledge of "our best efforts" to help the poverty stricken masses "in the huts and villages of half the globe" "not because the communists may be doing it . . . but because it is right. If a free society cannot help the many who are poor, it cannot save the few who are rich." Toward Latin America, Kennedy issued a "special pledge," a "new alliance for progress" in an effort to "assist free men and free governments in casting off the chains of poverty" through a "peaceful revolution of hope." Yet there was ambivalence: The revolution "cannot become the prey of hostile powers. Let all our neighbors know that we shall join with them to oppose aggression or subversion anywhere in the Americas." This was followed by a blatant threat to the Soviets regarding Cuba: "And let every other power know that this Hemisphere intends to remain the master of its own house." In speaking for the "Hemisphere," Kennedy sounded a customary note of U.S. imperialism and hegemony attending Cold War doctrine and discourse.

Kennedy reserved nine paragraphs for "those nations who would make themselves our adversaries." To those nations he would "offer not a pledge but a request: that both sides begin anew the quest for peace." But the peace would be won through strength. On the one hand, he assured his U.S. audience and the allies that he would not "tempt" the Sino-Soviet bloc with "weakness": "For only when our arms are sufficient beyond doubt can we be certain beyond doubt that they will never be employed." On the other hand, he said: "But neither can two great and powerful groups of nations take comfort from our present course"— where the cost of modern weaponry, the spread of atomic weapons, and the "uncertain balance of terror that stays the hand of mankind's final war" all conspire against a peaceful future.

These circumstances, explained the new president, require new plans, programs, and relationships. "So let us begin anew—remembering on both sides that civility is not a sign of weakness, and sincerity is always subject to proof. Let us never negotiate out of fear. But let us never fear to negotiate." Here the new chief executive seemed open, moderate, reasonable, and circumspect. The negative campaign images of youth—impulsiveness and inexperience—seemed somehow diminished by the reasoning of the argument and by the antithetical phrasing, which echoed a capacity for leadership—knowing what to do and how to do it.

Using the parallel phrase "Let both sides," "explore," "formulate," "invoke," "heed," Kennedy embodied Sorensen's earlier campaign call for discursive display of action, purpose and resolve through public address. In this section of the address, Kennedy not only continued to sound the key foreign policy notes Stevenson suggested but expanded their range: a spirit of cooperation, a call for arms inspection and control, and joint ventures in science, technology, the arts, and commerce. This is expressed metaphorically in the president's desire that "a beachhead of cooperation may push back the jungle of suspicion."

Constraints and Renewal. Kennedy also expressed his dependence on the American people. Acknowledging the limits of his proposals and the constraints of the executive office, Kennedy predicted: "All of this will not be finished in the first one hundred days. Nor will it be finished in the first one thousand days, nor in the life of this Administration, nor even perhaps in our lifetime on this planet. But let us begin." Moreover, the ultimate achievement would be that of the people rather than their leader: "In your hands, my fellow citizens, more than mine, will rest the final success or failure of our course." This fulfilled a normative expectation in inaugural address; the new president must express humility in his investiture. He must lead but he must always keep in mind those he serves and he must express an understanding of exactly from where his mandate and powers derive. He heads a government and rules a nation of, by, and for "the people."

In ritually placing his faith in and deriving his powers from the people, the president rekindled symbolically the interdependent relationship between governor and governed in a participatory democracy. In this renewal of the covenant, the reparation of the social contract between the president and the people can be expressed in many ways. Kennedy asked the people to revalue what he had found in their tradition—to find courage, strength, and conviction through selflessness and personal sacrifice on behalf of a larger national purpose that encompassed the wider community of nations. It was this idealism that proved so attractive in his reformulation of the traditional compact: "The energy, the faith, the devotion which we bring to this endeavor will light our country and all who serve it — and the glow from that fire can truly light the world." Pointing the index finger of his right hand toward the crowd, Kennedy would pose his most famous counsel: "And so, my fellow Americans: ask not what your country can do for you—ask what you can do for your country." "My fellow citizens of the world: ask not what America will do for you, but what together we can do for the freedom of man." The eloquence of the antitheses was made more powerful by the audience's enthymemic participation in the hope that what was expressed was not just an inspired way to discuss problems but rather a wise, broad-based insight into national and international solutions.

People within the nation and without were instructed to hold the new administration accountable—another sign of effective leadership: "[A]sk of us here the same high standards of strength and sacrifice which we ask of you." Kennedy uttered the magic alchemy of speech. He "Let the Word go Forth," that the "torch ha[d] been passed to a new generation of leadership." In the triumph of the short-lived moment between promise and performance, the themes of renewal and change reassured rather than alarmed. Kennedy addressed a nation that wanted to believe again; he found the right tone and doctrine—and placed this latest version at the altar where priest and people celebrate the magnificent grandiloquence of politics as national religion.

In closing, Kennedy stressed the moral nature of his new leadership and his dependence on historical circumstance. And bowing gloriously to his and the nation's newfound fate—in perhaps the preeminent public demonstration of humility employed by an American president—gave the obligatory expression of his dependence upon a higher power. As the first Catholic ever to attain the presidency of the United States, that obligation took on added meaning. Kennedy had once again asked all Americans to help him "get this country moving again":

"With a good conscience our only sure reward, with history the final judge of our deeds, let us go forth to lead the land we love, asking His blessing and His help, but knowing that here on earth God's work must truly be our own."

Immediate reaction to the speech both in the United States and abroad was overwhelmingly positive. As critical biographer Thomas C. Reeves noted, "The address won praise from foreign diplomats, politicians of both parties, editorialists, and the public at large." Even Khrushchev, who, of course, had been a major target of the address, saw "constructive things in the speech" and ordered the Soviet newspapers to "print the full text." The print-mediated praise mirrored a speech that had generated high expectations. As *New York Times* columnist James Reston observed, "Like all true expressions of the American ideal, this was a revolutionary document" that provided an impetus to "begin transforming our national life" and our international "relations." At the time, it seemed as if Kennedy was advocating a Pax Americana, if not an American Century—and if it was heady, it was not unnatural: "[T]his speech carries us back a century and more to a time when our predecessors on this continent thought of American democracy as something that would by its very virtues and allurements sweep the earth."[52]

According to David Burner and Thomas R. West, the inaugural "set the tone for a presidential administration as few such addresses have ever done." These authors observed that the sometimes chilly and at once solemn appeals to freedom and peace were "curious" because the "moment . . . was no grimmer than any other in the era of the cold war." We believe that this mystery is solved if one understands that Kennedy felt the need to rally the forces on foreign policy issues because it was easier than dealing with divisive domestic concerns. The emphasis on foreign policy suited Kennedy's temperament and political predicament. The thin margin of victory would require mass arousal to focus cohesiveness. Isolating foreign adversaries who pose challenges is a time-honored method of courting public favor—in the United States, if not with the allies. While the word "crisis" never appears, such a situation is certainly implied in this address. As Murray Edelman notes, "A domestic or foreign crisis is invaluable in maintaining the leader's symbolic appeal." However, in avoiding almost any mention of domestic affairs—save the small carrot thrown out to civil rights advocates who were thrilled to hear that human rights was a proper question "at home and around the world"—we believe Kennedy shirked a bit of his duty.[53]

While we are not advocating that he should have presented a full-blown domestic policy speech on an epideictic occasion, the daunting domestic problems that the country faced at that time did seem to deserve at least general symbolic treatment. Kennedy forces, perhaps rightly, reasoned that without the prior identification with foreign policy, audiences and constituencies important for domestic affairs would turn a deaf ear. The idea seemed to be that in the opening rounds, it is best to lead with your strongest jab. Interestingly, one might also take what appears at first glance to be an opposite viewpoint. Since Kennedy was perceived in the campaign as untested and perhaps weak in the foreign policy arena, he made the decision to take the issue on directly. In this he appears to have been successful. Only by first dispensing with the perceived softness on this issue could he hope to make inroads on domestic policy. Whatever the case, and however correct his political instincts might have been, it would soon become clear that for all his moralistic pledges and prescriptions, he intentionally placed the nation's most divisive domestic issue—civil rights—on the back burner.

CONCLUSION

At Houston, Kennedy met the most formidable challenge to his election by going on the offensive concerning the religious question. In so doing, the candidate demonstrated a cool, confident courage and reinforced an image of reasonableness and rationality. In displaying these traits, of course, Kennedy also played into the public's desire to feel that he was both competent and levelheaded. Thus, even at Houston in defusing the religion question, Kennedy also had defused the larger question of his youth and inexperience.

We agree with Allen J. Matusow's view that Kennedy's inaugural address was his best campaign speech. Tailored to assuage lingering concerns regarding his youth, inexperience and competence, it triumphantly closed the campaign and opened his presidency—requisite functions of all inaugural addresses. His rhetoric ambivalent, at times teetering between grandiose bombast and highly styled eloquence, Kennedy's inaugural address both met and created the high expectations of the time—pushing them to an apogee that probably could never have been fulfilled by mere mortals.[54]

NOTES

1. For interesting and useful studies on both speeches see David Henry, "Senator John F. Kennedy Encounters the Religious Question: 'I Am Not the Catholic Candidate for President,'" in *Oratorical Encounters: Selected Studies and Sources of Twentieth-Century Political Accusations and Apologies*, ed. Halford Ross Ryan (New York: Greenwood Press, 1988), pp. 153-173, and Theodore Otto Windt, Jr., "President John F. Kennedy's Inaugural Address, 1961," in *The Inaugural Addresses of Twentieth Century American Presidents*, ed. Halford R. Ryan (Westport, Conn.: Praeger, 1993), 181-193.

2. Jamieson echoed a similar observation when she maintained that concern for a candidate's Catholicism had been relegated to "marginal status at the fringe of the American political system." See Kathleen Hall Jamieson, *Dirty Politics: Deception, Distraction and Democracy* (New York: Oxford University Press, 1992), 72; "Campaign '60: 43 Days Before Election Day," *Newsweek*, September 26, 1960, 41. Kennedy was not, of course, the first Catholic to run for president as the nominee of a major party. New

York Governor Al Smith was soundly defeated by Hoover in 1928, and it was an axiom of American politics that Hoover's victory was in large measure attributable to Smith's Catholicism. For further discussion on Kennedy see Theodore C. Sorensen, *The Kennedy Legacy* (New York: Macmillan, 1969), esp. pp. 64-67.

3. Sorensen, *Legacy*; Jamieson, *Dirty Politics*, 142.

4. "Campaign '60: 43 Days Before Election Day," 41; Marquis Childs, "Kennedy's View of Church Issue," *Washington Post*, September 14, 1960, A20; "The Issue That Just Won't Die," *Newsweek*, September 12, 1960, 61; "Campaign '60: 43 Days Before Election Day," 42; "The Issue That Just Won't Die," 62; "Sticky Issue," *Newsweek*, October 31, 1960, 21.

5. Patricia Barrett, *Religious Liberty and the American Presidency: A Study in Church-State Relations* (New York: Herder and Herder, 1963), 33; and see Kathleen Hall Jamieson, *Packaging the Presidency: A History and Criticism of Presidential Campaign Advertising* (New York and Oxford: Oxford University Press, 1984), 128.

6. Theodore C. Sorensen, *Kennedy* (New York: Harper and Row, 1965), 110.

7. Sorensen, *Kennedy*, 137; "The Tilt Toward Kennedy," *Newsweek*, April 18, 1960, 14; "Politics: The Catholic Issue," *Time*, April 18, 1960, 16.

8. Sorensen, *Kennedy*, 110.

9. Memorandum on the Religious Issue from Theodore C. Sorensen, August 15, 1960, Theodore C. Sorensen Papers, Campaign Files 1959-1960, Religious Issue, Campaign Materials, Box 25, JFK Library; "The Campaign: The Power of Negative Thinking," *Time*, September 19, 1960, 21.

10. The text for both statements is taken from "Protestant Groups' Statements," *New York Times*, September 8, 1960, 25.

11. Julius Duscha, "Jackson Asks for Help in Tracing Source of Anti-Catholic Material," *Washington Post*, September 15, 1960, A2.

12. Duscha, "Jackson Asks," A2. When informed of Peale's statement, Kennedy said he preferred to think of it as a compliment. The secretive nature of the meeting was maintained even after the release of the conference's public statement. Donald Gill, the executive director of the Conference, "repeatedly refused requests from reporters for the names of the persons who drafted the statement as well as the names of the 150 persons who attended the meeting." "The Campaign: The Power of Negative Thinking," 21.

13. As evidence for this observation the National Conference statement cited a situation in Ohio—"a state with a Roman Catholic Governor"—as an example where Catholics had "seized control of the public schools [and] staffed them with nun teachers wearing their church garb." *Time* magazine pointed out that the Ohio situation was the result of a 1958 decision by the Ohio attorney general during the administration of Protestant Governor C. William O'Neill. As part of an effort to "ease a grave teacher shortage," Ohio attorney general William B. Saxbe ruled that the public schools could continue the forty-year practice of hiring nuns and allowing them to wear habits in class. Ohio's Catholic governor, Mike DiSalle, demanded a personal apology from Peale. "The Campaign: The Power of Negative Thinking," 21.

14. This final point was seen by many as relating to an incident in 1951 when Kennedy withdrew as a speaker at a fund-raising dinner in Philadelphia. The event was scheduled to raise funds for an interfaith chapel that would be dedicated to four Army chaplains who died in 1943 on the transport Dorchester. One of the deceased was Daniel Poling's son, Lieutenant Clark Poling. Kennedy had accepted the invitation but backed

out when he learned he was invited "as the spokesman for the Catholic Faith." As *Time* magazine reported, "Poling has never forgiven Kennedy—and he has never let Protestants forget the incident." "The Campaign: The Power of Negative Thinking," 21.

15. Hermann G. Stelzner, "John F. Kennedy at Houston, Texas, September 12, 1960," in *Rhetoric and Communication: Studies in the University of Illinois Tradition* ed. Jane Blankenship and Hermann G. Stelzner (Urbana: University of Illinois Press, 1976), 225-226; Berton Dulce and Edward J. Richter, *Religion and the Presidency: A Recurring American Problem* (New York: MacMillan, 1962), 194.

16. David Halberstam, *The Powers That Be* (New York: Dell Publishing, 1979), 457.

17. Kenneth O'Donnell Oral History, Interview One, with Paige E. Mulhollan, July 23, 1969, JFK Library. And see Robert C. Albright, "Kennedy Affirms Stand on Religion to Texas Pastors, Senator Pledges Separation of Church and State," *Washington Post*, September 13, 1960, A16. According to O'Donnell, Kennedy made up his mind while preparing for a speech one evening. "Tell them I'm going to do it," the candidate told O'Donnell. "This is as good a time as any to get it over with. I've got to face it sooner or later." Kenneth P. O'Donnell, David F. Powers, and Joe McCarthy, *"Johnny We Hardly Knew Ye": Memories of John Fitzgerald Kennedy* (Boston: Little Brown, 1970), 207.

18. Halberstam, *The Powers*, 457. Roderick P. Hart observes that "in any speaking situation a metastatement is made. That statement is the product of who has agreed to speak and who has agreed to listen, what they have decided to discuss, for how long, and within what set of procedural constraints. In the political arena, decisions often turn on this sociology of persuasion . . . as when John Kennedy faced the Houston ministers to address the religion issue during his 1960 presidential campaign." Roderick P. Hart, *The Sound of Leadership: Presidential Communication in the Modern Age* (Chicago: University of Chicago Press, 1987), 61; Alvin Spivak, "Kennedy Asks Faith Talk End," *Washington Post*, September 12, 1960, A2; James Reston, "Dallas: Economic and Religious Coalition in Texas," Editorial, *New York Times*, September 14, 1960, A42; "Test of Religion," *Time*, September 26, 1960, 21-22; *Houston Chronicle*, cited in Dulce and Richter, *Religion*, 182-183.

19. The candidate also was informed by Bishop John Wright of Pittsburgh that "contrary to public belief, no public act of a President [could possibly] lead to his excommunication," "and that he, as a Catholic, had not sworn allegiance to the Pope." Sorensen, *Kennedy*, 175; Lawrence H. Fuchs, *John F. Kennedy and American Catholicism* (New York: Meredith Press, 1967), 180.

20. Sorensen, *Kennedy*, 190-191; quotation, 190. The Houston speech that follows is taken from "John F. Kennedy, Speech to Greater Houston Ministerial Association, September 12, 1960, Delivery Copy," JFK Pre-Presidential Papers, Senate Files, Speech Files, Rice Hotel, Houston Texas, September 12, 1960, Box 911, JFK Library. Reprinted in the "Collected Speeches" section of this volume.

21. This line in the speech reportedly originated when Kennedy spoke in San Antonio on the way to Houston. He had wanted to know how many Catholics had died defending the Alamo. A search by campaign workers produced several Irish names among the dead Texans, but nothing concerning their religion. As Stelzner pointed out, the use of the term "shrine" to describe the Alamo probably identified Kennedy with his Texas audience, both those in the room and those watching the proceedings via the state-wide television broadcast. See Stelzner, "JFK at Houston," 230-231.

22. Sorensen, *Kennedy*, 191; Theodore H. White, *The Making of the President, 1960* (New York: Atheneum, 1962), 261; "Remarks of Senator John F. Kennedy, Question and Answer Period, Ministerial Association of Greater Houston, September 13, 1960," JFK Pre-Presidential Papers, Senate Files, Speech Files, Greater Houston Ministerial Association, Rice Hotel. Houston, Texas, September 12, 1960, Box 911, JFK Library; and see, e.g., Albright, "Kennedy Affirms."

23. Peter Braestrup, "Protestant Group Applauds Kennedy for Houston Speech," *New York Times*, September 14, 1960, A33.

24. W. H. Lawrence, "Kennedy Assures Texas Ministers of Independence," *New York Times*, September 13, 1960, A1, A22. And see Russell Baker, "Nixon Endorses Kennedy Pledge," *New York Times*, September 14, 1960, A1, A26; Lawrence E. Davis, "How Kennedy Is Being Received: The Texas and California Tours, Religious Issue Debated," *New York Times*, September 14, 1960, A1, A32; Charles Grutzner, "Poling Praises Kennedy's Stand on Religious Issue," *New York Times*, September 14, 1960, A34; Childs, "Kennedy's View," A20; "Enough Said," *Washington Post*, September 14, 1960, A20; "Test of Religion," *Time*, September 26, 1960, 21.

25. Halberstam, *The Powers*, 457-458.

26. Daniel J. Boorstin, "Our Only American Ritual," *U.S. News & World Report*, January 30, 1989, 35.

27. Karlyn Kohrs Campbell and Kathleen Hall Jamieson, *Deeds Done in Words: Presidential Rhetoric and the Genres of Governance* (Chicago and London: University of Chicago Press), 14-36, esp. p. 15.

28. See, e.g., Edward P. J. Corbett, "Analysis of the Style of John F. Kennedy's Inaugural Address," in *Essays in Presidential Rhetoric*, 3rd ed. ed. Theodore Windt and Beth Ingold (Dubuque, Iowa: Kendall/Hunt Publishing, 1992), 61-70; Dan F. Hahn, "Ask Not What a Youngster Can Do for You: Kennedy's Inaugural Address," *Presidential Studies Quarterly* 12 (1982): 610-614; Edward B. Kenny, "Another Look at Kennedy's Inaugural Address," *Today's Speech* 13 (1965): 17-19; Donald L. Wolfarth, "John F. Kennedy in the Tradition of Inaugural Speeches," *Quarterly Journal of Speech* 47 (1961): 124-132. An exception to this generalization can be found in Theodore Otto Windt, Jr., "President John F. Kennedy's Inaugural Address, 1961" in *The Inaugural Addresses of Twentieth-Century American Presidents*, ed. Halford Ryan (Westport, Conn.: Praeger, 1993), 181-193.

29. Kathleen Hall Jamieson, *Packaging the Presidency*, esp. pp. 122-168; William C. Spragens, "Kennedy Era Speechwriting, Public Relations and Public Opinion," *Presidential Studies Quarterly* 14 (1984): 78-86; quotations, 80-81.

30. "Conducting Political Campaigns Using the Media," Untitled Report, Theodore C. Sorensen Papers, Campaign Files, 1959-1960, Box 22, JFK Library; Memorandum for Speech Writers, Copies to TV Writers, Draft No. 1, July 23, 1960, Theodore C. Sorensen Papers, Campaign Files, 1959-1960, Speechwriters, Box 26, JFK Library.

31. The nation seemed to be taken up with its lack of direction. The recent launching of the Sputnik satellite, the so-called "missile gap," Khrushchev's 1959 visit and bellicose rhetoric, the embarrassment of the U-2 incident and the collapse of the Paris summit, a recessionary economy, and the seeming lack of any real plans to address pressing global and domestic issues all conspired to provide an occasion for national soul-searching. The assumed moral superiority of the American way of life had come into question. Studies

commissioned by the Rockefeller Fund, *Time* magazine, and even President Eisenhower all sought to address the idea of "national purpose." See, e.g., James M. Blum, *Years of Discord: American Politics and Society, 1961-1974* (New York: W.W. Norton, 1991); David Burner, *John F. Kennedy and the New Generation* (Boston: Little, Brown, 1988); Stephen P. Depoe, "Space and the 1960 Presidential Campaign: Kennedy, Nixon and 'Public Time,'" *Western Journal of Communication* 55 (1991): 215-233; White, *The Making*. Kennedy's article on "national purpose" augured "fresh ideas" guided by a renewed sense of American values. See Senator John F. Kennedy, "'We Must Climb to the Mountaintop,'" John F. Kennedy Pre-Presidential Papers, 1960 Campaign Files, General Speeches, Statements, and Sections, Box 1032, JFK Library.

32. "Statement of Senator John F. Kennedy (D.-Mass.), January 2, 1960," Theodore C. Sorensen Papers, Campaign Files, 1959-1960, Box 21, JFK Library; Memorandum from Archibald Cox to Senator Kennedy, August 31, 1960, Theodore C. Sorensen Papers, Campaign Files, 1959-1960, U-2 Incident, Box 26, JFK Library. It has been argued that "freedom" served as the "god-term" for the Kennedy presidency. "Peace" was the president's second-most favored and employed word. See Carol A. Berthold, "Kenneth Burke's Cluster-Agon Method: Its Development and an Application," *Central States Speech Journal* 27 (1976): 302-309.

33. Patrick Donaghy, "The New Frontier," Interview, *Catholic World*, November 1960, 80-86, quotation, p. 80; "The Presidency in 1960," Address by the Hon. John F. Kennedy, rpt. of *Congressional Record*, Pre-Presidential Papers, 1960 Campaign Files, Speeches, Statements, and Sections, The Presidency, Box 1031, JFK Library; "Remarks of Senator John F. Kennedy Accepting the Democratic Presidential Nomination Democratic National Convention, July 15, 1960," John F. Kennedy Pre-Presidential Papers, 1960 Campaign Files, Box 1032, JFK Library.

34. White, *The Making*, 350; for a detailed discussion of the election results see White pp. 350-365.

35. See, e.g., "The Kennedy Story," *U.S. News & World Report*, November 21, 1960, 46-55; "A Size-Up of Kennedy: An Interview With His Biographer James MacGregor Burns," *U.S. News & World Report*, November 28, 1960, 72-76; William S. White, "High Style in White House Politics," *Harpers*, January 1961, 99-102; Ernest K. Lindley, "The Switch," *Newsweek*, January 23, 1961, 32; "If the 'New Idea' Men Have Their Way," *Newsweek*, January 23, 1961, 38-40; "Operation Rooney," *Time*, January 6, 1961, 15; "Rooney's Rule," *Newsweek*, January 9, 1961, 24-25.

36. See, e.g., "What Kennedy Will Do As President," *U.S. News & World Report*, November 21, 1960, 40-45; "The Kennedy Strategy: Clues to the Next 4 Years," *U.S. News & World Report*, December 19, 1960, 38-41; "A New Leader," *Time*, November 16, 1960, 3; "Man of the New Frontier," *Time*, November 16, 1960, 5-7.

37. "The Kennedy Strategy," 38; "Washington: Handle with Care," *Newsweek*, January 2, 1961, 13-14; "Dawn of the New Congress," *Newsweek*, January 9, 1961, 19-20; "As Kennedy Takes Over," Photo Caption, *U.S. News & World Report*, January 23, 1961, 37; "Mr. Kennedy Today: The Change in Him," *Newsweek*, January 23, 1961, 16-20.

38. "Ring in the New," *Time*, January 6, 1961, 13-16.

39. Bloc Wire for Suggestions from Theodore C. Sorensen, December 23, 1960, Theodore C. Sorensen Papers, JFK Speech Files 1961-1963, Inaugural Address, 1/20/61, Memoranda, Speech Material Correspondence 12/10/60-5/23/61, Box 62, JFK Library.

40. Letter from Adlai E. Stevenson to Theodore C. Sorensen c/o Hon. John F. Kennedy, Theodore C. Sorensen Papers, JFK Speech Files, Inaugural Address, Box 62, JFK Library.

41. Letter from Douglas Dillon to Theodore Sorensen, December 29, 1960, Theodore C. Sorensen Papers, JFK Speech Files, Inaugural Address, Box 62, JFK Library; Letter from Allen Nevins to Theodore Sorensen, December 29, 1960, Theodore C. Sorensen Papers, JFK Speech Files, Inaugural Address, Box 62, JFK Library; Joseph Kraft, Oral History, Interviewed by John Stewart, 20, JFK Library.

42. Kathleen Hall Jamieson, *Eloquence in an Electronic Age: The Transformation of Political Speechmaking* (New York and Oxford: Oxford University Press, 1988), 97; Campbell and Jamieson, *Deeds Done in Words*, 229, note 22; Arthur M. Schlesinger, Jr., *A Thousand Days: John F. Kennedy in the White House* (Boston: Houghton Mifflin, 1965), 4.

43. Sorensen, *Kennedy*, 243, 241.

44. Jamieson, *Eloquence*, 209; Schlesinger, *A Thousand Days*, 163; Sorensen, *Kennedy*, 243.

45. See Sorensen, *Kennedy*, 242-243. The president's wish to be brief is perhaps reflected as well in an undated memorandum in the Sorensen Papers that lists slightly inaccurate word counts for the following inaugural addresses: Wilson 1913 (1,690) and 1917 (1,485); Roosevelt 1941 (1,281); Eisenhower (1,730). A "TCS" (Sorensen) draft was listed at 1,693 words, with a handwritten subtraction of 413, which left a remainder of 1,230 words. See Undated, Untitled, Unsigned Memorandum, U.S. Senate Letterhead, Theodore C. Sorensen Papers, JFK Speech Files, Inaugural Address, Box 62, JFK Library. Wolfarth lists the number of words Kennedy actually settled upon for delivery at 1,355. The briefest first inaugural was delivered by Theodore Roosevelt (983 words) and the longest was delivered by William Henry Harrison (8,578 words). The briefest inaugural address in history was Washington's second inaugural (134 words). See Wolfarth, "Tradition," 125.

46. Sorensen, *Kennedy*, 241; Theodore C. Sorensen, ed., *'Let the Word Go Forth': The Speeches, Statements, and Writings of John F. Kennedy 1947-1963* (New York: Bantam Doubleday/ Dell Publishing, 1988), 2; James L. Golden, "John F. Kennedy and the 'Ghosts,'" *Quarterly Journal of Speech* 52 (1966): 348-357; quotation, 349; Leonard L. Osborne, "Rhetorical Patterns in President Kennedy's Major Speeches: A Case Study," *Presidential Studies Quarterly* 10 (1980): 332-335.

47. Arthur Krock, "Inaugural Contrast: Kennedy Dramatizes the Change but the Basic Aspirations Remain," *New York Times*, January 22, 1961, 11E; Wallace Carroll, "A Time of Change Facing Kennedy," *New York Times*, January 21, 1961, A9.

48. Michael R. Beschloss, *The Crisis Years: Kennedy and Khrushchev, 1960-1963* (New York: Harper-Collins, 1991), 60-61.

49. Sorensen, *'Let the Word Go Forth,'* 11.

50. All citations are drawn from "The Inaugural Address of President John F. Kennedy—As Actually Delivered, January 20, 1961," Theodore C. Sorensen Papers, JFK Speech Files, Inaugural Address File, Box 62, JFK Library. Reprinted in the "Collected Speeches" section of this volume.

51. Schlesinger, *A Thousand Days*, 1-5; Sorensen, *Kennedy*, 240-245.

52. Thomas C. Reeves, *A Question of Character: A Life of John F. Kennedy* (New York: Free Press, 1991), 234; Beschloss, *Crisis Years*, 55; James Reston, "Washington:

President Kennedy's Inaugural—Speech on Policy," *New York Times*, Editorial, January 22, 1961, E10; "What Presidents Think About," Editorial, *New York Times*, January 22, 1961, E10.

53. David Burner and Thomas R. West, *The Torch Is Passed: The Kennedy Brothers and American Liberalism* (New York: Athencum, 1984), 95-96; Murray Edelman, *Constructing the Political Spectacle* (Chicago: University of Chicago Press, 1988), 64.

54. Alan J. Matusow, *The Unraveling of America: A History of Liberalism in the 1960s* (New York: Harper and Row, 1984), 30.

3

KENNEDY AND CIVIL RIGHTS

Civil rights fast became for President Kennedy, as it had for Eisenhower before him, a most thorny and recalcitrant domestic problem. In this chapter, we focus on two characteristic and critical national speeches concerning this issue—the September 30, 1962, radio and television address outlining events associated with the admission of James Meredith to the University of Mississippi and the June 11, 1963, radio and television address on civil rights. Each provides a representative narrative of the president's approach to civil rights. When viewed together, they provide a nexus for the wider discussion of presidential rhetorical governance in the civil rights arena.

Our historical and critical discussion of the Kennedy's civil rights address will isolate key characters and issues engulfing a legacy of power and prejudice and grassroots efforts to effect justice and equality for African Americans at home. Freedom's cause in the 1960s was, after all, a domestic as well as international wrangle; it had serious implications for both arenas. In his quest to export freedom abroad, Kennedy encountered a serious obstacle in the reports of racially motivated violence and injustice on the streets of America. As John F. Kennedy approached the presidency, at best he was considered a moderate. There were lingering "suspicions that [his] civil rights outlook was limned in political expediency." Even James MacGregor Burns, whom Kennedy himself had commissioned for an "authorized" pre-campaign biography in 1959, scored the candidate for a weak stand on civil rights.[1]

Kennedy recognized the need to shore up his image on civil rights and pledged his support in person by meeting with civil rights leaders prior to his presidential bid. With the onset of the campaign for the Democratic nomination, Kennedy worked to restore a more liberal image. Referring to the lunch-counter protests the candidate observed: "[I]t is in the American tradition to stand up for one's rights—even if the new way is to sit down."[2]

The 1960 Democratic party platform civil rights plank outlined "the toughest . . . pledges in party history," and it was politically expedient that the discourse of democratic candidates match. Privately, Kennedy felt the civil rights plank raised "unwarranted hopes" and "unnecessary fears" by being too specific. Publicly, Kennedy endorsed the platform; its civil rights plank had been written by Harris Wofford, Kennedy's adviser on civil rights. The party platform called for wide-ranging executive and legislative actions certain to raise the ire of Dixiecrats. Rather than being "ahead of its time," the platform merely reflected "new realities" that were "long since evident" but now newly reinforced by the February student lunch-counter sit-ins, which commenced one month after Kennedy declared his candidacy. The civil rights movement had become "far too advanced to be ignored by a political leadership seeking broad support."[3]

During the primary campaign, African Americans and Southern whites, each for different reasons, remained wary of Kennedy's stand on civil rights. The candidate, for his part, stepped up his emphasis on civil rights to attract more black votes. As Sorensen noted, "A normally Democratic vote among Negroes . . . was clearly in doubt in 1960 owing to their cynicism on civil rights in general, Kennedy's voting record and running mate in particular, and the influence of prejudiced protestant Negro preachers." Kennedy would combat the odds with evocative, sweeping appeals on race relations in the United States. In March 1960, he remarked:

> I come to you tonight from a Senate that has been locked in debate for [four] weeks over basic questions of democracy. In some respects the argument is unreal. Voting rights guaranteed almost a hundred years ago are being questioned. A Supreme Court decision is being challenged. Equality and justice are being given different values. But the facts are not unreal. The denial of rights is not unreal. The inequality is not unreal. And my determination to fight for strong effective civil rights legislation is not unreal.[4]

In June 1960, Kennedy made it clear that his domestic interests in civil rights also were linked to international affairs—specifically U.S. relations with the emergent nations in Africa: "We the people of the oldest nation ever founded on revolt from colonial rule welcome the nations of Africa—our newest partners in man's centuries-old struggle for individual freedom, national independence and human dignity. . . . This was the American dream in 1776; it is now the African dream—and together, Africa and America . . . must dedicate themselves to fulfilling that dream for all mankind." Kennedy viewed U.S. assistance in the development of Third World nations as crucial to his objective of competing with the Soviets. While denying that the emergent nations were "pawns" in the struggle of the two superpowers, Kennedy did admit: "We must help Africa because the ultimate survival of the Free World depends upon our ability to help construct a community of stable and independent governments—where human rights are valued and protected—and where people are given the opportunity to choose their own national course, free from the dictates or coercion of any other nation."[5]

Just prior to his nomination, Kennedy attended an NAACP rally in Los Angeles to discuss racial justice: "Our job is to turn the American vision of a society in which no man has to suffer discrimination based on race into a living reality everywhere in our land. And that means we must secure [for] every American equal access to all parts of our public life—to the voting booth, to the schoolroom, to jobs, to housing, to all public facilities including lunch counters."[6]

In his nomination acceptance address Kennedy would continue to raise expectations with observations on the party platform: "Pledges which are made so eloquently are made to be kept. 'The Rights of Man'—the civil and economic rights essential to the human dignity of all men—are indeed our goal and our first principles. This is a platform on which I can run with enthusiasm and conviction." These words, echoing the platform's call for "effective moral and political leadership . . . to make equal opportunity a living reality for all Americans," would soon become a centerpiece in Kennedy's presidential campaign appeals. The candidate raised hopes for new black appointees, initiatives in protecting voting rights, achieving desegregation in schools and housing, increasing employment opportunity, and implementing Justice Department enforcement in all applicable areas.[7]

Kennedy added to rising expectations during the general election. Not only did he pledge "moral and political" leadership on civil rights, he also demonstrated public sensitivity to the issue. In Wisconsin, Kennedy observed: "The Negro baby has one-half as much chance of finishing high school as the white baby, one third as much chance of finishing college, one fourth as much chance of being a professional man or woman, four times as much chance of being out of work." In California, he intoned: "Only a President willing to use all the resources of his office can provide the leadership, the determination and the direction . . . to eliminate racial and religious discrimination from American society."[8]

In the first debate against Nixon, Kennedy reiterated his striking statistics on disadvantaged minorities, making the point that the United States "can do better." In the second debate, Kennedy implied Eisenhower had a loose grasp of the Constitutional questions in the Supreme Court rulings related to Little Rock and indicated that federal marshals were preferable to regular army troops in enforcing court-ordered desegregation. Moreover, racial strife at home was, in Kennedy's view, becoming an international embarrassment. The civil rights crisis, Kennedy maintained, placed the United States in a "goldfish bowl before the world." During his presidency, Kennedy would be in that "goldfish bowl" more than once.[9]

It was becoming increasingly clear that this election campaign was "establish[ing] a new mood of executive engagement in the civil rights struggle, and signal[ing] an executive commitment to the morality of equal protection of the laws as a rule of independent, creative political action, rather than as merely an obligation to uphold the courts." On the other hand, given the realities of the new Congress, certain "commitments" made by candidate Kennedy "would be difficult for him to live up to as President."[10]

In this chapter we argue that Kennedy's presidential civil rights discourse relied upon both legal and moral argument, representing two different strands of thought characteristic of a representative democracy. In addition, we maintain that Kennedy's discourse was as much informed by international as domestic concerns. For Kennedy, this linkage was both functional and dramatic; it provided a key to his rhetorical and definitional consistency. By tracking chronologically Kennedy's civil rights rhetoric—culminating in his sustained rhetorical campaign on behalf of civil rights in 1963—we seek to uncover the changing demands and constraints placed upon the president and the administration as it responded to a series of crises in the arena of civil rights. Our goal is to contextualize Kennedy's civil rights discourse and extend present understanding of presidential domestic crisis discourse in a time of both national and international instability.[11]

BEGINNINGS: CIVIL RIGHTS DISCOURSE IN 1961

When Kennedy took office "he was confronted with a renaissance of black political action everywhere in the nation." In 1961 W.E.B. Du Bois "renounced his U.S. citizenship and moved to Ghana," and James Baldwin noted that "[A]ll of Africa will be free before we can get a lousy cup of coffee."[12]

On January 20, 1961, Kennedy delivered his Inaugural Address to the nation. Civil rights activists seemed heartened by these words:

> Let the word go forth from this time and place, to friend and foe alike, that the torch has been passed to a new generation of Americans . . . unwilling to witness or permit the slow undoing of those human rights to which this nation has always been committed today at home and around the world.

As indicated earlier, the Inaugural Address was crafted chiefly as a foreign policy address. Harris Wofford begged Kennedy to mention civil rights. At Wofford's insistence Kennedy added the phrase "at home" to the above passage. While there was no actual reference to "civil rights" in this address, the campaign discourse had suggested that Kennedy would be an activist president on this front. In generating "considerable excitement," critics have even suggested that the new, young and vigorous president had evoked an unrealistic euphoria.[13]

Ten days later, Kennedy delivered his State of the Union message to a joint session of Congress. In a speech dominated by foreign affairs, Kennedy offered only one line concerning civil rights: "[T]he denial of constitutional rights to some of our fellow Americans on account of race—at the ballot box and elsewhere—disturbs the national conscience, and subjects us to the charge of world opinion that our democracy is not equal to the high promise of our heritage." "But all these problems pale," he would note pointedly, "when placed beside those which confront us around the globe."[14]

Kennedy would directly link civil rights to international prestige. Since Kennedy viewed the United States as a fierce competitor with the Soviets for the allegiance of emergent Third World nations (with significant non-white majorities), it was critical to advance U.S. principles of freedom and democracy abroad. The domestic civil rights imbroglio presented Kennedy with a sizable and intractable credibility gap.

From the beginning of his term Kennedy would favor executive over legislative action. According to Harris Wofford, a top civil rights aide, "Kennedy grabbed at anything that would by-pass the legislative branch." Fearing that a Republican-Southern bloc coalition in Congress might obstruct civil rights initiatives or slow other crucial foreign and domestic legislation by filibusters and committee roadblocks, or even hand him an embarrassing defeat, Kennedy decided to litigate through the Justice Department, appoint sympathetic judges where possible, add blacks to high positions in the government, issue executive orders, execute presidential actions and directives, and use his persuasive presidential powers to negotiate trouble spots by issuing legal appeals. But by avoiding substantive civil rights legislation, Kennedy opened himself to justified, intensive criticism.[15]

Abuses in civil rights were so widespread and so bereft of remedy that Kennedy found himself mostly on the defensive—fending off questions concerning civil rights legislation and his failure to deliver on his campaign promise to remove housing discrimination "with the stroke of a pen." But there was a strong rationale for Kennedy's legislative timidity. Not only was Kennedy elected by a thin margin creating a weak political base, but he also faced specific opposition. Requesting new civil rights laws "would not only be futile, but would be lost in Howard Smith's Rules Committee or Jim Eastland's Judiciary Committee, while being sufficiently divisive to kill whatever other proposals had a chance of surviving." There were other bills to shepherd through Congress: trade, medicare, school appropriations, a jobs bill, and a proposed increase in the minimum wage, as well as other interdependent initiatives slated to aid minorities and improve the overall quality of their lives.[16]

Kennedy's strategic decisions were shaped in part by his cautious and circumspect sense of political realities and his belief that a liberal democracy works incrementally if at all. The President felt he was trying to implement a rational and reasonable plan of action. He reasoned that it would be counterproductive to challenge Southerners on the Hill, especially if he could find other means to get the job done.

In 1961, the Kennedys (including the Attorney General Robert Kennedy) "saw the struggle against racism as a conundrum to be managed, not a cause to be championed." Kennedy hoped to use the executive branch to do what he could to use existing law and resources as a bulwark against national and international political embarrassment. Thus, the high hopes civil rights activists had entertained would be dashed on the rocks of Kennedy's pragmatism. As civil rights advocate Clarence Mitchell exclaimed, what was once the "New Frontier," within months, now looked "suspiciously like a dude ranch with Senator James O. Eastland as the general manager and Howard Smith as the foreman."[17]

On February 8, 1961, Kennedy was asked at a press conference how he was going to use his "moral authority," as he had promised in the campaign, to convince white obstructionists in New Orleans that court-ordered desegregation was a good idea. The president replied: "All students should be given the opportunity to attend public schools regardless of their race, and that is in accordance with the Constitution." He gave no specifics beyond this appeal to obey the law.[18]

Kennedy's message to the Third Annual Conference on Schools in Transition, sponsored by the President's Commission on Civil Rights, argued that the "public school system must be preserved and improved" because "[o]ur very survival as a free nation depends upon it." And in a reference to school closings prompted by unrest over desegregation he commented: "This is no time for school[s] to close for any reason and certainly no time for schools to be closed in the name of social discrimination. If we are to give the leadership the world requires of us, we must be true to the great principles of our Constitution— the very principles which distinguish us from our adversaries in the world."[19]

On March 1, when asked what he thought of the Civil Rights Commission's recommendations that federal funds be withheld from colleges and universities that practiced discrimination, the president indicated this was not a part of the legislation he would send to Congress, but it was "under consideration" for executive order. The first action would "be in the field of employment." On March 7, 1961, the president signed an Executive Order establishing the President's Committee on Equal Employment Opportunity (PCOEEO).[20]

A week later Kennedy continued to promise legislative action: "when I feel there is a necessity" and "a chance of getting that Congressional action, then I will recommend it to the Congress." Yet specific actions that could be documented seemed cosmetic, such as "provid[ing] facilities and meeting places which ... do not discriminate on the grounds of race or color."[21]

By March 23 the press wanted to know why the president had not delivered on his campaign pledge to ban discrimination in federal housing by the "stroke of a pen." Kennedy's meek response was that this area was under consideration and that the matter was receiving "the continuing attention of this

Administration." By way of defense, the president added that he had issued the earlier executive order on employment and that the Justice Department was "moving ahead" on voting rights.[22]

From a rhetorical vantage point, thus far the president's expected frontal assault championing civil rights seemed a bit tepid. His chief definitional concerns focused on maintaining law and order and lamenting domestic events that might cause international embarrassment. Other legal initiatives would rest with Robert Kennedy's Justice Department. The moral leadership expected on civil rights had failed to materialize.

The president continued in this vein. When his Equal Employment Opportunity Committee met for the first time, Kennedy expressed ambivalence: "There [wa]s no intention to make . . . [equal employment] a harsh or unreasonable mandate" but neither was "there any intention to compromise the principle of equality in employment." Kennedy explained: "This is not only just in itself; it is one of the purposes for which we stand before the world. . . . All Americans can be satisfied today that . . . high moral purpose is in excellent hands." In the civil rights arena, the gulf between "high moral purpose" and effective policy initiatives and between intention and actual enforcement seemed to widen. Despite the increasingly shaky relationship between ideals and practices, Kennedy voiced encouragement that there was not "any more important domestic effort in which we could be engaged."[23]

The Freedom Rides

By far the most serious and highly publicized civil rights events of 1961 revolved around the Freedom Rides, sponsored by the Congress of Racial Equality (CORE) and led by James Farmer. In testing the desegregation of bus terminal facilities (from Washington, D.C. to New Orleans) these civil rights activists were beaten and mobbed, while in city after city the local police watched idly. There was some question as to whether Kennedy would be willing to send in federal troops to protect the riders. As Robert Weisbrot indicates, "In May 1961 the Kennedy administration seemed more prepared to suffer with these reformers than to save them."[24]

From the vantage point of the Oval Office, the Freedom Rides were viewed as matters of "dreadful" timing and political "embarrassment." The United States had just lost the first-man-in-space race to the Russians, the Cuban invasion had failed miserably, and in early June, the President was preparing for a meeting with European leaders and a summit with Khrushchev in Vienna. Kennedy knew that Russian propagandists still used the federally enforced desegregation of Little Rock High School as "proof" of America's racist policies. The United States seemed in a poor position to export the defense of freedom and human rights with domestic rancor bludgeoning national pride and complicating international diplomacy. As the President left for his European trip he "urged getting his 'friends off those buses,'" and questioned the students' shortsightedness for embarrassing him and the country at a vital moment. Civil rights had become entrenched rhetorically and ideologically "as a part of the battle against Communism abroad."[25]

In mid-May, Attorney General Robert Kennedy placed a call to Alabama Governor John Patterson to urge police protection for the Freedom Riders; although friendly with the Kennedys, Patterson ultimately refused. By May 20, the bloody encounters between demonstrators and the white mobs that met them became so brutal that President Kennedy issued a statement stressing his "deepest concern" about the situation; he called upon local and state officials in Alabama to "exercise their lawful authority to prevent any further outbreaks of violence." He added, "I hope that state and local officials in Alabama will meet their responsibilities. The United States government intends to meet its."[26]

On May 21, federal protection was finally authorized after Robert Kennedy's personal emissary in Montgomery, John Seigenthaler, was beaten unconscious, and a mob of 1,000 whites had trapped Martin Luther King and his followers who had convened inside the Reverend Ralph Abernathy's First Baptist Church in support of the Freedom Riders. Approximately 500 federal marshals restored order within hours.[27]

When the violence in Alabama threatened lives as well as American prestige abroad, Kennedy had little choice but to act. But both Kennedys reportedly still felt "the demands for Freedom now to be just as irresponsible as calls for segregation forever." The president, in particular, was said to be bothered by "idealists" and "romantics" whose "quixotic crusades interfered with his careful plans and cautious timetables." Thus, the president viewed civil rights activism, which threatened to "discredit" or "harm" the United States and subject it to ridicule in the foreign policy arena at a time when he needed "maximum unity," as a major impediment to larger national goals. This interpretation may account for the paucity of public presidential discourse concerning the Freedom Rides. Indeed, for many, Kennedy's civil rights discourse during his first two years in office reflected nothing more than quiet persuasion through the encouragement of private action. Even the promise of moral leadership had vaporized.[28]

Responding to a press conference question about the Freedom Riders in July, the president emphasized a utilitarian perspective based on legal and Constitutional rights: "We believe that everyone who travels . . . should enjoy the full constitutional protection given to them by the law and by the Constitution." In emphasizing that the freedom riders had the right to travel, Kennedy stressed the legal rather than the moral resolution of the problem. The latter, of course, was much more difficult and divisive.[29]

The president's tepid advocacy was combined with the fact that he still had not come up with any substantial legislation—neither a housing order nor a comprehensive civil rights package. He did, however, make inroads on voting rights, a particular venue reflecting the president's "go slow" approach. Moreover, Kennedy approved and secretly sustained the fledgling Voter Education Project. As Branch observes, however, these initiatives were conducted as "a forced march in the opposite direction of the Freedom Rides, in spirit if not in purpose."[30]

Some would criticize the administration for attempting to redirect and manipulate the movement "from buses to ballots, from civil disobedience to the Voter Education Project, thereby diverting the energy of civil rights workers from direct confrontation with Southern 'law.'" But the rule of law was viewed as preferable to the provocations resulting in bloody confrontations found in liberal civil rights reform activism.[31]

Our analysis of the president's civil rights discourse in 1961 reveals that John F. Kennedy placed a premium on human rights domestically and internationally—but he seemed most preoccupied with foreign affairs. In fact, violations of civil rights at home seemed to be an "embarrassment" that discredited the American government and its people before "world opinion." In pursuing executive over legislative action in the civil rights arena, Kennedy was, in his view, not demonstrating timidity, but instead a pragmatic "realism" concerning "reasonable" actions directed toward a national problem with significant international implications. Kennedy reinforced rhetorically that all Americans should be given an "equal opportunity" at school or on the job. This constitutional principle was employed by the president as a key line of definitional demarcation between the United States and its "adversaries around the world." Indeed, from campaign to inaugural through the first year in office, John F. Kennedy had thrown down the gauntlet: the U.S. mandate was to "stand tall before the world" on human rights. The president considered it impolitic when his own moral crusade for freedom world-wide was enervated by disruptions and demonstrations that palpably underscored the second-class status of African Americans at home.

Various laws and regulations were utilized to indicate that all citizens should respect and obey the law. Kennedy proved that if this norm was challenged by lawless mob action, he would, in fact, however belatedly, marshal the full powers of the federal government to restore order and stability. At times, the grudging gesture seemed much too little, too late. Kennedy's obsession with "law and order" grated on civil rights advocates. For Kennedy, the prospect of federal intervention posed a constitutional quagmire, and his political instincts told him to have little part in it.

The president's rhetorical weakness on the civil rights front in 1961 was matched by the administration's lack of progress with Congress. The sole civil rights legislation introduced in 1961 was a two-year renewal of the President's Civil Rights Commission attached as a rider to an appropriations bill.[32]

MORE OF THE SAME: CIVIL RIGHTS DISCOURSE IN 1962

From the perspective of Martin Luther King, Jr., 1962 seemed very similar to 1961. Chary of the emphasis placed on voting rights, King felt the Kennedy administration "neglect[ed] all other rights while one was selected for concentrated attention." As King saw it, Democrats and Republicans alike "[were] marking time in the cause of justice."[33]

John F. Kennedy's second State of the Union address on January 11, 1962 contained three paragraphs on civil rights—a substantial increase in message text when measured against the single line devoted to the same issue the year before. While pointing to "quiet but striking" administration advances in voting rights, interstate travel, and employment initiatives through executive actions, the president also spoke of "much more to be done."[34]

Rhetorically, in 1962, however, John F. Kennedy also seemed determined to avoid making a significant national call for moral rectitude. The president's encounter with Governor Ross Barnett over the court-ordered admission of James Meredith to the University of Mississippi would bring forth his most lengthy and serious public address on civil rights.

Meredith at the University of Mississippi

Kennedy's public rhetoric attending the admission of James Meredith to the University of Mississippi encapsulated Kennedy's legalistic rhetorical approach. As the most significant statement on civil rights by the president in 1962, the speech provides a recapitulation of the public values, commitments, and methods of rhetorical management that marked his first two years in office.[35]

Over national radio and television, the president assured the American people that "the orders of the court . . . [we]re beginning to be carried out" in the Meredith case. Moreover, this was proper because flaunting "the law is the surest road to tyranny." "Americans are free, in short to disagree with the law but not to disobey it." Moreover, in Lincolnesque terms, he warned: "If this country should ever reach the point where any man or group of men by force or threat of force could long defy the commands of our court and our Constitution, then no law would stand free from doubt, no judge would be sure of his writ, and no citizen would be safe from his neighbors."

Kennedy also defined his legal mission: "My obligation under the Constitution, and the United States, was and is to implement the orders of the court with whatever means are necessary, and with as little force and civil disorder as the circumstances permit." The president, addressing the South primarily and Mississippi in particular, expressed "deep regret" for federalizing the Mississippi National Guard and blamed a lapse of local police control. But he was also conciliatory, praising "those southerners who have contributed to the progress of our democratic development in the entrance of students regardless of race." In a display of empathy for southern tradition, the president noted "that the present period of transition and adjustment . . . is a hard one for many people." In the present state of national tumult, he counseled, any "failure" to achieve justice was a "responsibility" that "must be shared by us all, every State, by every citizen."

After praising Mississippians and their state heroes, the president appealed extemporaneously to the "patriotism and integrity" of the South, making it clear that the incidents at Mississippi had now become an international scandal. "The eyes of the nation and of all the world are upon you and upon all of us, and the honor of your University and State are in the balance." Finally, in closing, the president said plaintively:

> There is, in short, no reason why the books on this case cannot now be quickly and quietly closed in the manner directed by the court. Let us preserve both the law and the peace and then healing those wounds that are within we can turn to the greater crises that are without and stand united as one people in our pledge to man's freedom.
> Thank you and good night.

We know now, of course, that minutes before the president spoke the first tear gas canisters were fired at a white mob that had begun a night of violence that ended with the death of a French journalist and a juke-box repairman. To his credit, that night "the President stayed in his office at the other end of the telephone until dawn." Before events at the University of Mississippi had run their full course, however, between 60 and 70 people (and some estimate hundreds) had been injured; 23,000 federal troops were employed; and it had cost the federal government almost five million dollars—all in the effort to enroll one African American in an American university.[36]

Though the president had failed to stem the violence, his essentially moderate speech carried an ambivalent message: He "would play along with Southern officials trying to save face with segregationist constituents, but . . . would not tolerate violence and could not be intimidated by it."[37]

The political lesson derived by Kennedy through his imposition of federal troops was twofold: He became even more convinced that moral suasion was not enough to alter racial attitudes in the South and he revised his historical view of Reconstruction as an unnecessary federal intrusion. Governor Barnett's actions had shaken Kennedy's trust in the "honorable men" of the South. Kennedy felt betrayed by Barnett's broken promises regarding adequate protection for Meredith and viewed this failure as an act of disloyalty.[38]

Rhetorically, the president had reemphasized his commitment to law and order and his determination to employ "any means necessary" to end the threats to civil order, and reinforced his ongoing theme that such domestic crises weakened our national unity and international reputation. Kennedy may have been pleased with global media reports that were "startling in their similarity";

there was "substantially more understanding of U.S. racial progress" in world press readings of Oxford, Mississippi than there had been in coverage of Little Rock. The president was able to preserve the law, if not the peace, and according to some, his bold action helped build his personal reputation and credibility throughout the world and in Africa in particular.[39]

The Presidential equation for handling the Oxford crisis was, then, no different from his earlier rhetorical strategies. Thematically, he offered the following definition: Law and order equals peace and stability; peace and stability open the doors to progress and development; progress and development lead to the full flowering of freedom; and freedom is the key to a strong, unified country at home and abroad.

For their part, civil rights activists were pleased that the president had intervened but they were less than enthusiastic, even openly critical, of the president's televised address chiefly because he did not "bear down on the moral issue." His appeals to constitutional principle and emphasis on following the law and the courts seemed to deny or at least obstruct a more important principle—simple justice. Indeed, civil rights advocates were operating in a fundamentally different universe than the president. The man in the Oval Office was managing a political crisis and trying desperately to cool off all the "hotheads." Civil rights advocates heard a man too concerned about Southern sensibilities and too cautious to raise the real issue: the immorality of what was happening to Meredith and others like him. Impatient with platitudes and wary of the continuing bloodshed, there was little for civil rights advocates to cheer about after this address.[40]

Achieving racial justice and protecting human dignity were becoming increasingly difficult. Two events, in particular, would reinforce this notion—the Albany campaign and the issuance of Kennedy's long-awaited housing order. In October 1961, a massive city-wide attempt to desegregate Albany, Georgia was initiated, combining the efforts of the Southern Christian Leadership Conference (SCLC), the Student Nonviolent Coordinating Committee (SNCC), and the Congress of Racial Equality (CORE). By July 1962, 346 arrests had been made pursuant to that campaign. Albany officials had continuously refused to negotiate with civil rights activists.

On August 1, 1962, President Kennedy was asked to respond to the foundering Albany campaign. He indicated that Robert Kennedy had been in almost "daily" contact with the principals in attempts to aid negotiations and monitor the demonstrations and subsequent jailings. The president failed to mention that earlier the attorney general had sent a congratulatory note to Albany Police Chief Laurie Pritchett for his nonviolent handling of the situation. Civil rights activists became aware of this, however. President Kennedy, once again viewing the standoff through the analogic lens of international relations, told the assembled reporters: "I find it wholly inexplicable why the City Council of Albany will not sit down with the citizens of Albany, who may be Negroes, and attempt to secure them, in a peaceful way, their rights." He added: "The United States Government is involved in sitting down at Geneva with the Soviet Union. I can't understand why the government of Albany, City Council of Albany, cannot do the same for American citizens."[41]

Although the president promised to protect the rights of the citizens of Albany, it became very clear that "peaceful" demonstrations followed by "peaceful" arrests were not attracting media attention. Jails were filling with demonstrators without any tangible signs of progress. This was not only discouraging, it seemingly brought the modern civil rights movement to the lowest ebb in its history. Some blamed the administration for the deadlock, saying that as long as things remained "peaceful," the Kennedys would take no further action. This view reinforced movement forces' assumptions that Kennedy would remain passive and wait until more and more violence had been perpetrated before taking affirmative federal action. This, of course, gave some comfort to the white supremacists, who also watched the mass arrests and could relish the growing stalemate.[42]

Perhaps no issue haunted the president more than his campaign statement that he could remove discrimination in federal housing "with the stroke of a pen" through an executive order. After months with no action the high expectations dissipated and cynics began sending the president pens. Still fielding questions about this issue in July of 1962, the housing order symbolized Kennedy's "most specific contradiction between promise and performance," and became "a political embarrassment." In "heed[ing] the counsel of caution," the president fretted over the order, which some predicted might cause construction declines and, with them, a drop in the gross national product.[43]

When Kennedy finally issued the housing order, it lacked sufficient teeth and scope. In announcing it the president remarked: "Our national policy is equal opportunity for all and the Federal Government will continue to take such legal and proper steps as it may to achieve the realization of this goal." When questioned further, he added, "it's sound, public, constitutional policy and we've done it."[44]

In 1962, for the most part, the president found himself on the defensive, meekly responding to a host of questions on civil rights issues that were either points of continuing unrest or that highlighted the "good deal" left "undone." Indeed, as one of the "great unfinished tasks of democracy," the movement toward civil rights for all would now be caught up in the upcoming centennial year of Lincoln's Emancipation Proclamation. In calling for a year of celebration and remembrance, Kennedy observed: "The Emancipation Proclamation expresses our nation's policy, founded on justice and morality." With these words, he set the tone for 1963.[45]

Kennedy still found himself emphasizing law and order, due process, and equal opportunity for all Americans. His abhorrence of violence, black or white, was made painfully manifest, but there seemed little he could or would do to stop it. His reliance upon the system for change came at the cost of increasing unrest. Faith in constitutional principle also required faith that judges and juries would make equitable decisions—a faith that seemed unwarranted, if not naive.

In rhetorically reinforcing the themes of "much progress" and "much more to be done" the president sent a mixed message, causing many to question his veracity and commitment. This, of course, reflected poorly on his ability to portray an effective and consistent image in his rhetorical management of the domestic civil rights crisis and, by proxy, the international affairs he linked directly to the outcome of that struggle.

Thus, Kennedy was left with building a rhetorical case that was mostly ceremonial in nature. His activist words masked passive deeds. Simultaneously, he seemed to be on the defensive, facing multiple requirements to issue national statements in response to major crises, which either threatened violence, had become violent, or addressed the aftermath of violent action. Where lives had been lost, in particular, the discourse seemed palliative—too little, too late. While there were no deaths during the Freedom Rides, the same could not be said of events at Oxford, of the church bombings, nor the other violent acts that followed. The mob action and the violence perpetrated against those who demanded their civil rights, and the sporadic acts of violence by blacks outraged by the lack of federal protection, all contributed to an atmosphere of increased militancy—a militancy that both the president and civil rights leaders brooded over as they faced the new year. Kennedy's cautious approach to civil rights seemed to provide an explanation for why, in Martin Luther King's words, "the Negroes' 'Now' was becoming as militant as the segregationists' 'Never.'" Calls for order, civility, and peaceful change, and praise for "loyalty"—especially after bombings in the South—sounded thin and hollow. The civil rights movement was becoming increasingly disheartened. As January 1963 approached, a deeper, darker wind seemed to blow—and the president could not help but hear its strained and anxious sound. He must have wondered about the challenges that the new year would bring.[46]

A CHANGE IN STRATEGY: CIVIL RIGHTS RHETORIC IN 1963

Perhaps 1963 was like no other year the nation has faced in this century as images of violence and dreams of peace shared equal time in the national consciousness. Birmingham, George Wallace "standing in the schoolhouse door" at Tuscaloosa, the death of Medgar Evers, the August March on Washington, and Martin Luther King Jr.'s stunning depiction of his dream, all coalesced to etch a vivid national memory. One pivotal participant—the president of the United States—lent his eloquent and, finally, very clear voice to the cry for racial justice in the land. In the search for justice and human rights in the United States, 1963 would yield a level of hope and enthusiasm probably not found before or since.

In late February, President Kennedy sent a special message to Congress on civil rights. He told the legislators:

> Progress for the Negro has been too often blocked and delayed. Equality before the law has not always meant equal treatment and opportunity. And the harmful, wasteful and wrongful results of racial discrimination and segregation still appear in virtually every aspect of national life, in virtually every part of the Nation.

True to form, he was quick to add the national and international implications of such a state of affairs:

> Race discrimination hampers our economic growth by preventing the maximum development and utilization of our manpower. It hampers our world leadership by contradicting at home the message we preach abroad. It mars the atmosphere of a united and classless society in which this nation rose to greatness. It increases the costs of public welfare, crime, delinquency and disorder. Above all, it is wrong. Therefore, let it be clear, in our own hearts and minds, that it is not merely because of the Cold War, and not merely because of the economic waste of discrimination, that we are committed to achieving true equality of opportunity. The basic reason is because it is right.

Here, for the first time, in clear and certain terms, the president transcended all the prior appeals grounded in legal principle and clearly turned the civil rights question into a matter of morality. Kennedy finally had chosen moral suasion as a key definitional tactic in introducing his civil rights agenda to Congress. He outlined "existing and prospective action" including "important legislative as well as administrative measures." In particular, he introduced initiatives to improve voting rights, education, employment, public accommodations, the use of federal funds, and proposed extending the tenure of the Civil Rights Commission.[47]

In concluding this message, Kennedy emphasized that his proposals did "not constitute a final answer to the problems of race discrimination" but rather, "a list of priorities" meant to bridge "the gap between our precepts and our practices" without, at the same time, providing an "occasion for sectional bitterness." Some civil rights advocates considered this latest legislative proposal as "a narrow and limited afterthought, albeit a worthy one." Ever cautious, the president had yet to propose the comprehensive legislation demanded by civil rights reformers. Kennedy's political timidity would soon be shaken by upcoming events.[48]

Three events in 1963 tower above all others in shaping presidential discourse on civil rights—the Birmingham campaign, an encounter with George Wallace at Tuscaloosa, and finally, the March on Washington held in late August.

Birmingham

In Birmingham, Alabama Police Commissioner Eugene "Bull" Connor would garner national and international outrage as he unleashed with "gleeful vindictiveness" nightsticks, dogs, and firehoses on civil rights demonstrators. With many demonstrators exhausted or jailed, Martin Luther King, Jr. authorized the use of children as a new method to achieve racial justice. With this tactic, King hoped to "'subpoena the conscience of the nation to the judgment seat of morality.'"[49]

The brutality visited upon the children of Birmingham repulsed the president. He winced over the photos coming out of the segregated city and pined over the international scandal the demonstrations had wrought. According to Robert Weisbrot, Kennedy also became convinced that there was little he now could do to placate conservatives, who in any case opposed his "other reform measures. . . . So although a crucial tax bill was pending . . . Kennedy felt less incentive than earlier in his presidency to sacrifice civil rights in the hope of saving other liberal programs." Moreover, "the Birmingham campaign and the other protests it helped spark over the next seven months engaged over a hundred thousand people and led to nearly fifteen thousand arrests." Indeed, riots on the heels of the campaign threatened not only the fragile truce the administration helped secure between civil rights activists and local businesses in Birmingham but, more importantly, gave the president pause as "[t]he specter of open racial warfare invaded the Oval Office."[50]

The intransigence of the South, brutally displayed in Birmingham, seemed to harden the President's public resolve to attack the race relations issue on both legal and moral grounds. Before publicly rebuking George Wallace for "standing in the schoolhouse door," Kennedy would make a number of major addresses and press conference statements on civil rights. In our view these forays constitute a renewed and fortified rhetorical campaign directed at civil rights advocacy.

On May 18, the president went to Tennessee's Vanderbilt University and urged administration, faculty, and students to consider their special obligations: "Equality of opportunity does not mean equality of responsibility." "[F]or 'of those to whom much is given, much is required.'" In stressing the obligation to pursue learning, perform public service, and uphold the law, the president indicated "that only a respect for the law makes it possible for free men to dwell together in peace and progress." The educated, public-spirited person realizes that human beings "must be regarded with decency and treated with dignity," and that "to subvert the law, to suppress freedom, or to subject other human beings to acts that are less than human, degrades [one's] heritage, ignores [one's] learning, and betrays [one's] obligation." Kennedy concluded: "In these moments of tragic disorder, a special burden rests on educated men and women of our country to reject the temptations of prejudice and violence, and to reaffirm the values of freedom and law," and to realize that "in a time of tension, it is more important than ever to unite this country and strengthen these ties so that all of our people will be one." By praising learning, applied knowledge through public service, and lawfulness, and by upholding the unifying principle of human dignity through appeals rejecting prejudice and violence, Kennedy grafted traditional "law and order" values to those of moral suasion. As time went on, this hybrid appeal seemed more comfortable and natural to the president.[51]

On May 22, 1963, the president fielded a press conference question on George Wallace's threat to block admittance of two African American students at the University of Alabama. When asked whether he intended to use federal marshals as he did at Oxford, Kennedy replied, "I hope that would prove unnecessary," and expressed a desire that the matter could be settled by "local authorities." Although "very reluctant" to use such authority, the president pledged to enforce the pending court order as part of his constitutional obligation: "there is no choice in the matter. It must be carried out. . . . If it were a matter of choice, it would not be law." The president, asked if he was now considering civil rights legislation "as a result of recent developments down South," answered in the affirmative and indicated he was looking for a "legal remedy" on a number of fronts to prevent people from "tak[ing] to the streets."[52]

On June 6, 1963, the president delivered a commencement address at San Diego State University emphasizing and expanding upon themes developed at Vanderbilt. Kennedy reflected:

> American children today do not enjoy equal educational opportunities for two primary reasons: one is economic and the other is social. . . . [W]e must recognize that segregation and education, and I mean de facto segregation in the North as well as the proclaimed segregation in the South, brings with it serious handicaps to a large proportion of the population.

Kennedy maintained that federal, state and local government all played roles in providing additional educational opportunities to the citizens. Invoking a familiar theme, he concluded, "I believe that education comes at the top of the responsibilities of any government, at whatever level. It is essential to our survival as a nation in a dangerous and hazardous world, and it is essential to the maintenance of freedom at a time when freedom is under attack."[53]

By this time Kennedy's discourse privileged freedom atop his hierarchy of American values. Freedom, in turn, was linked to progress in education, jobs, and human rights. This progress was important to national and international interests, especially in a time of domestic and global "crisis."

Tuscaloosa

Defending human rights proved to be as difficult at home as it was abroad. On the same day Kennedy delivered his eloquent plea for international peace on

June 10 at American University, he was forced to send a telegram to Governor Wallace urging him not to interfere with the admittance of the two students at the University of Alabama. The next day, June 11, the president issued a proclamation urging Wallace to "cease and desist" in his attempts to bar integration. The president, steeled by his experience with Governor Barnett at Oxford, once again made it clear that federal authority would be used to enforce a court order to block Wallace's flaunting of the law of the land. Wallace's image-conscious obstructionist tactics would be met with calculated, effective, if not honest, negotiation by the administration. More importantly, Wallace's posturing gave President Kennedy an opportunity to make a public appeal on civil rights. Encouraged to make the address by his brother Robert and discouraged by all other advisers, the President hurriedly made notes and set Theodore Sorensen to work on a draft.[54]

Civil Rights as a Moral Issue: The June 11 Speech

At 8 p.m. on the night of June 11, with the final draft of a hastily prepared speech barely in hand, President Kennedy addressed the nation over television and radio. Seasoned by his earlier encounters with a stubborn Southern governor, and now irretrievably caught up in the morality of the civil rights drama, Kennedy combined themes tested during the campaign and throughout his presidency. Kennedy called upon Americans to "examine" their "conscience" and to reflect that the nation "was founded on the principle that all men are created equal, and that the rights of every man are diminished when the rights of one man are threatened." Kennedy stressed the moral imperative of the cause of human rights at home and abroad:

> Today we are committed to a worldwide struggle to promote and protect the rights of all who wish to be free. And when Americans are sent to Vietnam or West Berlin, we do not ask for whites only. It ought to be possible, therefore, for American students of any color to attend any public university they select without having to be backed up by troops.

Kennedy expanded upon a host of civil rights venues:

> It ought to be possible for American consumers of any color to receive equal service in places of public accommodation, such as hotels and restaurants and theaters and retail stores, without being forced to resort to demonstrations in the street, and it ought to be possible for American citizens of any color to register and to vote in a free election without interference or fear of reprisal.

He reinforced the case for equal treatment by restating his oft-used statistics on the status of black Americans whose competitive edge was diminished by racism. Calling this neither a "sectional" nor a "partisan" issue, Kennedy counseled: "It is better to settle these matters in the courts than on the streets, and new laws are needed at every level, but law alone cannot make men see right." For "we are confronted primarily with a moral issue. It is as old as the scriptures and as clear as the American Constitution. . . . The heart of the question is whether all Americans are to be afforded equal rights and equal opportunities, whether we are going to treat our fellow Americans as we want to be treated."

Having found a sure moral compass, Kennedy sought personal identification with the problem by asking Americans for renewed reflection and careful introspection. If black citizens, he reasoned, "cannot enjoy the full and free life which all of us want, then who among us would be content to have the color of his skin changed and stand in his place? Who among us would then be content with the counsels of patience and delay?" Indeed, while Lincoln may have freed the slaves, "their heirs, their grandsons, are not wholly free. They are not yet free from the bonds of injustice. They are not yet freed from social and economic oppression. And this Nation, for all its hopes and all its boasts will not be fully free until all its citizens are free." Again, this issue was related critically to America's mission as standard-bearer for the world community:

> We preach freedom around the world, and we mean it, and we cherish our freedom here at home, but are we to say to the world, and much more importantly, to each other that this is a land of the free except for the Negroes; that we have no second-class citizens except Negroes; that we have no class or cast[e] system, no ghettoes, no master race except with respect to Negroes?

Noting the mounting "cries for equality" and the "fires of frustration and discord . . . burning in every city," Kennedy spoke passionately of a "moral crisis" in the land. "Now the time has come for this Nation to fulfill its promise" by refraining from "token moves or talk." Calling for a "peaceful revolution," echoing a foreign policy theme in his Inaugural Address, Kennedy implored: "A great change is at hand, and our task, our obligation, is to make that revolution, that change, peaceful and constructive for all. Those who do nothing are inviting shame as well as violence. Those who act boldly are recognizing right as well as reality."

Kennedy informed the nation he would introduce civil rights legislation and Congress would be asked "to act, to make a commitment it has not fully made in this century to the proposition that race has no place in American life or law." Finally, the president pleaded for unity: "This is one country. It has become one country because all of us and all the people who came here had an equal chance to develop their talents." He added: "We have a right to expect that the Negro community will be responsible, will uphold law, but they have a right to expect that the law will be fair, that the Constitution will be color blind, as Justice Harlan said at the turn of the century."

For the most part the June 11 effort received widespread praise as immediate press reactions seemed to confirm that the president had reached a watershed on civil rights. The *Louisville Courier-Journal* observed that "the speech will surely rank as one of the landmark public documents." The *St. Louis Post-Dispatch* noted that the president's "moving appeal to the conscience of America should be regarded as one of the major achievements of the civil rights struggle." The one note of dissension had to do with timing. As the *Milwaukee Journal* pointed out, "If there can be any criticism of what the president said it is only that it should have been said sooner." Taking a similar tack, the *Daily Standard* of Celina, Ohio noted: "He should be a leader, molding new thoughts and ideas to be relayed to the citizens of this nation. Instead, he has been content, at least publicly, to let nature take its course, to follow each unfolding drama in silence, acting only when impelled to act, speaking only when it becomes safe to speak."[55]

The change in the president's public discourse seemed to confirm Theodore Sorensen's claim that by 1963 John F. Kennedy had seen enough of the "evils of racial discrimination," and was now "deeply and fervently committed" to civil rights and "to the cause of human rights as a moral necessity inconsistent with his political instincts." According to Alonzo L. Hamby, the speech was singularly more "blunt and idealistic" than any of the other presidential addresses on this issue that had preceded it. As Herbert S. Parmet notes, "No other Chief Executive had ever talked that way about human rights in America. [I]t was . . . [his] most eloquent speech and close to being his most spontaneous. His prepared remarks were not completely typed until he went on the air." Indeed, the president had extemporized his concluding statements.[56]

According to Carl M. Brauer the June 11 speech—"one of the most eloquent, moving and important addresses" of the Kennedy presidency—"marked the beginning of the Second Reconstruction, a coherent effort by all three branches of the government to secure blacks their full rights." Certainly events at Birmingham and the opportunity presented by Wallace's intransigence coalesced to help Kennedy mount a bold political foray that had been postponed for two years.[57]

We suggest that the speech could—in one sense—be considered rather conservative, merely repeating the traditional appeals to preserve law and order and extend equal rights to all persons as acts of patriotism and unity. Significantly, however, Kennedy jettisoned past pleas for incremental or piecemeal changes, and instead adopted a reformist language of moral resolve backed by a specific pledge to introduce substantive legislation. The president, no longer merely a "principled bystander," had now shifted the argument and upped the ante: government had both the ability and the responsibility to reorganize its priorities, to make human rights predominate, and to ensure that social injustices would be addressed in a pragmatic, systematic, and resolute fashion. Kennedy seemed intent upon diagnosing the system and proposing policies designed to effect an immediate legislative cure, and he was now willing to take the country along with him in his quest for racial justice. While Kennedy did not go into all of the particulars of the new legislation that night, he would do so eight days later in a Special Message to Congress on Civil Rights and Job Opportunities.[58]

An additional explanation for the shift combining both legal and moral argument appears in what we believe to be a speech draft crafted by the attorney general for the president for the June 11 address. Robert Kennedy provides a cogent rationale for the transformation in the President's public discourse:

> The shameful scenes of riot and bloodshed in Oxford last fall, and in Birmingham this spring—scenes so much more eloquently reported by the news camera than by any number of explanatory words—these events have done immeasurable harm to our country. Not only have they damaged our standing as a free nation in the eyes of the world, but—far more importantly—they have damaged our national conscience, our very ability to take pride in calling ourselves Americans.

This breach seems to have shaken the government to the core and President Kennedy's words reflected and refracted these considerations.[59]

In calling for a "moral" revolution at home and in introducing legislation to underwrite that call, Kennedy finally fused courageous talk with action. It was no accident that this address, unlike others preceding it, helped to complete a seamless garment, clothing pious calls for the protection of human dignity and the advancement of freedom as a specific U.S. role in the international community with the added raiment of unprecedented commitment to civil rights at home.

Gallup polls reflected a mixed response to the president's message; some felt he might be moving "too fast" on integration and his ratings in the South plummeted, but there was much more clarity in his intended direction than ever before. Martin Luther King, Jr. thought the speech the most "eloquent" and "profound" plea for "Justice and Freedom . . . ever made by any President." As Schlesinger observed: "It was a magnificent speech in a week of magnificent speeches." But many wondered why it had not come earlier. Moreover, it was to become painfully obvious that words alone would not stem the tide of hate and violence.[60]

On June 19, 1963, in a special message to Congress, President Kennedy would introduce his civil rights package by noting that "persisting inequalities and tensions make it clear that Federal action must lead the way, providing both the Nation's standard and a national solution." The president reiterated his call for legislation on voting, the Civil Rights Commission, and school desegregation. He warned Congress that "the result of continued Federal legislative inaction will be continued, if not increased, racial strife—causing the leadership on both sides to pass from the hands of reasonable and responsible men to the purveyors of hate and violence, endangering domestic tranquility, retarding our Nation's economic and social progress and weakening the respect with which the rest of the world regards us." Kennedy called for "a single omnibus bill" to "be known as the 'Civil Rights Act of 1963.'" Among other items, it was to cover public accommodations, employment, federally assisted programs, community relations, education, and job training. In a carefully crafted document, the president established what had already been done in these areas by executive action and also what was left to be done by these new legislative initiatives.

In the area of public accommodations, for example, the president again lamented the fact that African Americans had fought and died for their country, but could not be served equally in a public establishment. "No one," he said, "has been barred on account of his race from fighting or dying for America—there are no 'white' or 'colored' signs on the foxholes or graveyards of battle." Equal access to public facilities was, therefore, "the heritage of the melting pot, of equal rights, of one Nation and one people." Moreover, reinforcing his pleas for justice, Kennedy rejected the notion that property rights ought to take precedence over human rights. Kennedy pointed out that "property has its duties as well as its rights," and that the courts and tradition in other areas make it feasible as well as reasonable that the law "can require public accommodations to accommodate equally all segments of the general public." Kennedy noted one of the chief ideological dilemmas in a representative democracy: "Both human rights and property rights are foundations of our society—and both will flourish as a result of [these legislative] measure[s]." By mentioning the former before the latter, Kennedy privileged human rights over those of property—serving clear notice of his intention to pursue a more substantively moral reformist agenda.[61]

The legal remedies embodied in the President's civil rights bill were identified as "imperative" for ending "racial strife" and stemming the tide of "rancor, violence, disunity, and national shame" that "hamper our national standing and security." In overtly appealing to the American sense of justice, Kennedy also advanced the moral argument made on June 11. He transcended his traditional law and order stance and placed himself squarely in the reformist tradition of invoking moral authority. After carefully pointing out that 1963 was the centennial year of the Emancipation Proclamation, the president proclaimed unequivocally: "[J]ustice requires us to insure the blessings of liberty for all Americans and their posterity—not merely for reasons of economic efficiency, world diplomacy and domestic tranquility—but, above all, because it is right." The values of "efficiency," "diplomacy," and "tranquility" were subsumed under overriding ethical imperatives attached to the cause of freedom and justice for all. Appropriately, the president ended this address by quoting from Lincoln: "In giving freedom to the Negro, we assure freedom to the free—honorable alike in what we give and what we preserve."[62]

Indeed, Kennedy was "finally caught up in a revolution against the great cancer in American life." Even with its deficiencies, Kennedy had called for "the most comprehensive and far-reaching civil rights bill ever proposed." In seeking a single omnibus bill, Kennedy sought "a legislative victory on a moral issue." The legislative proposal was characterized as a "far cry from the eviscerated bill he had proposed in February."[63]

March on Washington

When Kennedy was first apprised of the March on Washington, he reportedly was "appalled," reflecting his concern that his new civil rights bill not be complicated by a "big show." Fearful that the march would threaten his new civil rights initiative by creating "an atmosphere of intimidation" sure to rankle the Congress—and mindful that his new stand was hurting him in the polls—the prospect of a massive, potentially violent march seemed palpable grounds for trepidation. After unsuccessfully pleading with the organizers to call it off, the president bowed to the inevitable, placed private political instincts aside, and decided to endorse the march.[64]

In a July 17 press conference, the president put the matter in the best light possible, predicting that the March on Washington would be "in the great tradition of public assembly for redress of grievances." While he "look[ed] forward to it," he also cautioned against any demonstrations which might lead to "violence" and "bloodshed." The president took secret measures to ensure that violence would be minimized and promised to meet with the leaders of the march, but decided against appearing with them in person.[65]

After the march, Kennedy, relieved that the largest demonstration in the nation's history up to that time had occurred without incident, expressed awe, pride, and gratitude: "One cannot help but be impressed with the deep fervor and quiet dignity that characterizes the thousands who have gathered . . . to demonstrate their faith and confidence in our democratic form of government." He added: "This Nation can be properly proud of the demonstration that has occurred here today. . . . The cause of 20 million Negroes has been advanced by the program conducted so appropriately before the Nation's shrine to the Great Emancipator, but even more significant is the contribution to all mankind." A relieved president now praised publicly what he had feared privately.[66]

During the last months of his life, President Kennedy continued publicly to link "equality of opportunity" to employment and educational issues, maintaining that sustained progress would demonstrate "to the world that a free society provides men and women the best chance for decent and fulfilled lives." Acknowledging that full realization "is going to take time," he stressed that the United States was engaged in "something much more difficult" than any other nation had previously undertaken.[67]

That the search for jobs, justice, and freedom from discrimination would not be won without further cost was dramatized in Kennedy's subsequent response to Governor Wallace's continued attempts to block integration in the schools in Alabama and the bombing murder of four children during a Sunday School class in September 1963 in Birmingham, Alabama. This latter event evoked the president's "deep sense of outrage and grief" and the president called for renewed reflection on "the folly of racial injustice, hatred and violence." He again expressed his hope for achieving "peaceful programs before more lives are lost." And once again Martin Luther King, Jr. asked for the intervention of federal troops, for in his view, Birmingham now had become a prime ignition point for "the worst racial holocaust this nation has even seen." On November 15, 1963, the president ratified the March on Washington's most prescient and primary point: "[E]conomic security is the number one issue today." He stated: "[T]he civil rights legislation is important. But to make that legislation effective we need jobs in the United States."[68]

On November 18, 1963, in his final public statement on civil rights, the president found prophetic voice:

> I believe that this is a matter that is going to be with us long after I have disappeared from the scene. No country has ever faced a more difficult problem than attempting to bring in 10 percent of the population of a different color, educate them, give them a chance for a job, and give them a chance for a fair life. That is my objective and I think it is the objective of the United States as I have always understood it.

This final statement indicates the changed tenor of Kennedy's resolve and shows the effects of the intransigence he had faced and faced down during his presidency.[69]

CONCLUSION

We close this chapter with some implications of our examination of Kennedy's civil rights rhetoric for (1) the discourses and philosophies of a representative democracy; (2) the consequences of rhetorical linkage of national and international goals; and (3) the nature of presidential domestic crisis discourse.

Discourses and Philosophies of a Representative Democracy

Perhaps no other president since Lincoln entered a term of office facing what would become such a sustained period of domestic crisis and challenge. A President who fired the imagination of a "new generation" of Americans, and who openly depended upon their sense of loyalty and patriotism, had for two years, by design and by inclination, failed the heady idealism associated with his earlier campaign discourse. Kennedy's rhetorical dependence on traditional constitutional principles of law and order, due process, and incremental change were at loggerheads with the strident demands for "social justice now."

Kennedy finally privileged appeals for morality over those for law and order, because the law did not include everyone in the 1960s—often leaving the unprotected prey to violence. There was a certain righteousness to this cause that no appeal to "peace" and "unity," however well-intentioned, could douse. Kennedy had to convince both hearts and minds and, finally, relinquish his innate political pragmatism in the face of harrowing events that made more narrow political interests pale. The President finally realized that he needed to speak to the moral strand of the American psyche. He may have been pushed or dragged, but he went, albeit not until peaceful assembly and the orderly redress of grievances were being assaulted on an almost daily basis. The violence challenged fundamental constitutional principles—reliance upon law and order and due process—and it destroyed the value base for rhetorical appeals based upon carefully timed, utilitarian, and incremental social change.[70]

The president premised his arguments on and defined his rhetorical stance with the legalistic constitutional principle of a "right to equal treatment" and only later grafted the moral equation onto his ongoing appeals. Here the emphasis shifted to what Ronald Dworkin has labeled the "right to treatment as an equal." This fundamental change in public discourse, if not personal preference, demonstrated Kennedy's rhetorical malleability and the suasive power of the civil rights movement, which seemed to influence the president's discourse over time.[71]

Dworkin aids in clarifying Kennedy's rhetorical shift by drawing a philosophical distinction between a liberalism based on neutrality versus a liberalism based on equality. "Liberalism based on neutrality takes as fundamental the idea that government must not take sides on moral issues, and it supports only such egalitarian measures as can be shown to be the result of that principle." Here we find the principle that guided Kennedy's discourse during his first two years in office. By taking sides on an issue of morality, Kennedy would violate the neutrality principle central to a traditional liberal approach. "Liberalism based on equality," on the other hand, "take[s] as fundamental that government treat its citizens as equals, and insists on moral neutrality only to the degree that equality requires it." Thus, an equality-based liberalism "rests on a positive commitment to an egalitarian morality." This positive commitment means that economic and social benefits must be distributed justly—not merely for purposes of procuring an "equality of result" but also to provide for vigilant scrutiny and action in ensuring that we meet basic rights as a concomitant of basic decency required by an egalitarian moral principle. It is precisely this ideal that civil rights advocates pressed upon the government and it is precisely this banner that Kennedy finally fully unfurled before the world most artfully in his June 11, 1963 address.[72]

Rhetorical Linkage of National and International Goals

For John F. Kennedy, civil rights concerns always played against the larger backdrop of foreign policy goals and objectives. Indeed, his preoccupation with foreign affairs seemed at times to cloud his judgment concerning civil rights. Kennedy's concern with international opinion drove him to make public comparisons of his delicate negotiations with Khrushchev at Geneva as a rationale and model for dealing effectively with domestic civil rights problems in Southern communities. For the first two years, the nonviolent demonstrations and the violent reactions to civil rights enforcement were argued to hamper both presidential effectiveness and U.S. prestige—"enemies" would take these eruptions as signs of U.S. instability and discord, all of which belied the strength of freedom and the presence of a just system in the United States. On this score, the president's leadership style actually seemed to exacerbate rather than ameliorate the situation. It also pitted a volatile domestic rancor against a preferred policy of presidential silence so that the president could conduct "his" foreign policy. Civil rights advocates reacted negatively when Kennedy's civil rights rhetoric seemed most concerned with preserving the preferred American image abroad.

Whether bemoaning racist treatment of foreign dignitaries or reacting to civil rights demonstrations and racist violence, Kennedy recognized the gross contradictions between American ideals and the reality of American race relations. From the president's perspective all of his directives and dispositions over the issue were quite reasonable and—until the introduction of his civil rights bill—politically circumspect. He had little patience with extremists on either side who did not conform to his carefully planned timetables and politically charged ambitions.

For African Americans, the dream of equality seemed, by 1963, to be turning into a nightmare. Here we believe that the civil rights crisis may have affected Kennedy's views of the "enemy" and this also had implications for foreign policy. The profound moral questions raised by discriminatory practices in the United States reinforced a rather unpalatable but nonetheless clear conclusion: "Evil" did not respect national sovereignty; it was a product that could be spawned in the United States as well as abroad. In this way also, then, the civil rights crisis engaged the contours of a global Cold War morality play.

Managing racial justice in America had seemingly enabled Kennedy to transcend rhetorically certain barriers in communicating with other nations— especially the Cold War rhetoric directed at the Soviets. In his highly acclaimed June 10 speech at American University concerning world peace, he pointed out the similarities between the actions of "nations and neighbors" in their relationship to one another. He stressed that all people thirst for dignity and freedom and that no government—East or West—had the right to block these legitimate aspirations.[73]

And so it may be that the civil rights activities of the early 1960s were indirectly responsible for a lessening of international tension, at least rhetorically on June 10, because direct and prolonged tensions on the domestic front seemed to have softened the foreign policy discourse of a president who had been privy to the best and the worst of human nature in both the domestic and international arena.

For President Kennedy, much of the process of governance had to do with image and sustaining prestige at home and abroad. By linking international and domestic human rights, Kennedy helped create a conundrum. As a result, for a significant time, Kennedy treated the civil rights unrest as a public relations problem that had to be carefully managed and controlled. Meanwhile, events were pushing him toward untested and unwanted decisions.

Presidential Discourse Concerning Domestic Crisis

At a less abstract level, this study suggests that domestic presidential crisis discourse (1) often relies upon appeals to the authority of the executive branch and the public duty to uphold national legal mandates; (2) depends upon perceived and evolving political and social situations and consequences; and (3) poses potential obstacles to foreign policy goals. It further demonstrates that there is utility in focusing on elites and their response to agitation for social change by grassroots elements. Kennedy's very public shift to moral argument suggests that "during a period of prolonged crisis and social discord, *even elites will modify their discourse.*"[74]

Scholars in the past who have criticized Kennedy for his lackluster role in the civil rights movement or who have argued that it was Robert Kennedy and his Justice Department who were key to any real progress in the Kennedy administration's civil rights record perhaps have not paid enough attention to President Kennedy's public discursive acts in 1963. The distribution of power is always hard-won, and in the Kennedy era, it was not bloodless; yet one wonders how much more blood might have been spilled had Kennedy not been so rhetorically malleable in the sustained campaign he began in the summer of 1963 and continued until his assassination.[75]

John F. Kennedy confronted constitutional, racial, and civil order problems in addressing the civil rights issues in America in the early 1960s. The rhetorical situation he faced drew him inexorably into face-to-face confrontations with governors, mayors, worried business persons, civil rights activists, and violent reactionaries. Using the cloak of the Constitution and the legal mandates shaping his role as president, Kennedy plied his persuasive powers to appeal to and sometimes cajole opponents of "unity" and "progress" from subverting "law and order" and threatening "liberty." At times these value appeals failed; at others, Kennedy seemed to win a kind of temporary peace.

As the violence escalated, Kennedy was given pause for serious reflection.

As injustice piled upon injustice in Birmingham and elsewhere, the television and newspaper images became harbingers of brutality that convinced him of the compelling need for change, not just because continued unrest was impolitic, but because an overriding goal of achieving justice and protecting human rights had now presented itself as the "right thing to do." The condition of African Americans in the United States was at first a national and international "political embarrassment" to the president; it was then transferred from legal to moral "outrage" requiring a renewed examination of the national conscience. The president finally undertook his persuasive efforts as both a Constitutional and a moral obligation, and the discourse of moral suasion was grafted to the Constitutional principle of "equality of opportunity" for all U.S. citizens.

By 1963, Kennedy spoke with the passion, measure, cadence, and deliberate speed of a civil rights advocate. Not since the days of Lincoln had the nation heard as passionate a plea on behalf of a minority group. The seeds of human rights Kennedy was intent to sew abroad finally took root on domestic soil as well.

NOTES

1. Carl M. Brauer, *John F. Kennedy and the Second Reconstruction* (New York: Columbia University Press, 1977), 23, 29; Herbert S. Parmet, *JFK: The Presidency of John F. Kennedy* (New York: Dial Press, 1983), 51; James MacGregor Burns, *John Kennedy: A Political Profile* (New York: Harcourt, Brace, Jovanovich, 1960).

2. Brauer, *Second Reconstruction*, 33.

3. Arthur M. Schlesinger, Jr., *A Thousand Days: John F. Kennedy in the White House* (Boston: Houghton Mifflin, 1965), 29; Brauer, *Second Reconstruction*, 35; Parmet, *The Presidency*, 51.

4. Theodore C. Sorensen, *Kennedy* (New York: Harper and Row, 1965), 150; quotation, p. 172; "Remarks of Sen. John F. Kennedy (D.-Mass.), Reception, Jewish Community Center, Milwaukee, Wisconsin, Wednesday Evening, March 23, 1960," JFK Pre-Presidential Papers, 1960 Campaign Files, Speeches, Statements and Sections, 3/19/60-3/31/60, Box 1028, JFK Library.

5. "Addendum to Excerpts from Speeches by Sen. John F. Kennedy, August 31, 1960," Pre-Presidential Papers, 1960 Campaign Files, Speeches, Statements and Sections, Foreign Affairs, Addendum and Excerpts, Box 1030, JFK Library; "Remarks of Sen. John F. Kennedy, Luncheon in Honor of the African Diplomatic Corp," JFK Pre-Presidential Papers, Press Secretary Subject File, Box 1044, JFK Library.

6. "Remarks of Sen. John F. Kennedy, NAACP Rally, Sunday June 10, 1960, Los Angeles, California," JFK Pre-Presidential Papers, 1960 Campaign Files, Speeches Statements and Sections, Civil Rights-Job Discrimination File, NAACP Rally, Box 1028, JFK Library.

7. "Remarks of Sen. John F. Kennedy Accepting the Democratic Presidential Nomination, Democratic National Convention, July 15, 1960," JFK Pre-Presidential Papers, 1960 Campaign Files, General, The New Frontier Acceptance Speech, Box 1032, JFK Library; Lawrence A. Sobel, ed., *Civil Rights: 1960-1966* (New York: Facts on File,

1967), 30; Victor S. Navasky, *Kennedy Justice* (New York: Atheneum, 1971), 97-98; Sobel, *Civil Rights*, 28; Parmet, *The Presidency*, 53.

8. Schlesinger, *A Thousand Days*, 929.

9. Brauer, *Second Reconstruction*, 43, 52, 44.

10. Aida DiPace Donald, ed., *John F. Kennedy and the New Frontier* (New York: Hill and Wang, 1966), 146; Brauer, *Second Reconstruction*, 59.

11. For background on Kennedy's presidential crisis discourse see Theodore Otto Windt, Jr., *Presidents and Protesters: Political Rhetoric in the 1960s* (Tuscaloosa and London: University of Alabama Press, 1990), esp. pp. 17-87. To appreciate Kennedy's discourse, it is useful to note the actual interventionist strategies available to the chief executive. At least seven presidential strategies can be utilized for enforcing civil rights: (1) litigation, (2) the presidential constabulary, (3) the government contract, (4) civil service employment, (5) administrative regulation, (6) withholding or withdrawal of federal funds, and (7) public appeals. Each of these strategies was in evidence during the Kennedy administration. The particular mix employed by the President will be recounted with an emphasis on his persuasive influence attempts. See Donald, *New Frontier*, 165-174.

12. James H. Turner, Richard Singleton, and David Musick, *Oppression: A Socio-History of Black-White Relations in America* (Chicago: Nelson-Hall, 1984), 99-100; Harvard Sitkoff, *The Struggle for Black Equality, 1954-1980* (New York: Hill and Wang, 1981), 83.

13. James Meredith was inspired to go to the University of Mississippi after hearing Kennedy's Inaugural Address. Brauer, *Second Reconstruction*, 66; Navasky, *Kennedy Justice*, 118.

14. "State of the Union Message of President John F. Kennedy," Presidential Office Files, Speech Files, Annual Message to Congress on the State of the Union, Drafts and Press Releases, 1/30/61, Box 34, JFK Library.

15. Parmet, *The Presidency*, 54; Steven R. Goldzwig and George N. Dionisopoulos, "John F. Kennedy's Civil Rights Discourse: From 'Principled Bystander' to Public Advocate," *Communication Monographs* 56 (1989): 179-198; Sorensen, *Kennedy*, 477.

16. Parmet, *The Presidency*, 93.

17. Sitkoff, *The Struggle*, 106; Brauer, *Second Reconstruction*, 64.

18. John F. Kennedy, *Public Papers of the Presidents of the United States: John F. Kennedy, 1961* (Washington, D.C.: U.S. Government Printing Office, 1962), 85, cited hereafter as *Public Papers 1961*.

19. *Public Papers 1961*, 124.

20. *Public Papers 1961*, 137. The PCOEEO was restructured by Kennedy's executive order. *See Public Papers 1961*, 150. A key program evolving from the committee's initiative came to be known as "Plans for Progress," a voluntary association of military and other governmental contractors who had pledged to curb discriminatory hiring and employment practices. The Equal Employment Opportunity Commission and its programs were judged successful. See Robert E. Gilbert, "John F. Kennedy and Civil Rights for Black Americans," *Presidential Studies Quarterly* 12 (1982): 386-399.

21. *Public Papers 1961*, 156, 217.

22. *Public Papers 1961*, 218.

23. *Public Papers 1961*, 256-257. The day after this last statement Yuri Gagarin of the U.S.S.R. completed the first manned space flight and a renewed U.S. space effort was

launched. See *Public Papers 1961*, 257. But most of Kennedy's public statements on civil rights until May were taken up with standard repartee; no, the White House news photographers ought not ban Negroes; yes, the president did indeed call for a new Department of Urban Affairs and Housing but it was not rhetorically linked to civil rights. Finally, the president issued a memo on his executive order on equal employment opportunity. He argued it must include federal employee recreational associations and their facilities. See *Public Papers 1961*, 263, 304.

24. Robert Weisbrot, *Freedom Bound: A History of America's Civil Rights Movement* (New York: Plume/Penguin Books, 1991), 60. At the time, Title 10 of the U.S. Code authorized the president to intervene—through the attorney general's office—when domestic violence deprived the citizenry of constitutional rights. See Parmet, *The Presidency*, 254.

25. William Manchester, *The Glory and the Dream: A Narrative History of America, 1932-1972* (Boston: Little Brown, 1973/1974), 935; Parmet, *The Presidency*, 186; Taylor Branch, *Parting the Waters: America in the King Years, 1954-1963* (New York: Touchstone/Simon and Schuster, 1989), 414.

26. *Public Papers 1961*, 391; and see, e.g., Branch, *Parting the Waters*, 417-418, 434-436.

27. Sobel, *Civil Rights*, 62; Schlesinger, *A Thousand Days*, 936; Brauer, *Second Reconstruction*, 105; Branch, *Parting the Waters*, 451-465.

28. Sitkoff, *The Struggle*, 106; Brauer, *Second Reconstruction,* 107; Manchester, *The Glory*, 935; Branch, *Parting the Waters*, 434, 439; Weisbrot, *Freedom Bound*, 58-66; Sitkoff, *The Struggle*, 107.

29. *Public Papers 1961*, 517. John F. Kennedy received legal help from the Justice Department in dealing with the Freedom Rides when, on May 19, 1961, Robert F. Kennedy asked the Interstate Commerce Commission (ICC) for "more stringent regulations against discrimination." See Brauer, *Second Reconstruction*, 108. This, of course, heartened the Freedom Riders. We also would like to emphasize that our critique focuses upon Kennedy's public address. We are not arguing that Kennedy's civil rights initiatives were absolutely barren. For an administration report on the first six months of office see "Administration Accomplishments in Civil Rights," Theodore C. Sorensen Papers, Subject Files 1961-1964, Civil Rights, Box 30, JFK Library. For an assessment see Gilbert, "Civil Rights." For a more recent positive assessment see Irving Bernstein, *Promises Kept: John F. Kennedy's New Frontier* (New York and Oxford: Oxford University Press, 1991), esp. pp. 44-117.

30. Branch, *Parting the Waters*, 482. In defending his civil rights record of 1961, one year after assuming office, Kennedy noted that "substantial progress" had been made on at least one front—that of voting. See *Public Papers 1961*, 703. This was Justice Department inspired and initiated. In fact, those initiatives revealed the primary civil rights strategy of the administration—litigating the vote. See Schlesinger, *A Thousand Days*, 935. In addition, voter education projects became key to the civil rights cause, but they were only one avenue of redress—and they were a slow, and for the voting rights workers, sometimes deadly, road to achieving human rights.

31. Navasky, *Kennedy Justice*, 21; Sitkoff, *The Struggle*, 113-114.

32. Sobel, *Civil Rights*, 102.

33. Martin Luther King, Jr., *Why We Can't Wait* (New York: Signet Books, 1963/1964), 20; Weisbrot, *Freedom Bound*, 65.

34. John F. Kennedy, *Public Papers of the Presidents of the United States: John F. Kennedy, 1962* (Washington, D.C.: U. S. Government Printing Office, 1963), 8, hereafter cited as *Public Papers 1962*. There seemed to be little advancement of civil rights in 1962. See Sobel, *Civil Rights*, 124, 136-137, 139, 142-143. The incidents of violence also mounted. For example, two churches were burned during voter registration drives near Sasser, Georgia. Between August and mid-September 1962, a total of four churches were torched in efforts to terrorize civil rights activists. In addition, several night-rider shootings were reported. Even without the overt violence, there were still ominous signs of recalcitrance. For example, the White Citizens Council of New Orleans offered "reverse" freedom rides—"free one-way rides [for African Americans] to Washington or any northern city of their choice." See Sobel, *Civil Rights*, 159.

35. See, e.g., Branch, *Parting the Waters*, 633-688; Goldzwig and Dionisopoulos, "Civil Rights Discourse." All subsequent citations are drawn from John F. Kennedy, "Radio and Television Address to the Nation on the Admission of James Meredith to the University of Mississippi, September 30, 1962," *Public Papers 1962*, 726-728. Reprinted in the "Collected Speeches" section of this volume.

36. Schlesinger, *A Thousand Days*, 948; Sobel, *Civil Rights*, 110; Navasky, *Kennedy Justice*, 227-228; Weisbrot, *Freedom Bound*, 66-67.

37. Harry S. Ashmore, *Hearts and Minds: The Anatomy of Racism From Roosevelt to Reagan* (New York: McGraw Hill, 1982), 346. In polls conducted after the speech, the president experienced a "transitory setback" in the South (65 percent approval in September, 52 percent in October). But outside of the South the president continued to hover at the 65 to 70 percent range and by November his approval rating in the South once again reached 65 percent. See Brauer, *Second Reconstruction*, 200-201.

38. Weisbrot, *Freedom Bound*, 67-68.

39. USIA Memorandum to the President, Presidential Office Files, Civil Rights, Mississippi, 10/1/61-11/1/62, Box 98, JFK Library; Schlesinger, *A Thousand Days*, 948.

40. Ashmore, *Hearts and Minds*, 346.

41. *Public Papers 1962*, 592-593.

42. King, *Why We Can't Wait*, 43; Brauer, *Second Reconstruction*, 176-177.

43. *Public Papers 1962*, 544; Parmet, *The Presidency*, 258; Brauer, *Second Reconstruction*, 205-207.

44. *Public Papers 1962*, 832, 835. The order was limited to housing "built or bought with federal aid or financed by private mortgages guaranteed or insured by federal agencies." Independent banks and savings and loans who had federally insured deposits were exempted. This latter provision proved a fatal weakness. See Sobel, *Civil Rights*, 149; Schlesinger, *A Thousand Days*, 948; Branch, *Parting the Waters*, 586-587; Weisbrot, *Freedom Bound*, 53-54.

45. The President fielded questions on Robert Weaver and the still unfilled new Housing and Urban Affairs cabinet position (*Public Papers 1962*, 62-63, 97, 153-154, 401) and civil rights legislation (*Public Papers 1962*, 95); made much out of new agreements on equal opportunity employment (*Public Papers 1962*, 117-118, 505-507, 544); responded to hearings on equal opportunity in housing by noting that when inequality persists in Washington, D.C. "in particular, it sometimes constitutes a personal affront to the diplomats of sovereign nations and always reflects upon our ability as a nation to live up to our Constitutional ideals" (*Public Papers 1962*, 324). Kennedy also found himself (1) issuing commentary on the "reverse" freedom rides as an issue that

"really doesn't merit very much comment" other than to say that "there is no city, traditionally, that has enjoyed a happier reputation than New Orleans.... And I would not let one man possibly blacken it" (*Public Papers 1962*, 380); (2) noting the eighth anniversary of the Supreme Court desegregation decision by responding to a question at a press conference that indicated "progress" had been made but that there was still "a good deal left undone" (*Public Papers 1962*, 407); (3) making reference to plans and a report on "100 Years of Progress" for the upcoming celebration of the Emancipation Proclamation in 1963 (*Public Papers 1962*, 497); (4) ordering a review of the status of equal opportunity in the armed forces (*Public Papers 1962*, 508); and (5) responding to a press conference question regarding Martin Luther King's suggestion that the president use more "moral persuasion" by reaffirming his commitment to "every American citizen['s] . . . Constitutional rights" and declaring that "this Administration has taken a whole variety of very effective steps to improve the equal opportunities for all Americans and will continue to do so" (*Public Papers 1962*, 572). Additionally, Kennedy was building the public record by issuing a memorandum on equal opportunity for women employed by the federal government (*Public Papers 1962*, 578); commemorating the one-year anniversary of "Plans for Progress" by giving his approval to the "feasibility of this approach" and reinforcing "the need to pursue our objective vigorously and without let up" (*Public Papers 1962*, 642). On September 13, 1962, he reacted to the burning of churches and the shooting of two young Mississippians who were involved in voter registration as "cowardly as well as outrageous" and he promised that the perpetrators would be "appropriately dealt with" (*Public Papers 1962*, 676). He pledged the "protection" of the U.S. government for people who chose to register to vote and stipulated that "if it required extra legislation and extra force, we should do that" (*Public Papers* 1962, 677).

Finally, the president issued two statements in 1962 commemorating the centennial of Lincoln's Emancipation Proclamation. On September 22, 1962, the president told the American people that the proclamation "was not an end but a beginning." Yet despite past civil rights problems and their attendant "humiliation and deprivation," the president praised African Americans for their loyalty to the United States "and for working for [their] own salvation." Kennedy said "progress" had been made, but, "the task is not finished" (*Public Papers 1962*, 702).

46. King, *Why We Can't Wait*, 21. Roy Wilkins has indicated that 1962 "was the lowest moment for the civil rights movement during the Kennedy years." As Arthur M. Schlesinger, Jr. records, King observed, "A sweeping revolutionary force [was] . . . pressed into a narrow tunnel." The president's leadership did little to aid activists to buck the trend. See Roy Wilkins (with Tom Mathews), *Standing Fast: The Autobiography of Roy Wilkins* (New York: Viking, 1982), 285; Schlesinger, *A Thousand Days*, 950; Branch, *Parting the Waters*, 650.

47. John F. Kennedy, *Public Papers of the Presidents of the United States: John F. Kennedy, 1963* (Washington, D. C.: U.S. Government Printing Office, 1964), 222-230, quotations, p. 222; cited hereafter as *Public Papers 1963*. On voting, Kennedy said, "In a free society, those with the power to govern are necessarily responsive to those with the right to vote" (*Public Papers 1963*, 223). Introducing his agenda for education, the president referred to *Brown v. Board of Education*: "That decision represented both good law and good judgment—it was both legally and morally right" (*Public Papers 1963*, 225). The president also told Congress that "Racial discrimination in employment is

especially injurious both to its victims and to the national economy. It results in a great waste of human resources and creates serious community problems. It is, moreover, inconsistent with the democratic principle that no man should be denied employment commensurate with his abilities because of his race, creed, or ancestry" (*Public Papers 1963*, 227). In referring to public accommodations the president seemed more forceful than ever: "No act is more contrary to the spirit of our democracy and Constitution—or more rightfully resented by a Negro citizen who seeks only equal treatment—than the barring of that citizen from restaurants, hotels, theaters, recreational areas, and other public accommodations and facilities" (*Public Papers 1963*, 228). The President assured "all members of the public" of his commitment to "equal access to all public accommodations," saying, "A country with a 'color blind' Constitution, and with no castes or classes among its citizens, cannot afford to do less" (*Public Papers 1963*, 229). The president went on to outline past and present executive action in this area. Finally, Kennedy articulated other executive actions undertaken by his administration and called for legislative extension of the Civil Rights Commission for four more years as a means of establishing a "national clearinghouse" to provide technical assistance and support for desegregation activities throughout the nation.

    48. *Public Papers 1963*, 229-230; Branch, *Parting the Waters*, 699.

    49. Weisbrot, *Freedom Bound*, 71, 70; Branch, *Parting the Waters*, 756-802. Over 950 people signed up to go to jail and 600 were incarcerated the first day, with up to 75 children placed in a single eight-person cell. The next day, Friday May 3, 1,000 children steeled themselves for a march. Some of the marchers were met with "special monitor guns that forced water from two hoses through a single nozzle, mounted on a tripod. . . . The . . . guns made limbs jerk weightlessly and tumbled whole bodies like scoops of refuse in a high wind . . . . [B]ystanders, horrified at such sights, threw bricks and rocks at the hoses" (Branch, *Parting the Waters*, 758-759). The Birmingham Campaign finally resulted in the bombing of A. D. King's home and Martin Luther King's hotel, whereupon riots broke out at Kelly Ingram Park (Branch, *Parting the Waters*, esp. p. 779). Kennedy once again feared that federal forces would be needed to quell the riots and this time the government faced the prospect of having to deal with violent blacks as well as whites (Branch, *Parting the Waters*, 797).

    50. Weisbrot, *Freedom Bound*, 72; Branch, *Parting the Waters*, 799.

    51. *Public Papers 1963*, 407-409.

    52. *Public Papers 1963*, 418, 423.

    53. *Public Papers 1963*, 447-448.

    54. The citations from the June 11 speech that follow are taken from the "Radio and Television Report to the American People on Civil Rights, June 11, 1963," Presidential Office Files, Speech Files, Box 45, JFK Library. Reprinted in the "Collected Speeches" section of this volume.

    55. Newspaper quotations drawn from Presidential Office Files, Speech Files, "Radio and Television Report to the American People on Civil Rights, 6/11/63," Box 45, JFK Library.

    56. Sorensen, *Kennedy*, 470; Alonzo L. Hamby, *Liberalism and Its Challenges: F.D.R. to Bush*, 2nd ed. (New York: Oxford University Press, 1992), 212; Parmet, *The Presidency*, 267; Branch, *Parting the Waters*, 824; Brauer, *Second Reconstruction*, 259. We have found at least two drafts of the June 11 speech in the files of the Kennedy library. For the most part, these drafts are in conformance with the final product, until the

extemporaneous concluding remarks, which, in our view, were insignificant modifications.

57. Brauer, *Second Reconstruction*, 259-260. Robert Kennedy argued that in 1962 "nobody was ready" for civil rights legislation. Moreover, the president's personal moral conscience did not necessarily get a boost from the Birmingham campaign. Rather, events at Birmingham strengthened the president's political hand and this emboldened him to seek civil rights legislation "which you could never have obtained prior to that time." See Robert F. Kennedy, *In His Own Words: The Unpublished Recollections of the Kennedy Years*, ed. Edward O. Guthman and James Shulman (New York: Bantam Books, 1988), 149.

58. Goldzwig and Dionisopoulos, "Civil Rights Discourse"; Brauer, *Second Reconstruction*, 260-262.

59. "From Attorney General," Printed Material, Undated, Theodore C. Sorensen Papers, JFK Speech Files, 1961-1963, Box 73, JFK Library.

60. Brauer, *Second Reconstruction*, 263; Branch, *Parting the Waters*, 824; Schlesinger, *A Thousand Days*, 965. A premonition of the violence that lie ahead occurred almost instantaneously. A few hours after the president's address, Medgar Evers was murdered near his home in Jackson, Mississippi. George Wallace's carefully staged, dramatic, but ultimately ineffective stand at Tuscaloosa would seem but a footnote to history when measured against the timelessness of Kennedy's striking words and the repugnant reality of mounting violence bred by racist attacks.

61. Further proof of the point comes by way of example. Kennedy finally rejected "voluntary" approaches to integration; instead he endorsed an "equal access" clause on public accommodations for his civil rights bill (*Public Papers 1963*, 486). Kennedy also lamented the delays in desegregation of schools. The right to equal education, he said, quoting the Supreme Court, was a "present right" not to be relegated "to some future enjoyment," and Kennedy proposed specific legislative remedies for the problem.

Unemployment relief was also a part of his civil rights package because unemployment fell "with special cruelty on minority groups" and because without "employment opportunities" the realization of all rights became less than "meaningful." Kennedy proposed funding for more jobs, education, and training and he also made sure he included an arm for detecting discriminatory employment practices. Always pragmatic, Kennedy argued: "Studies show . . . that the loss of one year's income due to unemployment is more than the total cost of 12 years of education through high school; and, when welfare and other social costs are added, it is clear that failure to take these steps will cost us far more than their enactment. There is no more profitable investment than education and no greater waste than ill-trained youth" (*Public Papers 1963*, 489).

In proposing, by executive order, to establish a federal community relations service, the president highlighted the need for the identification of "community tensions before they reach the crisis stage" (*Public Papers 1963*, 491). Furthermore, he indicated that spending federal dollars on any program ought not subsidize discrimination: "Simple justice requires that public funds, to which all taxpayers of all races contribute, not be spent in any fashion which encourages, entrenches, subsidizes, or results in racial discrimination" (*Public Papers 1963*, 492). Cautioning against the violence of "weeks past," the president implored all citizens "to exercise self-restraint" while Congress attended to the task he set before it (*Public Papers 1963*, 493).

62. *Public Papers 1963*, 483-494. Many within the administration would oppose the president's civil rights bill and were especially concerned with making it a "moral issue." Some argued that had it not been for Robert Kennedy, the initiative would have died a cautious death (Navasky, *Kennedy Justice*, 99). But the president reportedly "lobbied vigorously." Although some claimed certain provisions were omitted, such as banning employment discrimination, and others were criticized for not going far enough, with the announcement of this legislation Kennedy "had touched the most sensitive vein in American society," and having risked much, gave every indication publicly that he would stay the course (Parmet, *The Presidency*, 272).

63. Parmet, *The Presidency*, 354; Sorensen, *Kennedy*, 496, 498; Sitkoff, *The Struggle*, 158.

64. Manchester, *The Glory*, 982; and see, e.g., Brauer, *Second Reconstruction*, 291-292; Navasky, *Kennedy Justice*, 226.

65. *Public Papers 1963*, 571-572, 631; Sorensen, *Kennedy*, 504.

66. *Public Papers 1963*, 645; Goldzwig and Dionisopoulos, "Civil Rights Discourse," 192.

67. *Public Papers 1963*, 650.

68. *Public Papers 1963*, 661-662; Sobel, *Civil Rights*, 187; *Public Papers 1963*, p. 857.

69. *Public Papers 1963*, 868.

70. Walter R. Fisher, "Reaffirmation and Subversion of the American Dream," *Quarterly Journal of Speech* 59 (1973): 160-167.

71. Ronald M. Dworkin, *Taking Rights Seriously* (Cambridge, Mass.: Harvard University Press, 1977), 227, 267.

72. Ronald M. Dworkin, *A Matter of Principle* (Cambridge, Mass.: Harvard University Press, 1985), 205. Interestingly, it may be that the evolution of individual and collective "equal rights" as a moral mandate in America and the evolution of case law pursuant to this understanding received their greatest initial thrust in this century with the enactment of the Civil Rights Act of 1964, essentially a package initiated by John F. Kennedy and passed after his assassination.

73. *Public Papers 1963*, 461. This speech is explored more fully in the next chapter. The full speech text is included in the "Collected Speeches" section of this volume.

74. Goldzwig and Dionisopoulos, "Civil Rights Discourse," 194.

75. See, e.g., Parmet, *The Presidency*; Navasky, *Kennedy Justice*.

4

PRESIDENT KENNEDY'S FOREIGN POLICY DISCOURSE: A RHETORIC OF ROMANTIC PRAGMATISM

According to Theodore Sorensen, John F. Kennedy was more interested in foreign affairs than domestic and the bulk of his presidential time, talent, and energy was consumed with global concerns. The Kennedy era conjures up images of Cold War crises played against a backdrop of superpower confrontation in a nuclear age. It was a most sobering, harrowing, and provocative period. The stakes were high and the discourse was heated.[1]

As is widely acknowledged, much U.S. rhetoric presumed and countered a worldwide monolithic Communist menace. In the Kennedy era, the stark dualisms of freedom versus tyranny, capitalism versus communism, and West versus East provided polar references for a rhetoric of struggle and conflict. Kennedy's rhetoric during the presidential campaign was premised on his belief that totalitarian states have a distinct advantage over democracies in enforcing their political agenda: "The hard, tough question for the next decade . . . is whether any free society . . . can meet the singleminded advance of Communism. . . . Have we the nerve and the will?" His presidential rhetoric focused upon an affirmative answer to this question.[2]

As indicated previously, two days before Kennedy's inauguration Khrushchev publicly advocated a policy in which "wars of national liberation" would commence in earnest. That the comments were targeted more toward China than the United States was lost on the president-elect, who distributed the speech to top advisers and told them to "read, mark, learn, and inwardly digest" the words, which according to Robert McNamara, would come to be "a significant event in [their] lives."[3]

Kennedy's first State of the Union Address provided a substantive response matching Khrushchev's perceived bellicosity. The president's returning shot had its own share of heated rhetorical flourish. As Robert S. Thompson indicates, "most of his words were harsh." Indeed, "Even more than the inaugural address, the speech to Congress in late January 1961 was the kickoff of the Kennedy foreign policy drive—a drive intended to show the world, America, and perhaps Kennedy himself that he was tough." The alarmist, confrontational tone of Kennedy's first State of the Union Address would continue throughout the first two years of his presidency. "I speak today in an hour of national peril and national opportunity." The president declared an "hour of maximum danger" in which "hostile forces grow stronger" while "the tide of events has been running out and time has not been our friend," as the Communist juggernaut continued its "ambitions for world domination."[4]

Privately, the president's advisers drew a less bleak picture. Kennedy was crafting not only a definition of the international threat but also a domestic political message—the evocation of crises and the isolation of "flashpoints" would provide ample opportunity to demonstrate his leadership against the challenge of global Communism. In particular, the State of the Union speech provided Kennedy with an opportunity to announce plans for military expansion. Although this announcement was accompanied by concomitant commitments to increase international economic aid and pursue agreements with the Soviets concerning negotiated disarmament and nuclear testing, as Beschloss observes, "Khrushchev almost surely thought Kennedy's State of the Union address a deliberate slap in the face." During the first two years of his presidency, Kennedy's resolve would be most vigorously tested in acute confrontations with the Soviets over Cuba and Berlin.[5]

In this chapter we will argue that John F. Kennedy's foreign policy rhetoric displayed a pattern that alternated between confrontation and conciliation, or what Sorensen characterized as the President's "arrows" and "olive branches." This discourse addressed multiple audiences strategically, responding to what Kennedy perceived as a complex and increasingly dangerous political environment. We believe the character of Kennedy's foreign policy discourse is best described and understood as romantic pragmatism—combining liberal idealism with what he viewed as a pragmatist's sense of realism. Kennedy concerned himself with defining and presenting the "facts" of the global situation within the wider interpretive context of the American ideals he employed lavishly—especially in the tense struggle to win the allegiance of developing nations to Western-style democracy. In this pursuit Kennedy was unabashedly nationalistic, jingoistic, and at times xenophobic. This, of course, suited the times. We will argue that this particular mix of foreign policy rhetoric produced mixed results and an ambiguous legacy.[6]

THE COLD WAR AS A "BACKDROP"

To understand the rhetorical strategies guiding Kennedy's foreign policy discourse we offer a brief discussion of the rhetoric of the Cold War. Cold War rhetoric has both resulted in and fended off armed conflict. It has served as a barometer of U.S. foreign policy, influenced domestic affairs, facilitated increased defense spending, emphasized military solutions to diplomatic problems, determined our notion of the geopolitical terrain, brought us to the precipice of both nuclear annihilation and hopes for peace, and, finally, lifted rhetorical propaganda to an art form.[7]

All of these outcomes have been experienced as a result of the "overarching goal" of avoiding a nuclear confrontation between the Soviet Union and the United States. While attempting to prevent the disaster of a "hot war," the superpowers focused on continuing their various spheres of political, economic, and social influence. This Cold War "chess board" diplomacy—with its moves and countermoves—was indeed a delicate, perilous game, but one to which the superpowers felt fully subscribed as a matter of survival. Its gambits help explain both Kennedy's idealism—intended to extend global influence—and his pragmatism—in seeking to avoid a global conflagration. However, like all Cold War rhetoric, there were limitations to its efficacy. As Martin Medhurst observes: "In Cold War discourse five constraining factors are always present: the history of superpower relations, domestic political concerns, the status of both domestic and world economies, present diplomatic negotiations, and the ever-present possibility of a military engagement." Kennedy would be required to walk a delicate tightrope under these constraints. On the one hand he felt the United States must take a key role in protecting freedom by advancing democracy against the ideological and material advances of the Soviets while, on the other, he was haunted by a nuclear specter that required careful negotiation, conciliation, and overtures for peaceful coexistence. His concern for winning these dual wars was complicated by both an arms and technology race borne of fear, and by a concern over a loss of American prestige in the world community. For Kennedy, the ultimate failure was for the United States to be revealed as weak in either military preparations or peace negotiations. Thus, the familiar Cold War platitude of "peace-through-strength" created a political and rhetorical double-bind that accounted for some of the ambiguity, if not inconsistency, in Kennedy's foreign policy address. As Sorensen has observed: "Of all the Churchill phrases John Kennedy liked to quote, his favorite was: 'We arm to parley.'"[8]

Additionally, in eschewing the Eisenhower era's Manichean worldview of "good versus evil," Kennedy augured a "new age" in U.S. foreign policy. Pluralism would replace dualism and multilateralism would be championed over unilateralism. It was heady and seemed right for the times—a new openness to a changing world. The trick was in the details. What seemed certain in the early 1960s was that the new policy would not only bring renewed hopes and expectations but also even greater and graver responsibilities.[9]

In the post-World War II Cold War environment, a candidate for the presidency in the United States had to demonstrate "statesmanlike qualities" and "the preferable credentials were those of authority in foreign policy." What

Kennedy lacked in experience in this area he made up for in interest and enthusiasm concerning diplomatic history. Despite service on the Senate Foreign Relations Committee—which he sparsely attended between 1957 and 1960—Kennedy felt that his youth and inexperience would be most sorely tested in the area of diplomacy and military preparedness, which at the time were often seen as synonymous.

During the campaign Kennedy distributed *The Strategy of Peace*, a collection of his foreign policy statements that would serve as "the literary centerpiece of his campaign" as well as the precursor and guide to his foreign policy speeches as president. For Kennedy, the problem in foreign policy was one of recovering the American mission and reformulating the American purpose, which would require sacrifice. This relied upon the full flowering of the American character through realization of characteristic American ideals. Kennedy urged his audience to understand that the nations of the world looked to the United States as a beacon of "personal and natural liberty, of the natural equality of all souls, of the dignity of labor, of economic development broadly shared. Yet we have allowed the Communists to evict us from our rightful estate at the head of this world-wide revolution." Thus the U.S. mission was premised upon "human freedom" as "an enriching, ennobling, practical achievement. . . . [O]ur purpose is not only to defend the integrity of this democratic society, but also to help advance the cause of human freedom and world law—the universal cause of a just and lasting peace." Therefore: "This generation does not have to find new purposes. The old American purposes are still wholly relevant. What this generation needs to do is to face its problems—at home and abroad. They cannot be divided." The problem was not one of principle but of action. There was no room for "soft sentimentalism." A strategy was required that would produce "tough-minded plans and operations" to "rescue" the American character "from the sea of fat in which it has been drowning." The candidate summoned his audience to once again be "true to the work of a Choosing People—a people who voluntarily assume the burden and the glory of advancing mankind's best hopes." The American role "in these crucial years of our world leadership" was to ensure that our policies promoted "freedom" and "world peace." These twin goals required "that we recapture our national purpose and redouble our energy. For we seem to have both the sense of the promise of America and the will to fulfill it."[10]

For Kennedy, however, this mission required increases in both conventional and nuclear forces. Part of the challenge ahead lay in facing up to Soviet incursions—both ideological and material. This meant heating up the propaganda war, developing "flexible response" plans for "wars of national liberation," and repairing the so-called "missile gap." Kennedy also was concerned that war could come by intention or miscalculation, and found historical parallels useful in making this cautionary point:

[O]ur experience with the illogical decisions of Adolph Hitler should have taught us that . . . [negative world opinion] might not deter the leaders of a totalitarian state—particularly in a moment of recklessness, panic, irrationality, or even cool miscalculation. . . . [Nuclear holocausts by inadvertence] are very real possibilities. . . . For many years now we have been living on the edge of the crater.[11]

The promise and the peril of the Cold War outlined in *The Strategy of Peace* was meant to assure Americans of Kennedy's grasp of global affairs and his resoluteness in transcending the national malaise many felt. His rhetoric was strategically designed to communicate that he would not only continue the policy of containment initiated by Truman, but also respond imaginatively to threatened U.S. interests in a changing world. According to the candidate, both vision and practical plans of action had been blunted in the complacency and surfeit attending the Eisenhower administration's eight years of torpid diplomacy. The discourse, of course, implied Kennedy's idealism and youthful vigor. His leadership would promise innovative ideas and plans of action that would translate into swift, effective foreign policy implementation.

The resulting narratives were typical of the liberal rhetoric of the time, naming and celebrating the values of a capitalist democracy. As Alonzo L. Hamby notes:

John Kennedy's critique of Eisenhower's diplomacy epitomized the divided mind of Democratic liberalism in its effort to couple an idealistic encouragement of peaceful economic development and social revolution with greater military strength. The liberals suffered from intellectual tensions similar to those of the conservatives — they shrank from the unpleasant and dangerous implications of the Cold War, yet because they visualized the United States as the world's primary defender of the values of liberal democracy, they could not escape the urge to wage it more vigorously.

The first two years of Kennedy's foreign policy address are best described as a rhetoric of confrontation. In the final year of his presidency, Kennedy adopted a more conciliatory tone.[12]

A RHETORIC OF CONFRONTATION—1961-1962

Cuba and the Bay of Pigs

In 1959, just prior to the collapse of the dictator Fulgencio Batista, many American voices accorded Fidel Castro high standing as the revolutionary savior of Cuba. But by 1961 the climate was much different and the dominant American view was that he was too friendly with the Soviets, seemed to be supporting armed revolution in other Latin American countries, and perhaps most importantly, by being located 90 miles off the coast of Florida, became the chief symbol of the threat "wars of national liberation" posed in the Western hemisphere. Arguably, repressive U.S. policies were partially responsible for Castro's shift to the sphere of Soviet influence—a move viewed by many Cubans as a matter of economic and political survival.[13]

According to James N. Giglio, Cuba would remain, until Kennedy's death, his greatest foreign policy concern. As Herbert S. Parmet noted, "Castro had become a 'bone' in the American throat." Eisenhower had handed over his watch with a chilling directive—he had already initiated plans to overthrow Castro and counseled Kennedy to implement them. The press too, for its part, fanned the fires of public sentiment, increasing both diplomatic and public pressures to "get Castro."[14]

Early in the 1960 campaign Kennedy had characterized the Batista rule as a "bloody and repressive dictatorship." *The Strategy of Peace* hailed Castro as "part of the legacy of Bolivar" and attributed some of his more extreme and unwelcome actions to U.S. perfidy in propping up Batista. As the election drew near, Kennedy genuinely felt that Castro had broken his promises of free elections and now was unalterably in the Soviet sphere of influence—casting an ominous shadow over the Caribbean. The candidate fretted over the possibility that Eisenhower would overthrow Castro, "electing" Richard Nixon in the process, which is exactly the kind of scenario Nixon had in mind. As a result, Kennedy heated up his discourse against Castro.[15]

During the campaign Kennedy had praised a policy of U.S. support for anti-Castro "freedom fighters," but, fearing adverse world opinion, was privately and publicly unwilling to commit U.S. ground forces to the cause. Kennedy also made partisan arguments against the Republicans for allowing "a Communist menace" to spread its tentacles "only eight jet minutes from Florida." Nixon reportedly was incensed with the thought that Allen Dulles had informed Kennedy of the Eisenhower administration's plans to train and equip Cuban exiles as guerrilla forces. Ironically, in the fourth televised Kennedy-Nixon debate, Nixon claimed he found himself in the unenviable position of having to publicly deny his endorsement of the covert Eisenhower administration plan to overthrow Castro. "The bizarre result was that many Americans who did not wish to intervene in Cuba voted for Nixon, who was privately prodding the CIA to get the job done before Election Day. Many Americans who wanted more militancy against Castro voted for Kennedy, who was privately ambivalent at best about ousting Castro by force."[16]

According to Trumbull Higgins, when Kennedy took office "American relations with Cuba had deteriorated to the level of those with Japan in July 1941." In renewing the appointment of Allen Dulles as CIA director, Kennedy became both inheritor of and a player in the prior administration's covert schemes. Richard Bissell, deputy director for plans at the CIA, urged McGeorge Bundy, national security adviser to the president, to implore Kennedy to authorize an "executive action" with the goal of overthrowing the Castro regime; such plans anticipated U.S.-assisted, covert, armed invasion and even assassination attempts.[17]

The day before Kennedy's inauguration, Eisenhower told him that the secret Cuban operation was proceeding in an orderly fashion and that it was Kennedy's "responsibility" to provide "whatever is necessary" for its continued success. Dulles and the CIA assured Kennedy that a Cuban invasion could be successful. On March 11, the Joint Chiefs approved an invasion plan. On Wednesday, March 15, Operation Zapata was introduced, focusing on a "quiet" landing at the Bay of Pigs, with the proviso that if there was a "failure" in the operation, the Cuban exiles would "melt into the mountains." This proved to be a flawed, if not fatal assumption.[18]

Kennedy was adamant that U.S. forces ought to steer clear of the Cuba operation: "The minute I land one Marine, we're in this thing up to our necks. I can't get the United States into a war and then lose it, no matter what it takes. I'm not going to risk an American Hungary. And that's what it could be, a fucking slaughter. Is that understood gentlemen?" On April 12, Kennedy reassured the press of the same intention: "[T]here will not be, under any conditions, an intervention in Cuba by United States armed forces." On April 17, a brigade of Cuban exiles would land on the beach at the Bay of Pigs.[19]

As the fiasco unfolded "four volunteer [U.S.] airmen were shot down and killed . . . thus invalidating the administration's last pretense that the United States was not involved in the invasion." Kennedy, always cautious, had approved six Navy jets to serve as air cover for ammunition supply flights and their escorts, but they arrived too early. The hapless invaders were left defenseless; four supply planes were chased away and two of their B-26 escorts were downed. In all, 114 exiles died and 1,189 surrendered. Kennedy placed the blame on his military and state advisers as well as the CIA for misinformation; his trust in the intelligence community was shattered for the rest of his presidency. As the details of the incident unfolded, they provided grounds for international embarrassment, especially in parts of Latin America where the invasion was seen as an example par excellence of "Yankee imperialism." American embassies were stoned in New Dehli, Warsaw, Cairo, and Tokyo.[20]

Address to the American Society of Newspaper Editors

Despite the enormity of Kennedy's foreign policy gaffe, he seemed militantly unrepentant. On April 20, 1961, the president addressed the American Society of Newspaper Editors in a hurried attempt to fend off the political negatives of the Cuban misadventure. Ted Sorensen had worked through the night preparing a draft of the speech. As the president saw it, his task was to douse domestic calls for violent reprisals against Castro's regime, secure world opinion of the United States as a prudent policy maker, and convince the Soviets that his restraint in the operation was neither a sign of weakness nor complacency. The rhetorical problem was perhaps best crystallized in Arthur M. Schlesinger, Jr.'s comment that after the Bay of Pigs, "The New Frontier looked like a collection of . . . stupid, ineffectual imperialists." Kennedy's address was intended to adopt a "fighting stance" without prodding anyone to "reckless action," and we suggest that he employed two simultaneous definitional strategies in pursuit of these goals: establishment of a transcendent context and the articulation and defense of U.S. foreign policy goals and objectives.[21]

Establishing a Transcendent Context. In his opening remarks Kennedy said he sought to "present the facts . . . with candor." As framed by the president, what had happened in Cuba was emblematic of "the eternal struggle of liberty against tyranny"—just one flashpoint "in so many other arenas of the contest for freedom." In Kennedy's narrative, Cuba served as a synecdochic representation of global Communist repression. Kennedy reinforced this point through an implied historical analogy: "This is not the first time in either ancient or recent history that a small band of freedom fighters has engaged the armor of totalitarianism. It is not the first time that communist tanks have rolled over gallant men and women fighting to redeem the independence of their homeland." While the comparison to Hungary in 1956 left much to be desired, it served Kennedy's transcendent strategy well.[22]

Each of the three "lessons" Kennedy drew from the failed operation also emphasized the larger struggle taking place between the two superpowers:

> First, it is clear that the forces of communism are not to be underestimated, in Cuba or anywhere else in the world. . . . Secondly, it is clear that this nation, in concert with all the free nations of this Hemisphere, must take an even closer and more realistic look at the menace of external communist intervention and domination in Cuba. . . . Third, and finally, it is clearer than ever that we face a relentless struggle in every corner of the globe that goes far beyond the clash of armies or even nuclear armaments. . . . [T]hey serve primarily as a shield behind which subversion, infiltration, and a host of other tactics steadily advance, picking off vulnerable areas one by one in situations which do not permit our own armed intervention.

Having defined this transcendent context, Kennedy minimized the specifics of the exact U.S. role in the operation, thus overlooking American complicity in the failure. Instead, Castro's regime was scapegoated: "[W]e will not accept Mr. Castro's attempts to blame this nation for the hatred with which his one-time supporters now regard his repression." And the president almost seemed to promise that grassroots attempts to overthrow Castro would continue: "The Cuban people have not yet spoken their final piece—and I have no doubt that they and their revolutionary council . . . will continue to speak up for a free and independent Cuba."

Kennedy denied that those involved in the uprising were "mercenaries" and pledged his support for "countless other guerrilla fighters" who have now "determined that the dedication of those who gave their lives shall not be forgotten, and that Cuba must not be abandoned to the Communists. And we do not intend to abandon it either." In making this promise the president reinforced the impression of a popular uprising of "Cuban patriots against a Cuban dictator." He thus deflected attention away from the "covert" facts that the operation was planned by U.S. military and intelligence communities and approved by the State Department, and that the landing force was CIA-trained in Guatemala.

Rearticulating and Defending U.S. Policy. For those who felt that the United States should have committed ground forces to help the "freedom fighters" or who were now calling for reprisals against Castro, Kennedy reinforced earlier public policy statements: "Any unilateral American intervention, in the absence of an external attack upon ourselves or an ally, would have been contrary to our traditions and our international obligations." At the same time, Kennedy warned, "our restraint is not inexhaustible," and the doctrine of inter-American "noninterference" could be trumped if the nations of the Western hemisphere "should fail to meet their commitments against outside Communist penetration." Such an interpretation was, in the president's view, clearly the prerogative of the United States. If a "failure" were to occur, Kennedy said: "then I want it clearly understood that this government will not hesitate in meeting its primary obligations which are to the security of our Nation."

We view this rhetorical strategy as particularly ambivalent. Kennedy seemed to be saying that the United States was bound by tradition and international obligation not to act unilaterally, while simultaneously arguing that that is exactly what the United States would do if its national security interests were perceived to be in jeopardy. We believe this ambiguity may be explained by considering the rhetorical goals of this address. Kennedy's tough talk may have been motivated by his fear that the Soviets interpreted as weakness his failure to commit U.S. forces during the invasion. However, because unilateral action would be perceived negatively in many international quarters, especially in Latin America, Kennedy also had to speak against it. The result, of course, was rather ambiguous.

Kennedy was intent upon reinforcing U.S. rights. If intervention was deemed necessary as a matter of national security or in the fulfillment of treaty obligations, then so be it. The president struck a defiant pose with the Soviets and all those who violently disagreed with what had been revealed by the press as an American-sponsored operation. He drew the relevant "lessons" from history. To the U.S.S.R., he said: "We do not intend to be lectured on 'intervention' by those whose character was stamped for all time on the bloody streets of Budapest." In a reference to anti-American protests, Kennedy cautioned: "Those who staged automatic 'riots' in the streets of free nations over the effort of a small group of young Cubans to regain their freedom should recall the long roll call of refugees who cannot now go back—to Hungary, to North Korea, to North Vietnam, to East Germany, or to Poland, or to any other lands from which a steady stream of refugees pours forth, in eloquent testimony to the cruel oppression now holding sway in their homelands."

In the "new age" of foreign policy, the United States was to take the lead in defending against an adversary whose slow but steady incursions on freedom—"piece by piece"—threatened the security of all nations. Therefore, "Only the strong, only the industrious, only the determined, only the courageous, only the visionary who determine the real nature of our struggle can possibly survive." In rearticulating this mission in both idealistic and survivalist tones (which for the chief executive constituted the pragmatic realities of the situation—at least in his public stance), Kennedy employed parallelism to sketch the nature of the challenge in stark tones: "We dare not fail to see the insidious nature of this new and deeper struggle. We dare not fail to grasp the new concepts, the new tools, the new sense of urgency we will need to meet it, whether in Cuba or South Vietnam. And we dare not fail to realize that this struggle is taking place every day." "History," said Kennedy, "will record the fact that this bitter struggle reached its climax in the late 1950s and early 1960s." And he closed: "Let me then make clear as President of the United States that I am determined upon our system's survival and success, regardless of the cost and regardless of the peril."

The tough talk masked a disastrous foreign policy adventure. In pointing out the inadequacies and sorry legacies of the Communist system, Kennedy portrayed the Cuban incident as part of a global struggle, emblematic of the operational ideals of the international U.S. mission. It was a rhetorical alchemy intended to transform a politically embarrassing defeat at the Bay of Pigs into Cold War propaganda chips by suggesting that the policy remained pristine and idealistically apace with events on the world stage.

The fearless, sometimes apocalyptic, words directed at the newspaper editors would be supplemented one week later in an address to the American Newspaper Publishers Association. Kennedy argued that given the nature of the present worldwide struggle against a monolithic communist menace—a piecemeal struggle marked by covert forms of intimidation and subversion—the nation's press also would have to review its grave responsibilities. This hour of maximum danger required a kind of special circumspection on the part of a free press. He called for voluntary self-restraint so that no further aid or comfort would be given to our adversary through published reports of covert U.S. activities.

Once again Kennedy would outline a program that seemed ambivalent, if not, in his own words, "contradictory." On the one hand he called upon the press to provide "far greater public information" and, on the other, "far greater official secrecy." Because the press reported "details of the nation's covert preparations to counter the enemy's overt operations," it was now time to consider the following question: "Is it in the interest of national security?" But as it stood, the question smacked of blatant political self-interest. The nation was not at war and there was no reason for the press to suppress its constitutional freedoms—especially as a nod to presidential foreign policy goals identified as identical to "national security." Thus, despite the fact that in a press conference on April 21—the day after the speech to the editors—Kennedy seemed to lay some blame on his own doorstep by saying: "There's an old saying that victory has one hundred fathers and defeat is an orphan. [And] I'm the responsible officer of the Government," he now found a new scapegoat in the press. It was neither Kennedy's failed policy nor his intemperate words, but rather Communism, Castro, and the press that were blamed for the disaster at the Bay of Pigs. Kennedy was not about to admit personal weakness and foreign policy misjudgment in public. As a former journalist, he should have known better. His addresses to the newspaper editors and publishers contained rather bold words for a man who had just signed off on one of the most hare-brained secret missions in modern military history, and his rhetorical justifications seemed to provide a pretext to continue along the same path. Kennedy's public addresses concerning the Bay of Pigs merely added to the sorry legacy of this whole affair.[23]

Kennedy's political and foreign policy objectives were sometimes at loggerheads: He did not want to be seen as soft on Communism, but he also did not want to unduly rankle the liberal establishment nor inflame the Latin American and Third World nations with imperialistic designs and actions in Cuba. Moreover, he feared that tougher action in Cuba might precipitate Soviet reprisals in Berlin. Herein, also, lie reasons for his ambiguous public statements and, of equal importance, the ambivalence in his personal policy decisions. Further, as a political tactician, Kennedy attacked foreign and domestic policy issues as a seamless garment, and a stain in one area could leak through to the other. The fact that he did not receive domestic political fallout from the failed Cuban invasion also may have encouraged him toward continued unsavory covert Cuban adventures and further confrontations with the Russians.[24]

Rhetorically, the address to the newspaper editors was important for what it symbolized concerning the kind of foreign policy that was being shaped in the early months of the Kennedy administration. As Lewis J. Paper observed, it was "probably the most eloquent exposition of Kennedy's deep-seated drive to thwart the communist menace." In shifting the context to the wider frame of ideological warfare between the United States and the Soviet Union, Kennedy found a means of dissembling that was useful to his political interests but hardly helpful to the nation or the international community. The stage was set for further conflict and divisiveness between the superpowers.[25]

The Berlin Crisis

In a February 1960 campaign speech Kennedy ominously remarked: "No issue confronting the next president of the United States will be more complex or more difficult than the issue of Eastern Europe." He critiqued present policy in the region as based upon "empty slogans and impractical formulas" that had excluded a policy of "real hope." Whatever specific new initiatives Kennedy had in mind, he talked in very general terms in his public address. What was clear was his proclaimed resolve to make a stand against world communism.[26]

The clear symbol of his determination was Berlin, a divided city that was to become the ideological fulcrum of the Cold War. Kennedy's rhetoric was no mean contributory factor in this development. In March 1960 candidate Kennedy directly addressed Berlin's symbolic importance: "Berlin is more than a symbol of personal liberty. It is a living contradiction of the Soviet dogma that only a communist society can bring material prosperity. For the people of East Berlin, and East Germany, and all of Eastern Europe can look up from their bare, drab, toilsome existence and see in their midst the buoyant, vital, expanding economy of West Berlin . . . which has rebuilt a war-torn city and returned prosperity to its people." Berlin was "perhaps the chief symbol of the free world's determination not to yield to Russian threats and Russian pressure." Accordingly, our stake in the city was considerable "and the dangers of maintaining that stake are very great. . . . But we should not despair. For as Francis Bacon said, many years ago, 'there is hope enough to spare, not only to make a bold man try, but also to make a sober-minded and wise man believe.'" Kennedy would make himself over into the "bold man" who would "try" and many "wise" men and women would come to "believe." However, the actual cost was as yet undetermined, and clouded by the ever-present specter of nuclear warfare. By the time the fall campaign began, Kennedy had grown much more silent on Berlin.[27]

Nevertheless, Berlin provided the linchpin for Kennedy's foreign policy during his presidency. As Herbert S. Parmet notes, "No single issue commanded as much of Kennedy's attention. All other global irritations were peripheral, all related, and each and every one a test of whether the Soviets would somehow use that situation as a device for dissolving Western commitments to the city. Russian motivations were beside the point."[28]

As the Vienna summit approached, foreign policy defeats in Cuba, Laos, and in the space race made State Department officials feel that a meeting could be ill-advised. The United States felt that the chief concern should be an atmospheric test ban treaty, with Laos and Berlin as secondary issues. The Soviets, however, were determined to create "two Germanys" by signing a peace treaty with the East German government by year's end. The Western powers feared their rights of access to Berlin—located 110 miles inside the border of East Germany but pledged to protection by the Allied powers—would be summarily abrogated. The arguable strategic relevance of Berlin was overshadowed by its symbolic importance. At a news conference in Paris on June 2, 1961, referring to talks with General de Gaulle on West Berlin, Kennedy said the two leaders would take a dim view of "statutory rights . . . changed by force or threat of force."[29]

A new Berlin "crisis" silently spewed forth from Vienna. Khrushchev said he would sign a treaty giving the German Democratic Republic authority over the entire city; the Western powers would have to evacuate in six months. Kennedy viewed this as an unacceptable position because it severed Western access rights. The bellicosity increased until Khrushchev ultimately threatened war. Kennedy came away from Vienna feeling that he could not negotiate with Khrushchev, and probably should have waited on the summit talks. According to Beschloss, "Khrushchev's Berlin ultimatum had thrown the two great powers into the most potentially dangerous confrontation since the early 1950s."[30]

On June 6 the president went on national television to report on his European trip. He described a "sober, intensive" set of discussions with Mr. Khrushchev—but falsely claimed that there had been "no threats or ultimatums by either side." At a press conference on June 28, Kennedy sought to educate the public on the renewed tensions over Berlin. Referring to a June 10 aide memoire in which the Soviets had publicly announced treaty intentions with East Berlin, Kennedy outlined the history of the Berlin crisis as "Soviet-manufactured" and recited a series of events all the way back to the 1948 Soviet blockade. The "obvious purpose" of the treaty, said the president, "is not to have peace but to make permanent the partition of Germany." Moreover, any unilateral signature by the Soviets with East Germany "would bring an end to Allied rights in West Berlin and to free access for that city." Therefore, "Such action would simply be a repudiation by the Soviets of multilateral commitments to which they solemnly subscribed and have repeatedly reaffirmed. . . . No one can fail to appreciate the gravity of this threat. No one can reconcile it with Soviet professions of a desire to coexist peacefully." In his July 19 press conference Kennedy maintained that the proposed treaty would actually "curb West Berlin's communications with the free world and . . . suffocate the freedom it now enjoys."[31]

Report to the Nation on the Berlin Crisis

In a report commissioned by the president, Dean Acheson recommended that the United States stand fast in a test of wills over Berlin by declaring a national emergency, initiating a military buildup in Central Europe, and refusing to include an offer to negotiate. This hard-line stance was tempered by Kennedy's July 25 speech, which tried to strike a delicate balance between confrontation and conciliation. The president opted to increase conventional military preparations and include a plea for negotiations. Each of these measures was dramatically introduced against the more chilling backdrop of Kennedy's intent not to retreat from a thermonuclear challenge. He felt the need to convince Khrushchev of American determination to defend Berlin.[32]

We suggest that this address again shows Kennedy's appeal to principle as a foundation for policy. The speech also strikes an ominous, fearful chord in its discussion of civil defense. But as a text, it seems uncharacteristically unfocused for a nationally televised speech crafted by Sorensen and Kennedy—containing in the middle a discussion of the domestic economy that seems out of place. Our analysis of the address reveals the president (1) establishing a rationale for the present Berlin crisis on both legal and moral grounds; (2) impressing upon the world, and upon the Soviets in particular, the willingness of the United States to risk nuclear war to fulfill its solemn commitments to Berlin; (3) announcing preparations for a long-term military buildup and an increase in funding for civil defense; and (4) issuing an appeal for cooperation in this venture from all free nations, but especially the Atlantic Alliance and reinforcing U.S. commitment to and preference for peaceful negotiation. A summary of each of these definitional strategies follows.[33]

Establishing a Rationale. A somber, nervous and tense president—flags draped on each side of his massive desk, which was once again covered in felt to cut down on the glare of the television lights—addressed the nation at 10:00 P.M. Eastern Standard Time. By the time he had concluded, the national mood would reflect that of the president.

Kennedy first reminded the American people of his trip to Europe and the Vienna summit, then summarized the problem with Premier Khrushchev as follows: "In Berlin, as you recall, he intends to bring an end, through a stroke of the pen, first our legal rights to be in West Berlin—and secondly our ability to make good on our commitment to the two million free people of that city. That we cannot permit." Rhetorically, the problem of exercising U.S. legal rights and upholding earlier agreements and commitments had as much to do with creating a rationale for the present crisis as it did with describing Khrushchev's malevolent designs. In a memorandum to Theodore Sorensen regarding a revised version of the address, General Maxwell D. Taylor observed:

> In the first part of the redraft, I feel there is perhaps too much legalistic rehearsal of the quadripartite agreements and post-war actions which underlie the occupation status of Berlin and our rights derived from them. I question this because, in the first place, it seems to me a little abstruse for a Presidential nationwide speech, and, further, I feel we should stress our duty to maintain the freedom of West Berlin at least as much as we stress those rights.

The president, for his part, seemed to acknowledge this point in his framing of Khrushchev's intention.[34]

Next, Kennedy confidently assured his audiences: "We are clear about what must be done—and we intend to do it." The president called upon all Americans to support his actions through "sacrifice," "courage," and "perseverance" so that "both peace and freedom will be sustained." In the third paragraph, Kennedy tried to widen the rationale for the military buildup he would announce in the speech:

The immediate threat is to free men in West Berlin. But that isolated outpost is not an isolated problem. The threat is world-wide. Our effort must be equally wide and strong, and not be obsessed by any single manufactured crisis. We face a challenge in Berlin, but there is also a challenge in Southeast Asia, where the borders are less guarded, the enemy harder to find, and the danger of communism less apparent to those who have so little. We face a challenge in our own hemisphere, and indeed wherever else the freedom of human beings is at stake.

Thus, Berlin was just one flashpoint on the frontier of freedom and its defense was in concert with actions in other areas. The rationale for this definitional strategy may perhaps be located in a discussion provided by W. W. (Walt) Rostow in a July 20 memorandum to Theodore Sorensen, which contained the following advice for the upcoming speech: "If possible, the buildup of our forces should be related to contingencies in Southeast Asia as well as in Central Europe—and perhaps to contingencies elsewhere as well." Rostow explained: "This form of projecting the action would give the State Department the chance to explain to the governments in Southeast Asia and elsewhere that this American buildup provides increased contingency support for them and is not associated exclusively with Berlin or with a Europe First mentality in Washington." But in the address this kind of concern for careful balancing of foreign policy concerns would get short shrift.[35]

The president displayed a map of the disputed territory and proceeded to explain the legal rationale for "both our presence in West Berlin and the enjoyment of access across East Germany." He declared that "our rights there are clear and deep-rooted. But in addition to those rights is our commitment to sustain—and defend, if need be—the opportunity for more than two million people to determine their own future and choose their own way of life." Thus the rationale of rights and commitments became pivotal to the opening section of the address. As Edward R. Murrow of the United States Information Agency advised Secretary of State Dean Rusk prior to the speech, "emphasis should be placed on the illegal and unilateral nature of the Soviet action which has precipitated the crisis" and "the absence of any current crisis in Berlin unless the Russians choose to create one." Murrow felt that the "abnormal situation" of a "divided city and a divided country," persisted "simply because of the Soviet denial of self-determination for the German people." He felt, then, that "Mention might be made of the 'magnet of freedom' represented by West Berlin and the Western zone—1,200 Germans a day 'voting for self-determination with their feet.'"[36]

Risking Nuclear War. Beyond rights and commitments, West Berlin now symbolized "a great testing place of Western courage and will." In providing for the security of Berlin, said Kennedy, "we cannot separate its safety from our own." He rejected the view that Berlin was indefensible and backed it with historical examples where courage overcame the odds. "I hear it said that West

Berlin is militarily untenable. And so was Bastogne. And so, in fact, was Stalingrad. Any dangerous spot is tenable if men—brave men—make it so." The saber-rattling sounded dashing until one realized what was at stake.

Yet Kennedy persisted in this path: "We do not want to fight—but we have fought before." Adversaries would error mightily in believing the West "too selfish and too soft and too divided to resist invasions of freedom in other lands. Those who threaten to unleash the forces of war on a dispute over West Berlin should recall the words of the ancient philosopher: 'A man who causes fear cannot be free from fear.'" The president was steadfast: "We cannot and will not permit the Communists to drive us out of Berlin, either gradually or by force." This stance transcended rights and commitments and spoke directly to the United States' ability "to maintain the confidence of other free peoples in our word and in our resolve." Kennedy was determined to win the war of wills by pledging his willingness to risk a nuclear exchange.[37]

Military Buildup and Civil Defense. The necessity of being "ready to resist with force, if force is used upon us" prompted Kennedy to announce a military expansion program "to meet a world-wide threat . . . which stretches far beyond our present Berlin crisis." In outlining the seriousness of the new policy initiative Kennedy reiterated earlier defense buildup requests and actions as well as new measures to meet the new challenge. The president reminded the nation that he had already asked Congress for supplementary "defense buildups" that included adding personnel to the Marine Corps, activating more reserves, increasing air and sea lift capacity, procuring new weaponry, expanding missiles and missile systems, and placing one-half of U.S. B-52 and B-47 bombers on "ground alert" so they could be airborne within fifteen minutes.[38]

In addition, the Berlin crisis helped focus the need for a "flexible response" doctrine. As Kennedy put it: "[W]e need the capability of placing in any critical area at the appropriate time a force which, combined with those of our allies, is large enough to make clear our determination and our ability to defend our rights at all costs—and to meet all levels of aggressor pressure with whatever levels of force are required. We intend to have a wider choice than humiliation or all-out nuclear action."

This became the rationale for the announcement of additional military preparations including: a request for an increase in funds for the armed forces; increasing active-duty forces; increasing draft calls; activating more reserves; improving airlift, sealift and antisubmarine capacities, and requesting $1.8 billion for conventional weaponry, munitions, and equipment. Kennedy's requests for a big stick came with the acknowledgment that the new preparations would weigh heavily upon "American families." "But," Kennedy argued, "these are burdens which must be borne if freedom is to be defended—Americans have willingly borne them before—and they will not flinch from the task now." The president's inaugural pledge to "bear any burden, pay any price" was fast becoming a self-fulfilling prophecy. As the president would himself point out, since the January inauguration the defense budget was increased by an amazing $6 billion.

The apocalyptic nature of the new crisis, however, was perhaps best underscored in Kennedy's harrowing discussion of civil defense. On July 5, the president had sent a memo to McGeorge Bundy directing him to get an "emergency program" from Civil Defense. He queried: "What could we do in the next six months that would improve the population's chances of surviving if a nuclear war should break out?" In the address, Kennedy told the nation that another of his responsibilities was to inform the citizenry "what they should do and where they should go if bombs begin to fall." Therefore, beginning "tomorrow," he would ask Congress for funds "to identify and mark space in existing structures . . . that could be used for fall-out shelters in case of attack." He would also pledge to find means of stocking the shelters "for survival," and seek improvements in air raid warning and fallout detection systems. In words conjuring visions of world holocaust, Kennedy startled the nation with an unnervingly chilly forecast: "In the event of an attack, the lives of those families which are not hit in a nuclear blast and fire can still be saved—if they can be warned to take shelter and if that shelter is available." It was a bald, unsheltered discourse. As Michael Beschloss observed, "No President had ever spoken so directly about the possibility of nuclear attack."[39]

Cooperation and Peaceful Negotiation. Kennedy's Cold War diplomacy is perhaps best encapsulated in his inaugural catchwords "never negotiate out of fear, never fear to negotiate." He intended to use the military buildup as a strategy to negotiate from a position of strength and this speech was not without its olive branches. "Our peacetime military posture is traditionally defensive; but our diplomatic posture need not be." Therefore, said the president, "We do not intend to abandon our duty to mankind to seek a peaceful solution." Kennedy indicated that the United States was "willing to consider any arrangement or treaty in Germany consistent with the maintenance of peace and freedom, and with the legitimate security interests of all nations." He even mentioned his cognizance of "the Soviet Union's historical concerns about their security in Central and Eastern Europe, after a series of ravaging invasions—and we believe arrangements can be worked out which will help to meet those concerns." "In short," said Kennedy, "while we are ready to defend our interests, we shall also be ready to search for peace—in quiet exploratory talks—in formal or informal meetings." But the discourse of peaceful negotiation was vague—and no new ideas were coming from either the State Department or from our allies who had failed to reach agreement over what to do about Berlin. In addition, the words rang particularly hollow when measured against the preponderant stridency of the bulk of the address.

Kennedy concluded the address on a personal (and hand-written) note that underlined the seriousness of the present challenge and his need for ongoing support. As a candidate, he said grimly, he could not really have foreseen "how heavy and constant" the "burdens" of the presidency would become. He solemnly reminded the audience that when war had come in the past, it was always a "case of serious misjudgments . . . on both sides." In a "thermo-nuclear age, any misjudgment on either side about the intentions of the other could rain more devastation in several hours than has been wrought in all the wars in human history." Seemingly humbled by this prospect, Kennedy asked the nation and the community of nations "for your help, and your advice," for "your goodwill, and your support—and above all, your prayers."

Kennedy's advisers were pleased with the speech, and over 70 percent of respondents reported a willingness to go to war to defend freedom in Berlin. While Khrushchev bridled over the tough talk, his chief response was to authorize the construction of the Berlin Wall, which was first erected August 13. Over time, the wall had the effect of lessening tensions by stanching the East German refugee problem. The July 25 speech may have actually encouraged Khrushchev to go forward with the barricade. There was no reference to the 1945 Potsdam agreement guaranteeing "free access" between West and East Berlin. Had Kennedy spoken more ambiguously—using the term "Berlin" rather than "West Berlin"—perhaps Khrushchev would have been more cautious. Kennedy briefly considered using the wall as a symbol for Western superiority, but mostly kept silent—preferring instead to have administration spokespersons express the president's shock at these events.[40]

Although Kennedy was briefly questioned as to why he had allowed the wall to be built, in the long run he received very little critique concerning it, and adopted a public posture of hand-wringing whenever the subject came up. The best solution to the problem seemed to be to do nothing to upset the newly balanced status quo, thus averting the domestic political fallout that inevitably would have attended a more hard-line stance. More to the point, in closing the border in relative silence, both Kennedy and Khrushchev helped diffuse direct confrontation between the superpowers. Khrushchev formally withdrew his treaty proposal deadline with East Germany on October 17 in a six-hour address to the Soviet Twentieth Party Congress.[41]

The July 25 address was successful in convincing Khrushchev of Kennedy's willingness to employ the U.S. nuclear arsenal in defense of Berlin, but the cost was a dramatic increase in superpower tensions and an avowed policy of escalation. Kennedy's rhetoric converted a foreign policy concern into a crisis by saying to the Soviets and the world community—in Edward R. Murrow's words (some of which were paraphrased and incorporated into the speech) in his earlier memorandum to Rusk—"So far as we are concerned, our national honor has been pledged, our future has been mortgaged, we will not flinch or falter." Berlin thus provided a pretext and rallying point for expanding the arms race, baptizing the administration's flexible response doctrine, and setting the superpowers upon an even more dangerous course in which room for negotiation had again been dramatically narrowed. Kennedy's supporters claimed that the press was responsible for increasing tensions because it paid little attention to the call for peaceful negotiation also offered July 25. While there is some truth to this observation, the press can hardly be blamed for focusing on the more strident sections of the speech—especially since it was the president himself who chose this occasion to discuss civil defense and bomb shelters. The tough words, new military policy initiatives, and the expressed concern for national survival in a post-holocaust setting do not appear to us to be flexible rhetorical grounds for bolstering hopes for peace or diplomacy. On July 25, Kennedy seemed to be arming instead of parleying. Despite an idealistic defense of freedom, Kennedy fell prey to immediate, pragmatic plans of action that augured preparations for Armageddon.[42]

Kennedy's definition of the situation opened the doors to further and more serious conflict in an escalation of words and deeds that would lead to the resumption of U.S. atmospheric nuclear tests and The Missiles of October. Thus, the failed summit at Vienna, the presumed demonstration of weakness in the negotiated accords on Laos, the disastrous Cuban invasion, and the Gagarin space flight had fused to inspire the president to inaugurate a brinkmanship diplomacy of waging peace while preparing for thermonuclear war.

Showdown: The Cuban Missile Crisis

It is not unseemly to suggest that the Missiles of October represented a defining moment in the history of the Cold War. As studies and analyses multiply—and as revisionist histories reconfigure what we now know about the crisis, especially with the recent meeting of U.S. and Soviet principals in 1989 and the opening of Soviet archives containing key documents—prospects have improved immeasurably for a more balanced picture of what actually occurred and why. In this light, it also would seem wise to return to Kennedy's public discussion of the crisis to see if there is anything more to learn.[43]

Ever since the Bay of Pigs fiasco, Kennedy had seemed even more obsessed with ousting Castro. On January 20, 1962, Major General Edward Lansdale took over Operation Mongoose—a phased plan of covert operations directed against Cuba designed to destabilize and eventually overthrow its leader. Covert operations mounted against the regime included espionage, sabotage, paramilitary raids, counterfeiting, and other forms of political and psychological warfare.[44]

Meanwhile, relations between the superpowers continued to deteriorate. In late March 1962, Stewart Alsop penned an article for the *Saturday Evening Post* entitled "Kennedy's Grand Strategy," which attempted to stir enthusiasm in Western Europe for the "flexible response" doctrine. The article interpreted Kennedy as declaring that a first strike on the part of the United States was not inconceivable. This bold public pronouncement heightened Khrushchev's fears of U.S. intentions and the Soviet military was placed on alert. With the United States perhaps at its zenith in nuclear strength, Khrushchev may have calculated that—rather than waiting for parity—America was preparing to launch an immediate preemptive strike.[45]

In addition, Kennedy's comments during an earlier March 7, 1962, press conference may have inadvertently encouraged Khrushchev to believe that placing offensive missiles in Cuba would not upset the strategic balance of power. The president observed: "If you have a missile that can carry a bomb 5,000 miles, does it really make . . . a significant difference, if you don't have a bomb stationed in this area but you have it 5,000 miles behind, which can cover that area." However, while placing missiles 90 miles from Florida may not have altered the strategic balance, it certainly carried the potential to upset the American domestic political situation.[46]

In the spring of 1962, relying on his latest intelligence estimates, Castro began preparations for war with the United States. Simultaneously, the United States increased military maneuvers and, paradoxically, presented its most comprehensive outline yet for a disarmament treaty at Geneva. To the surprise of no one, Cuba had become pivotal to the off-year election campaign. Republicans made it a key campaign issue. In September, the House and Senate passed a joint resolution pledging to use force against the tiny island if any of its activities proved a threat to the vital interests of the United States. Kennedy went on the campaign trail and assured the nation that there were no offensive nuclear weapons in Cuba and that he would never permit the Soviets to install them. If by some accident of chance the Russians did manage to install them, he pledged appropriate and effective countermeasures. As early as August 22, however, intelligence reports had indicated the presence of offensive missiles, and by August 30 Kennedy reportedly had received "hard" evidence. At his August 29 press conference, the president observed that reports of Communist troops flowing into Cuba were wrong and that the Communists that were there were merely offering technical assistance. When asked whether the United States should invade Cuba, the president, still haunted by the implications for Berlin, replied: " I'm not for invading Cuba at this time. . . . I think it would be a mistake . . . because I think it would lead to . . . very serious consequences for many people." On August 31, the United States filed a protest after a Navy plane was fired upon 15 miles from the Cuban coast. To protect its rights, the United States made plain that any more incidents would result in retaliation by all necessary means.[47]

The tough talk between the superpowers continued in the first two weeks of September. The Soviets announced that because of threats against Cuba, they would now supply more technical and arms specialists. Kennedy activated 150,000 reserves. The Russians interpreted this as an "act of aggression" and maintained that the Cuban buildup was for defensive purposes only. Meanwhile, a Cuban pilot who had defected reported that Cuba now had over 200 Soviet MIGs at its disposal. These events prefaced the president's press conference of September 13. Charging Castro with "monumental economic mismanagement" that had led "his own followers . . . to see that their revolution ha[d] been betrayed," Kennedy told the nation that he did not find it "surprising that in a frantic effort to bolster his regime [Castro] should try to arouse the Cuban people with charges of an imminent American invasion, and commit himself still further to a Soviet takeover in the hope of preventing his own collapse." While the increased Soviet support had been placed under "most careful surveillance," it did "not constitute a serious threat" and there would be no "unilateral military intervention on the part of the United States." The president warned, however, that "if Cuba should ever attempt to export its aggressive purposes by force or threat of force against any nation in this hemisphere, or become an offensive military base of significant capacity for the Soviet Union, then this country will do whatever must be done to protect its own security and that of its allies." Kennedy was unequivocal: "As President and Commander in Chief I have full authority now to take such action." Eight days later on September 21, Andrei Gromyko, the Soviet Foreign Minister, would inform the U.N. General Assembly that any form of U.S. attack on Cuba would result in war with the U.S.S.R.—a position confirmed in October by *Izvestia*.[48]

The Cuban Missile Crisis Address

On October 16, 1962, the president's Executive Committee (Ex Comm) advisory team poured over U-2 photographs of West Central Cuba, revealing the presence of medium-range ballistic missiles, which did not as yet appear to be equipped with nuclear warheads. Other sites were later identified as incomplete intermediate-range missile installations. This gave the president and his administration crucial time to react. But the presence of the missile sites had a shocking and immediate political impact. The president, after all, had promised in September that he would not allow this to happen. Gradually, Ex Comm consensus emerged around two different courses of action: either direct air strikes against Cuba or a naval blockade, which came to be called a "quarantine"—a term taken from the 1937 "Quarantine the Aggressor" speech by Franklin Roosevelt. Either option had disadvantages and each could be interpreted by the Soviets as an act of war.[49]

At 12:00 P.M. on October 22, Press Secretary Pierre Salinger telephoned Robert Fleming, the committee chair of network presidential air time requests, to inform him that the president would like time to address "'the highest national urgency.'" Salinger secured a 7:00 P.M. air time. The completed speech "served as the basic briefing document in all capitals of the world and in a series of ambassadorial meetings in the State Department. Photographs were provided as well." Soviet ambassador Anatoly F. Dobrynin, upon being informed of the address at 6 P.M. in Secretary of State Dean Rusk's office, was later depicted by Rusk as having "aged 'ten years in front of my eyes.'" As 7 P.M. approached, Kennedy fingered the reading copy of "the most serious speech" to be delivered in his lifetime.[50]

Our analysis of the address reveals the president painting a rhetorical portrait of the Soviet Union as an outlaw actor in the world community. As the president framed his address, the Russian attempt to install offensive missiles in the Western Hemisphere posed a threat to the entire human community. It also violated international treaties, their own public statements, and repeated warnings from the United States. Thus, after introducing the world to new and overwhelming evidence of Soviet arrogance and deception, the president set for himself a systematic course—with the intent of both proving and reinforcing the enormity of the present international breach. Second, the president used the international outlaw theme as a context for and justification of a new turn in present policy with the discursive delineation of "initial steps" the United States would take to meet its presumed obligations. Finally, in closing his address, the president chose to say some special words to the people of Cuba and the United States, a definitional strategy that celebrated U.S. ideals and reconfigured the whole episode as one more instance of bearing any burden and paying any price for freedom. The gravity of the events was matched by the emotional tone of the words used to describe them.[51]

An Outlaw Actor in the World Community. The president would give no hint of any U.S. responsibility for or complicity in the provocative state of the status quo. Indeed, his main rhetorical strategy was to define the Soviet Union as a legal and moral pariah. In opening his address, Kennedy maintained that the U.S. government, in keeping its commitment to monitor Soviet actions in Cuba, had uncovered a "new crisis." Kennedy was careful to point out that the threat involved the entire Western Hemisphere. The medium-range missiles were "capable of striking Washington, D. C., the Panama Canal, Cape Canaveral, Mexico City, or any other city in the Southeastern part of the United States, in Central America or in the Caribbean area." "[I]ntermediate range ballistic missiles" could travel "twice as far"—"capable of striking most of the major cities in the Western hemisphere, ranging as far North as Hudson Bay, Canada, and as far South as Lima, Peru." Moreover, "jet bombers, capable of carrying nuclear weapons, [we]re now being uncrated in Cuba." While the ranges described were arguable, the activities on the island were interpreted by the president as "an urgent transformation of Cuba into an important strategic base" and "an explicit threat to the peace and security of all the Americas."

Having outlined the specific threat, Kennedy reinforced the perfidy of these developments by describing the Soviets as violators of law, presidential admonition, morality, and human decency. Legally, the installations represented a "flagrant and deliberate defiance of the Rio Pact of 1947, the traditions of this Nation and this Hemisphere [perhaps an oblique reference to the Monroe doctrine, in which Kennedy put little faith], the Joint Resolution of the 87th Congress, the Charter of the United Nations, and my own pubic warnings to the Soviets on September 4 and 13." Having put on record the Soviet transgressions, Kennedy moved to issues of integrity and the world's ability to trust the Soviets by taking them at their word.

As the president framed it, the Soviets gave "repeated assurances . . . both publicly and privately" that the military buildup was of a "defensive character." Kennedy was determined to demonstrate that such assurances were intentionally deceptive: "I quote the government, 'The Soviet Union has [such] powerful rockets to carry these nuclear warheads there is no need to search for sites for them beyond the boundaries of the Soviet Union.' That statement was false." "Only last Thursday," Kennedy argued, he had been informed by Soviet Foreign Minister Gromyko that Soviet military aid was "'pursued solely [for] the purpose of contributing to the defense capabilities of Cuba' . . . and that 'if it were otherwise . . . the Soviet Government would never become involved in rendering such assistance.' That statement also was false." Thus, the president corroborated his charges of "deliberate deception" regarding the "offensive threat." He further reinforced the righteousness of the U.S. position in contrast to the Soviets by pointing out: "Our own strategic missiles have never been transferred to the territory of any other nation, under a cloak of secrecy and deception; and our history . . . demonstrates that we have no desire to dominate or conquer any other nation or impose our system upon its people." The United States did place missiles in Turkey that pointed at the Russian border—but these were known to all parties. The contrast in histories highlighted post-World War II Soviet aggression.

Kennedy advanced his arguments against the Soviet initiatives by negative attribution: It was a "secret, swift and extraordinary buildup," a "sudden, clandestine decision," a "deliberately provocative and unjustified change in the status quo." And while in the past the United States was "determined not to be diverted . . . by mere irritants and fanatics," the Russian leadership had now revealed itself engaged in an action so invidious that it was analogous to Munich prior to World War II: "The 1930s taught us a clear lesson: aggressive conduct, if allowed to go unchecked and unchallenged, ultimately leads to war." Kennedy then made his purpose clear: "Our unswerving objective, therefore, must be to prevent the use of these missiles against this or any other country, and to secure their withdrawal or elimination from the Western Hemisphere."

Counter-Force: Preventive Policy Measures. To achieve his objective, Kennedy outlined seven "initial steps." The first three measures included imposing a "strict quarantine on all offensive military equipment under shipment to Cuba"; continuing and increasing "close surveillance of Cuba" and U.S. armed forces preparations and readiness; and announcing categorically: "It shall be the policy of this Nation to regard any nuclear missile launched from Cuba against any nation in the Western Hemisphere as an attack by the Soviet Union on the United States, requiring a full retaliatory response upon the Soviet Union." The quarantine could have been considered an act of war against Cuba and, by proxy, the Soviet Union. The continued surveillance indicated that the United States had in the past and would in the future violate Cuban air space with spy missions. The new policy sounded an unnerving declaration of

114 "In a Perilous Hour"

war against the Soviets should anyone in Cuba by miscalculation or mistake launch a guided missile. This was the most profoundly disturbing foreign policy discourse ever to emanate from a Cold War rhetorician.

Other measures included reinforcing the U.S base at Guantanamo and evacuating dependents, placing other troops on alert; requesting an "immediate" meeting of the Organization of American States and an "emergency" meeting of the U.N. Security Council to condemn and take action against the Soviets, with a call for U.N. monitoring of the "dismantling and withdrawal of all offensive weapons in Cuba"; and asking Premier Khrushchev "to halt and eliminate this clandestine, reckless, and provocative threat" and to "abandon this course of world domination" in favor of "a search for peaceful and permanent solutions." These measures, of course, were meant not only to strengthen the U.S. position in the ongoing conflict, but also to sway world opinion as to the steadfastness and righteousness of the president's actions.

Other policy proclamations included a declaration of a willingness to "present [the] case against the Soviet threat to peace, and our own proposals for a peaceful world, at any time and in any forum." The president added a final warning: "Any hostile move anywhere in the world against the safety and freedom of peoples to whom we are committed—including in particular the brave people of West Berlin—will be met with whatever action is needed." These latter two policy statements spoke to Kennedy's refusal to call for a specific summit with Khrushchev and his fear that the blockade action against Cuba might precipitate Soviet retaliation in Berlin—or elsewhere. The global nature of the conflict as defined and enacted by the president made the choices frightening and the options for encountering a theater of war legion.

Bearing the Burden—Paying the Price. Having focused the attention of his multiple audiences on the nature of the threat, the Soviet duplicity involved, and the policy initiatives he would undertake to meet U.S. responsibilities, Kennedy also had, simultaneously, succeeded in defining himself as leader of the Free World, defender of the Western Hemisphere, Commander-in-Chief of the United States Armed Forces, and moral agent in a universe polluted by the Soviet Union. Both the threat and the announced remedies provided Kennedy a pragmatic context for invoking preferred values. We believe the idealism expressed in this speech was consistent with Kennedy's earlier foreign policy addresses, and we believe it was particularly traceable to the Inaugural Address. This became most evident when, toward the end of his address, the president isolated on two key audiences: the Cubans and his "fellow citizens."

Kennedy reaffirmed his commitment to the value of freedom in his specific remarks to the "captive people of Cuba." The president said he shared their "aspirations for liberty and justice for all." He argued that the United States had no wish to cause suffering or impose its system, but rather: "We know that your lives and land are being used as pawns by those who deny you freedom." He encouraged the Cubans to overthrow Castro's regime and find their rightful place among the "free nations" of this hemisphere. He recited First Amendment freedoms enjoyed and enjoined in the United States as the preferred model for protecting and exercising liberties. Thus Cuba was depicted by the president as a nation that aspired to U.S. principles and ideals and that, if left to its own devices—"free from foreign domination"—would realize the full flowering of its national interests and potential.

In words directed to the U.S. audience, Kennedy augmented the freedom theme with acknowledgment that the nation was now set on a "difficult and dangerous" course that would require "sacrifice," "self-discipline," and "patience." "But the greatest danger of all," said Kennedy, "would be to do nothing." The policy the president had chosen was argued as "consistent with our character and courage as a nation and our commitments around the world." Kennedy boasted: "The cost of freedom is always high—but Americans have always paid it. And one path we shall never choose, and that is the path of surrender and submission." He closed in high-minded, moralistic tones, employing his familiar antithetical appeals: "Our goal is not the victory of might, but the vindication of right—not peace at the expense of freedom, but both peace and freedom, here in this Hemisphere, and, we hope, around the world. God willing, that goal will be achieved. Thank you and good night."

If one looks at the latter part of this speech, the Cuban missile crisis is portrayed as simply one more instance of U.S. efforts to fulfill its self-ordained global mission—a mission requiring courage, self-sacrifice, and a national resolve that refuses to succumb or surrender. This, of course, is nothing less than the mission in the international community Kennedy had clearly articulated in his Inaugural Address. He defined the U.S. role in the Cuban missile crisis as the enactment of a consistent foreign policy doctrine that had been enunciated from the beginning.

After the speech the U.S. citizenry seemed to be in a warlike mood, "almost rejoicing" as they pondered prospects of invading Cuba and overthrowing Castro. An October 23 Gallup poll revealed that 84 percent of U.S. citizens approved of the blockade. Congressional leaders telephoned their support. A minority protested the action vociferously. Linus Pauling labeled it "an act of utmost irresponsibility." Bertrand Russell appealed to U.N. Secretary General U Thant for "swift condemnation of [this] tragic U.S. action." But another, even more important impact of the address and events it signified is perhaps best summed up in a memorandum Columbia University professor and presidential adviser Richard E. Neustadt sent to Theodore Sorensen October 27:

> The reaction among students here to the President's speech of Monday last was qualitatively different from anything I've ever witnessed before in moments of crisis since I started to teach nine years ago: this time these kids were literally scared for their lives and were astonished, somehow, that their lives could be risked by an American initiative. In short, what they have heard and said ad infinitum about the hazards in our era suddenly came home to them; for the first time, apparently, awareness of the real world got transferred from their heads to their guts.

Kennedy's announced policy, then, had played well to the jingoistic mood of the country, infuriated the pacifists, and scared most of the rest of the global village. Within weeks after the blockade the president obtained an agreement to dismantle and remove the missiles—and was widely perceived as having bested his Cold War nemesis. The crisis improved Kennedy's political standing. The press began to compare the president to Wilson and Roosevelt—two earlier "wartime" chief executives.[52]

In a very real sense, then, the October 22 speech was not merely a natural response to a perceived threat, it was also seized upon by Kennedy's speechwriters as an opportunity to develop a portrait of leadership under trying circumstances. Having irrefutable evidence of Soviet duplicity, Kennedy was free to tarnish them as world outlaws, specify immediate policy actions to counteract their aggression, and return to the central ideals of mission, purpose, and sacrifice to unify the country around his proposed response.

A number of things were unclear at the beginning of this speech. First, it was unclear whether the placement of the missiles in Cuba was indeed a provocative act. Even if it was, it was unclear whether Kennedy's proposed intervention through blockade was not itself a provocation to war. Another problem Kennedy faced (and chose to ignore) was enacting a blockade without the consent of Congress. This was in line with his view of an active presidency in which the contours of power were shaped by his expansive view of executive privilege. Moreover, since the difference between offensive and defensive weapons is difficult to determine unless actually employed, Kennedy's labeling of the site as "offensive" was at least arguable. And even if the missiles could rightfully be labeled offensive, it made little difference strategically but considerable difference politically. The president had pledged in September he would intervene if events took the course they did, and it was politically impossible for him to back down in October. The angry, fomenting anticommunist tides in the country at the time led Kennedy to comment afterward that, had he ignored the events in Cuba, he would have been impeached. Kennedy's public discourse had backed him into a political corner of brinkmanship diplomacy. The president could cling only to the hope that the responsible person on the other side of the globe would blink first. The stakes, of course, were incalculable.[53]

Pratt maintained that the October 22 address did not appeal to national unity. We suggest, however, that latter sections of the President's speech addressed to the Cubans and to his "fellow citizens" indirectly made that very appeal. In telling the American people that "many months of sacrifice and self-discipline lie ahead," Kennedy implicitly acknowledged the need for national unity as a force for supporting his announced policies and for confronting the new terror. He told the nation that the path "we have chosen" is "most consistent with our character and courage as a nation," and that it represented the "cost of freedom . . . Americans have always paid." So while the individual value appeals (e.g., sacrifice, self-discipline, bearing the cost of freedom) were instrumental to Kennedy's specific purposes, taken together, they represented consummatory appeals to unity as insurance in a precarious time. Merely labeling a political event a "crisis" entailed an appeal for unity and sacrifice. Danger was itself a unifying factor, and Kennedy had just announced the most dangerous discovery and reaction in Cold War history. Thus, positive Gallup polls after the speech were hardly surprising. During periods of foreign policy crisis—as after the Bay of Pigs and the Berlin crisis—Americans support their president.[54]

THE RHETORIC OF CONCILIATION: A SHAFT OF LIGHT IN THE DARKNESS

Kennedy's successful closure on the Cuban missile crisis not only enhanced his reputation but also buoyed his spirits and those of the nation. As 1963 approached, he renewed his hopes for detente with the Soviets and eventual world peace. In his third State of the Union Address, the president reflected: "[H]aving witnessed in recent months a heightened respect for our national purpose and power—having seen the courageous calm of a united people in a perilous hour—and having observed a steady improvement in the opportunities and well-being of our citizens—I can report to you that the state of this old but youthful union is good." The president added: "But complacency or self-congratulation can imperil our security as much as the weapons of our adversaries. A moment of pause is not a promise of peace." He forecasted "a year of obligation and opportunity." One "special avenue" he selected was "the search for worldwide peace."[55]

Kennedy once again announced increased expenditures on military equipment and conventional and nuclear armaments in pursuit of his peace-through-strength policy, adding pointedly:

> But our commitment to national safety is not a commitment to expand our military establishment indefinitely. We do not dismiss disarmament as an idle dream. For we believe in the end that it is the only way of insuring the security of all without impairing the interests of any. Nor do we mistake honorable negotiation for appeasement. While we shall never weary in the defense of freedom, neither shall we abandon the pursuit of peace.

Toward the end of the address Kennedy seemed in a genuinely conciliatory mood: "For we seek not the world-wide victory of one nation or system, but a world-wide victory of men. The modern globe is too small, its weapons are too destructive, they multiply too fast, and its disorders are too contagious to permit any other kind of victory." A confident chief executive closed on an upbeat metaphorical note: "[N]ow the winds of change appear to be blowing more strongly than ever, in the world of communism as well as our own. For 175 years we have sailed with those winds at our back, and with the tides of human freedom in our favor. We steer our ship with hope, as Thomas Jefferson said, 'leaving fear astern.' Today we still welcome those winds of change—and we have every reason to believe that our tide is running strong. With thanks to Almighty God for seeing us through a perilous passage, we ask His help anew in guiding the 'Good Ship Union.'" Despite the overextended metaphor, the content of the discourse augured—more than at any previous time in Kennedy's presidency—the ideational, predispositional, and mechanical structure for a lasting peace.

The March Toward Detente

Judging Kennedy at his word and through corroborating historical accounts, the missile crisis had given the president an even greater realization of the necessity to increase efforts on behalf of peace. The country and the world could no longer afford to drift from crisis to crisis, something Kennedy, ironically, had accused the Eisenhower administration of during the campaign. Having stared into the abyss, Kennedy renewed his efforts toward peaceful coexistence with the Soviets. The negotiations with Khrushchev on resolving the missile crisis helped open up wider discussions on disarmament.

By December 10, 1962, the Soviet Union had announced that it would be amenable to a test ban treaty that included international verification using an electronic "black box" system for detecting underground nuclear explosions. While this seemed to signal a softening of the hard-line Soviet position on verification, three days later, at Geneva, they rejected a U.S. proposal for international inspection. By December 18, both the United States and the U.S.S.R. announced publicly they had dropped their goal of a January 1 test ban treaty. Nonetheless, the Soviets asked the administration to halt tests by that date. The next day the United States rejected this appeal, viewing it as a call for an unpoliced moratorium. On December 22, the Soviets exploded another bomb.

But by January 20, 1963, Khrushchev had publicly announced he was amenable to two or three on-site inspections a year. In his press conference of January 24, President Kennedy indicated that talks on these issues were ongoing. When asked whether France and China also should be signatories on the treaty, Kennedy replied: "The first step is to see whether the British and the Americans can work out an effective test ban treaty with the Soviet Union. Once that's done, then I think we can move on to these other questions." When questioned about the disparity between Khrushchev's offer of two to three yearly inspections and the U.S. preference for eight to ten, Kennedy indicated that he would let his arms control negotiators pursue the matter, but added: "There is not only the question of on-site inspections, but the location and number of the automatic devices, and all this has to be meshed in kinds of inspection, [and] how free the inspectors will be." Characteristically, Kennedy had pointed out the complexity of the matters under negotiation, thus stanching hopes for a quick resolution of outstanding questions.[56]

This strategy seemed especially appropriate when, on January 26, the United States announced the suspension of underground testing in an effort to encourage test ban negotiations. But by January 31 test ban talks disintegrated with the Soviet demand to integrate them into the wider disarmament talks in Geneva—raising a troubling negotiation point that had stalled test ban talks in the past. On February 1, Kennedy ordered the resumption of plans for underground tests and resumed testing in Nevada on February 8. On February 12, the Geneva disarmament talks reopened with a Soviet call for the United States to withdraw its nuclear forces from foreign lands. This proposal was condemned by the United States and Great Britain as a political ploy—more propaganda against the West.

In mid-February, the Soviets announced that they would accept three yearly on-site inspections and the installation of black boxes in their territory—but that any further movement on the test ban should come from the United States or Great Britain. For his part, Kennedy continued to stress the importance of ongoing talks and rejected a suggestion by Hubert Humphrey that if things were not settled by April 1, the chances of ever getting a meaningful agreement were nil. The president would press ahead regardless of an arbitrary date because "the alternative is the spread of these weapons to governments which may be irresponsible, or which by accident may initiate a general nuclear conflagration." Indeed, Kennedy observed: "[T]he major argument for the test ban treaty is the limiting effect it might have on proliferation."[57]

The stalemate dragged on through the spring, and Kennedy faced increasing criticism. A pensive commander-in-chief would observe: "I am haunted by the feeling that by 1970, unless we are successful, there may be ten nuclear powers instead of four and by 1975, fifteen or twenty." The prospects were horrifying: "I regard that as the greatest possible danger and hazard." And so the president would press ahead, dogged in the face of multiple obstacles. In April, he observed, "I am not overly sanguine about the prospects for an accord." "[T]ime is running out." By May the president was losing hope, but promised one last "push" through July, pledging he would test "every forum to see if we can get an agreement."[58]

"The Strategy of Peace": Transcending the Cold War at American University

True to his word, Kennedy exploited tirelessly every venue in his pursuit of a test ban treaty. His determination to mount a "last push" was best reflected in his June 10 address at American University. In the spring of 1963, in direct response to moribund prospects for an agreement, the president determined that after the latest series of U.S. atmospheric tests, he would deliver a major "peace" address proposing to halt testing and pledging once again not to be the first to resume; he would encourage the Soviets to do likewise. Kennedy assigned the draft to Sorensen, with the charge to "put forward a fundamentally new emphasis on the peaceful and the positive in our relations with the Soviets. . . . [The president] did not want [the] new policy diluted by usual threats of destruction, boasts of nuclear stockpiles and lectures on Soviet treachery." Since the latter comment seemed to serve as an adequate, if not telling, assessment of Kennedy's discourse up until that point, it remained to be seen exactly how the post-Cuban missile crisis environment may have influenced Kennedy's discursive public diplomacy.[59]

Kennedy's decision to use the epideictic occasion of a commencement ceremony to deliver a major deliberative address concerning foreign policy presented him with an interesting rhetorical task in that he had to develop a hybrid discourse that would successfully combine appropriate values and policies. Since epideictic address usually celebrates present values through praise and blame, Kennedy would be provided an excellent opportunity to reassess values used in policy decisions as a way of embarking upon a new course in the future. These new values would establish a context for new policy decisions. The result would be an attempt, at a rather late hour, to reverse previous Cold War rhetoric and blaze a path transcending his own discourse and that of other presidents in the post-World War II era. Thus, Kennedy would provide renewed reflections on the ideals necessary to guide a future post-Cold War policy of detente to a group of students who were themselves in the process of divining their future. Both message and occasion seemed fitting and proper.[60]

When the president arrived at Reeves Field to receive an honorary doctoral degree and deliver his commencement address to the 991 graduates of American University, he climbed an outdoor platform that had been baking in 96 degree heat. The Marine band, red coats blazing, and commencement dignitaries including the president, fully robed in academic regalia, had no shade for comfort. As in similar situations when Kennedy delivered a nationally televised major policy address, he would finger the reading copy of the speech. On the second page of the delivery copy, in an effort destined to become a classic model of diplomacy for addressing the question of world peace, the following words appeared: "not merely peace for Americans but peace for all men—not merely peace in our time but peace in all time." In a hand-written insert placed above the words "all men," the president added "and women." It was the only substantive change he made to the delivery copy used for the address.[61]

We believe that this address was unique in the annals of Cold War history. Its distinguishing features included a masterful interpolation of self-reflexiveness, magnanimity, and humanity. These qualities set the tone and context for a discussion of peace that would both signal and embody a foreign policy shift that pledged genuine detente between the superpowers and renewed hopes and expectations for world peace.

A Self-Reflexive Mood

Kennedy used the ritual of the commencement ceremony as a symbolic backdrop for the announcement of a new definition of and attitude toward world peace. Noting that American University was first opened by Woodrow Wilson in 1914 and that Wilson had encouraged university students to be public-minded, Kennedy praised the university, quoting John Masefield, who had "'admired [its] splendid beauty'" and revered it as "'a place where those who hate ignorance may strive to know, where those who perceive truth may strive to make others see.'" Kennedy proclaimed for himself a like-minded mission: "I have, therefore, chosen this time and place to discuss a topic on which ignorance too often abounds and the truth too rarely perceived—and that is the most important topic on earth: peace."

Having dispensed with the formal duties enjoined by the specific occasion, Kennedy set for himself the following goals: defining what he meant by peace; calling for a reexamination of U.S. attitudes toward peace, the Soviets, and the Cold War while reassuring allies of U.S. intent to honor present commitments; announcing new political initiatives to foster peace; and finally, examining attitudes toward peace and freedom among U.S. citizens as exercised in their sometimes intemperate relations with one another. Each of these objectives was interconnected. Each demonstrated a self-reflexive mood, injecting a previously unheard but welcome note of humility into the Cold War era.

In developing his "strategy of peace," Kennedy shaped four major rhetorical arguments: (1) peace is a rational human end; (2) peace is the noble aspiration of all peoples; (3) pursuing peace is a plausible political philosophy yielding positive political outcomes; and (4) peace is crucial to and an enactment of the flowering of human rights.

Peace as a Rational Telos. The president's new definition of peace offered: "Not a Pax Americana enforced on the world by American weapons of war. Not the peace of the grave or the security of the slave" but a "genuine peace—the kind of peace that makes life on earth worth living—the kind that enables men and nations to grow and to hope and to build a better life for their children—not merely peace for Americans but peace for all men and women—not merely peace in our time but peace in all time." Using parallelism, alliteration, rhyme, and the poetics of contrapuntal phrasing, Kennedy's definition was at once visionary and magnanimous. It held out hope for all humanity. Its raison d'etre was, of course, "the new face of war" with its "explosive force," "expenditure of billions of dollars," and "idle stockpiles—which can only destroy and never create." But the president argued forcefully that peace must be valued in an even more transcendent light: For the first time in his presidency, Kennedy argued that peace had a natural telos—it comprised "the necessary rational end of rational men." In providing this entelechial motive, the president transferred and elevated the argument from one of Cold War necessity to human purpose—by employing a god-term of the modern age—"rationality." Peace, he maintained, is the only path open to thinking human beings in the nuclear era.

In arguing for peace as a rational telos, Kennedy directly targeted those who felt unable in principle to negotiate with the Communists because by definition they were too evil or treacherous. He may have been coaching his own attitudes as well as others: "Too many of us think it is impossible. Too many think it unreal. But that is a dangerous, defeatist belief." Rational people know "our problems are manmade—therefore they can be solved by man. . . . No problem of human destiny is beyond human beings. Man's reason and spirit have often solved the seemingly unsolvable."

In following a telos that could effect a "genuine peace," Kennedy qualified the argument—he was "not referring to the absolute, infinite concept of universal peace and goodwill," which might only "invite discouragement and incredulity" if it were made "our only and immediate goal," but rather he was evoking "a more practical, more attainable peace—based not on a sudden revolution in human nature but on a gradual evolution in human institutions—on a series of concrete actions and effective agreements which are in the interests of all concerned." Here, while the telos is sure, it also requires an active human hand and the cooperation of political institutions to achieve fruition. "So," said Kennedy, "let us persevere. . . . By defining our goal more clearly—by making it seem more manageable and less remote—we can help all people to see it, to draw hope from it, and to move irresistibly toward it." The entelechy of peace, then, was as much a communal process as it was a product. It called for "mutual tolerance" and an openness to potential "surprising changes between nations and neighbors." This was a fresh, and, at the time, novel approach.[62]

Peace as the Noble Aspiration of the People. Kennedy's attempt to effect a revaluation of Cold War attitudes also extended to recasting the important characters in the ongoing narrative. Instead of focusing on U.S.-U.S.S.R. conflicts—between the two leaders, the two governments, or their policies—which had been a past grand strategy of Cold War rhetoric, the president featured a narrative about the people residing in those nations and their commonalities. By so doing, Kennedy found yet another rhetorical mode of transcendence. He pleaded with his audience "not to see only a distorted and desperate view of the other side." He was determined to assuage the ravages of Cold War discourse that had dehumanized our concept of the Russians. He observed pointedly: "No government or social system is so evil that its people must be considered as lacking in virtue. As Americans, we find communism profoundly repugnant as a negation of personal freedom and dignity. But we can still hail the Russian people for their many achievements—in science and space, in economic and industrial growth, in culture and in acts of courage."

Kennedy continued to put a human face on the once inhuman adversary. He tried to demonstrate a common bond between the people of the United States and the Soviet Union by referring to their "mutual abhorrence of war," their suffering in World War II, and the fact that, should a war "break out again," both nations would be "primary targets" of devastation. Moreover, each nation was having to "bear the heaviest burdens" of the Cold War—"devoting massive sums of money to weapons" rather than human needs such as "ignorance, poverty, and disease." It was now time to end "a vicious and dangerous cycle" of "suspicion" where "new weapons beget counter-weapons." Neither advocating "blind[ness] to our differences" nor unmindful of our "common interests," Kennedy proposed: "[I]f we cannot now end our differences, at least we can help make the world safe for diversity. For in the final analysis, our most basic common link is that we all inhabit this small planet. We all breathe the same air. We all cherish our children's future. And we are all mortal." The human biological link, Kennedy argued, must overcome the fearful technological one. In this larger frame of commonality, the president pleaded, prospects for peace were best visualized.

Peace as Plausible Political Philosophy and Utilitarian Policy. Kennedy also encouraged a new political philosophy to sustain the new attitude: "We are not distributing blame or pointing the finger of judgment. We must deal with the world as it is, and not as it might have been had the history of the last eighteen years been different." Moreover, the impact of the missile crisis seemed to have influenced that philosophy: "Above all, while defending our own vital interests, nuclear powers must avert those confrontations which bring an adversary to a choice of either a humiliating retreat or a nuclear war. To adopt that kind of course in the nuclear age would be evidence only of the bankruptcy of our policy—or of a collective death-wish for the world." Thus, Kennedy called for "self-restraint" and avoidance of "unnecessary irritants"—rhetorical or otherwise.

The president reassured the Allies that his new political course sought "a relaxation of tensions without relaxing our guard." There would be "no deal" with the Soviets "at the expense of other nations." Nevertheless, "interests converge . . . not only in defending the frontiers of freedom, but in pursuing the paths of peace." Up until this point Kennedy had not used the word "freedom"—and its use in this context reveals the privileged status of peace in this address. Peace and freedom would not be linked again until later, when Kennedy addressed human rights in the United States with an eye toward civil rights unrest. In our view, such word use suggests a humble stance in keeping with the self-reflexive quality of this address.

The new philosophy also was argued as utilitarian. Its practicality would be revealed in "a new effort to achieve world law—a new context for world discussions." As a symbol of the advance in political thought represented by the change in attitude, Kennedy announced a hot-line between Washington and Moscow to prevent "dangerous delays, misunderstandings, and misreadings . . . at a time of crisis." In addition, while the ultimate goal was to institutionalize agencies and structures that would "by stages" produce disarmament—especially at present at Geneva—one area where a "fresh start [wa]s badly needed" was the test ban treaty negotiations. Thus Kennedy announced trilateral agreement on "high-level" discussions that would begin in Moscow on a comprehensive test ban treaty. The United States—in a "good faith" effort to jump-start the stalled talks—also would not test in the atmosphere "as long as other states do not do so." These measures symbolized what rational human beings could do in pursuit of rational ends.

Peace as a Human Right. Toward the end of the address, Kennedy turned his attention to the homefront, where strife over civil rights was severing the delicate strands of national comity and undermining national and international interests. This unrest threatened both "peace and freedom" in the United States, and it was the duty of "all citizens . . . to respect the rights of others and to respect the law of the land." The topic was "not unrelated to world peace": "The quality and the spirit of our own society must justify and support our efforts abroad." The president queried: "And is not peace, in the last analysis, basically a matter of human rights?" Having struck at the foibles of his own nation in upholding human rights and having encouraged its citizens to do better, Kennedy appealed on behalf of all humanity: "While we proceed to safeguard our national interests, let us also safeguard human interests." It was therefore incumbent upon the United States, and by implication all human beings, to denounce "a strategy of annihilation" and work "toward a strategy of peace."

The president's interdependent set of peace narratives provided powerful visions of the potential rewards of working for peace: rationality, respect for all persons, enlightened government and policy, and the protection and defense of human rights and interests. In extending his olive branch, John F. Kennedy had inverted past Cold War rhetoric, which had extolled individual and nationalistic freedom, often at the expense of communal and global peace.

Significantly, and perhaps tellingly, Sorensen believed that the address at American University was "the first Presidential speech in eighteen years to succeed in reaching beyond the cold war." By that standard, this speech may be singled out as the one foreign policy address that actually fulfilled the high expectations attending the inaugural—the promise having been long-delayed by one rhetorical-political crisis after another. The address also served as the opening for a replenished and substantive focus on the test ban treaty.[63]

While the speech had major impact in the international community and received favorable press coverage, it was somewhat overshadowed in the United States by events in Tuscaloosa—and Kennedy's own subsequent speech on June 11—another masterful demonstration of the triumph of idealism over pragmatism. The text of the American University speech suggests that Kennedy's involvement with civil rights questions at home affected positively his view of global human rights.

There has been some complaint that what the president said may have been too little too late. He recognized that the address was his first significant overture on world peace since an address to the United Nations in 1961. For Kennedy, timing was important—and he might have argued that events such as the missile crisis opened up an opportunity that was previously unavailable. Our analysis of this speech, however, reveals a president who was keenly aware of the epideictic nature of this occasion. Posturing himself as national moralist, educator, and even, at times, a revivalist in the tent-pole tradition, Kennedy used the commencement address as a forum for coaching new attitudes to forge a "practical" peace. Noble in tone and content, Kennedy's words would soar eloquently and plead righteously before introducing the pragmatic policy initiatives also meant to produce a Cold War breakthrough.

We believe this address will continue to be revered as a monumental model of diplomacy, a shining moment in which Kennedy transcended the rhetorical and political shackles of the Cold War. By replacing the trenchant discourse of competition between the superpowers with the wider dialogue of cooperation and by refocusing the narrow vision of East-West bipolar conflict with conciliation, Kennedy was able to effect a uniquely different tone and atmosphere. Here the U.S. posture was not reactive but self-reflexive. The crafted message was less a statement of narrow national self-interest than a magnanimous diplomatic gesture defending human interests. Kennedy's choice to bypass regular State and Defense Department channels resulted in an address remarkably free of bureaucratese. This contributed, somewhat ironically, to a more eloquent appeal on behalf of humanity.

Using the values of applied reason and innate human rationality as pathways to peace, humankind could form political institutions useful in safeguarding its freedoms and engaging its responsibilities. Since humankind had used its rational powers to create its technological nightmare, Kennedy argued, those same powers could be brought to bear to undo it. To the degree that this was accomplished, and there were no guarantees, save a rhetorically defined teleology, we would fulfill our human destiny. To do otherwise was to turn from our own humanity. In this speech, then, we believe Kennedy reestablished hopes for peace, recaptured the attractive appeal of the heady, can-do attitude and philosophy that had swept him into the White House, and set up prospects for movement on a test ban treaty that for all practical purposes had been declared dead. Kennedy's last-ditch effort had accomplished something of a resurrection.

Address on the Nuclear Test Ban Treaty

The Soviets were impressed with the American University address and had it published in its entirety in *Izvestia*. Most of the speech went out in an uncensored broadcast to the Russian people. More importantly, Khrushchev—labeling the American University effort as "'the greatest speech by any American president since Roosevelt'" and finding it "'notable for its sober appraisal of the international situation'"—announced on July 2 his interest in discussing a limited test ban treaty. The president had dispatched Averell Harriman as his chief negotiator for the Moscow talks with plans for negotiating a comprehensive test ban. A difficult road lie ahead. The treaty had to be negotiated, signed, and ratified by the Senate, but none of this proved insurmountable.[64]

One small dampening in Soviet ardor accompanying the June 10 speech occurred during Kennedy's triumphant trip to Europe. In Bonn, Germany at a June 24 press conference, Kennedy promoted the Moscow talks as an effort to stanch the proliferation of nuclear powers: "When Pandora opened her box and the troubles flew out, all that was left in was hope. . . . [I]f we have a nuclear diffusion throughout the world, we may even lose hope." But two days later, as he stood in Rudolph Wilde Platz in West Berlin, before throngs of wildly enthusiastic well-wishers, caught up in the symbolism and emotion of the moment, he seemed to revert to a bellicose, intimidating pre-American University Cold War rhetoric. Seemingly content again with drawing the line between East and West—and almost comfortable in the belligerent and boastful posture that had tainted U.S.-Soviet relations countless times before—Kennedy painted his adversaries as standardbearers for an "evil empire." In West Berlin, Kennedy's tentative march toward detente derailed.[65]

"Two thousand years ago, two thousand years ago the proudest boast was 'Civitas Romanus Sum.' Today, in the world of freedom, the proudest boast is 'Ich bin ein Berliner!'" He continued:

> There are people who really don't understand, or say they don't, what is the great issue between the free world and the Communist world. Let them come to Berlin! There are some who say that communism is the wave of the future. Let them come to Berlin! And there are some who say in Europe and elsewhere we can work with the Communists. Let them come to Berlin! And there are even a few who say that it's true communism is an evil system, but it permits us to make economic progress. "Lasst sie nach Berlin kommen!" Let them come to Berlin!

The speech also marked Kennedy's first direct public condemnation of the Berlin Wall—whose symbolism had, in this moment, all but overrun his political judgment. The president verged on gloating: "Freedom may have many difficulties and democracy is not perfect, but we have never had to put a wall up to keep our people in, to prevent them from leaving us." While this was a masterful manipulation of a crowd in an emotionally charged setting—and while the audience at hand was both thrilled and titillated by the young American President to whom they had given a hero's welcome—there was nothing in this speech that supplied reassurance of a new attitude of peaceful coexistence. We doubt that Moscow could detect anything suggesting an effort to "make the world safe for diversity" in Kennedy's remarks at Rudolph Wilde Platz.

Nonetheless, the long-derailed test ban treaty talks proceeded on track and, despite some setbacks, by July 17 all three powers had announced agreement on some of the provisions of the treaty draft. On July 19, Khrushchev delivered a major policy address endorsing the test ban treaty. The next day the United States, the Soviet Union, and Great Britain announced tentative agreement on a limited treaty—banning atmospheric, outer space, and underwater testing. On July 25 the tentative agreement was signed by delegates in Moscow.[66]

President Kennedy decided to use the national airwaves to make his case for a treaty destined to face a tough Senate ratification. Kennedy crafted four major arguments for a limited test ban: It would (1) reduce world tension and lead to wider disarmament initiatives; (2) protect the world from radioactive fallout; (3) prevent nuclear proliferation; and (4) limit the nuclear arms race and strengthen national and world security. Because he was defending a pact that had already been initialed as an international agreement, Kennedy was at pains to describe the terms and conditions of the agreement while, simultaneously, attempting to demonstrate that it would work adequately for all parties. Thus, one valid reading of this speech reveals a president defining the parameters of the content of the treaty (with regard to what it could and could not do) conducive to his rhetorical situation, anticipating and deflecting arguments that could be used against the agreement while simultaneously tempering unrealistic expectations. Moreover, since this speech seems to enact a deliberative mode of address, its pragmatism seemed destined to overshadow its idealism. Under such an interpretation, we can justifiably conclude that Kennedy relied more upon pragmatic than idealistic appeals.

In light of the American University address, the test ban treaty speech can be interpreted as the second step in the president's campaign for peace. Kennedy's efforts in this regard would not advance without ratification, so he employed a political strategy intended to pressure the Senate through popular opinion. It is our view that the test ban treaty speech continued self-reflexive arguments begun at American University. In this way Kennedy was able to reinforce an improbable, if not fantastic vision—a world at peace.

Self-Reflexivity in the Major Arguments. Kennedy argued that a limited test ban could reduce tensions and lead to more meaningful disarmament initiatives. But he also heightened the importance of the treaty by offering a visualization of what might happen if the efforts to build a more peaceful world failed:

> A war today or tomorrow, if it led to nuclear war, would not be like any war in history. A full-scale nuclear exchange, lasting less than 60 minutes, with the weapons now in existence, could wipe out more than 300 million Americans, Europeans and Russians, as well as untold numbers elsewhere. And the survivors, as Chairman Khrushchev warned the Communist Chinese, "the survivors would envy the dead." For they would inherit a world so devastated by explosions and poison and fire that today we cannot even conceive of its horrors. So let us try to turn the world from war. Let us make the most of this opportunity, to reduce tension, to slow down the perilous nuclear arms race, and to check the world's slide toward final annihilation.

Kennedy's visualization was heightened by his use of contrasting metaphors within the speech. Without the treaty the world continued to face "the darkening prospect of mass destruction on earth." But while past meetings had "produced only darkness, discord or disillusion," the new agreement was "a shaft of light [that] cut into the darkness." Images of light signifying a future of hope contrasted against dark images of nuclear despair and helped reify the necessity of taking an "important first step" to control the unspeakable. This helped Kennedy build popular support. The president invited the audience to reflect upon the terror of a future without the treaty so that they, too, could feel the necessity of opening "new doorways to peace."

In arguing that the treaty would reduce the dangers of radioactive fallout, Kennedy was, of course, particularly concerned with the negative effects of atmospheric testing. As at American University, Kennedy would point to the human issues involved: "Continued unrestricted testing by the nuclear powers, joined in time by other nations which may be less adept in limiting pollution, will increasingly contaminate the air that all of us must breathe." Kennedy would fortify his argument by expanding upon its human dimensions:

> Even then, the number of children and grandchildren with cancer in their bones, with leukemia in their blood, or with poison in their lungs might seem statistically small to some, in comparison to natural health hazards. But this is not a natural health hazard—and it is not a statistical issue. The loss of even one human life, or the malformation of even one baby—who may be born long after we are gone—should be of concern to us all. Our children and grandchildren are not merely statistics toward which we can be indifferent.

Such a narrative defined the treaty as a bulwark against the tide of a technologically-induced nightmare. Not one human being could be written off.[67]

In his arguments for the efficacy of the treaty in curbing the spread of nuclear weapons to other nations, Kennedy again resorted to a personalist appeal for self-reflection:

> I ask you to stop and think for a moment what it would mean to have nuclear weapons in so many hands . . . scattered throughout the world. There would be no rest for anyone then, no stability, no real security, and no chance of effective disarmament. There would only be increased chance of accidental war, and an increased necessity for the great powers to involve themselves in what otherwise would be local conflicts.

Finally, in making the argument that the limited test ban treaty would improve both national and international security, the president assured the nation that the United States had and would maintain "the strength that we need." In addition, rather than relying on the "good faith" of our adversary, any "secret violations" could and would be detected. Moreover, under treaty provisions, the

United States was able to "withdraw" and "resume all forms of testing," if required. But one should not conclude that this limited ban could or would be "quickly broken." In essence, said the president, "careful judgment" reveals the treaty provisions "safer by far for the United States than an unlimited nuclear arms race." By focusing on U.S. security interests enhanced by the test ban, Kennedy again adopted a self-reflexive, if more selfish, mode of argument. But in so doing, and by explaining the personal stake Americans had in the outcome, Kennedy was summoning all responsible citizens to "make every effort to test our hopes by action."

The conclusion of the address combined a reflexive posture with a call for support from the people. After reminding the audience of the "ancient Chinese proverb, 'A journey of a thousand miles must begin with a single step,'" Kennedy implored his fellow Americans to "take that first step. Let us, if we can, get back from the shadows of war and seek out the way of peace. And if that journey is one thousand miles, or even more, let history record that we, in this land, at this time, took the first step."

Each of the four arguments, including their self-reflexive components, was marshaled on behalf of ratification. The treaty debate that lay ahead was a part of the constitutional process and, therefore, "as it should be." For, "A document which may mark an historic and constructive opportunity for the world deserves an historic and constructive debate." The four arguments, then, also supported a call to action as the final step in the president's appeal.

Self-reflection was employed as a method of self-actualization. Kennedy would have Americans speak out on behalf of humanity through practical action. No longer alone in defense of the frontiers of freedom, but, rather, a joint partner with the people, Kennedy issued the following summons: "It is my hope that all of you will take part in this debate, for this treaty is for all of us. It is particularly for our children and grandchildren, and they have no lobby here in Washington. This debate will involve military, scientific, and political experts, but it must not be left to them alone. The right and the responsibility are yours." Thus did the President reestablish himself as a leader who both cared about and depended upon "the people."

Kennedy's appeals to self-reflexivity on behalf of the limited test ban treaty represented a continuation of efforts begun at American University—a serious and sometimes profound attempt by the president to coach a new national and international moral imagination. He sought to transcend Cold War thought and actions by asking all to envision a world without nuclear arms. Kennedy had, in his words, introduced a policy of hope and a diplomacy of action in the face of a spiraling arms race. The discourse was also a ringing affirmation of the president's own humaneness, demonstrating his public regard for humanity.[68]

Kennedy's efforts to define parameters, anticipate arguments, and temper expectations were helpful. His rhetorical performance would neither reach the heights of eloquence nor the flights of humanity of his American University address—nor do we believe it should have. For Kennedy was announcing the fruits of labor lost and begun again in the spring of 1962 and, finally, reinvigorated again in June of 1963. Thus, the Limited Nuclear Test Ban address was mostly an attempt to launch the second step in his campaign for peace—a ratification of previous efforts. At American University he offered a vision of peace. With this address he induced the nation and Senate to give peace a formal legal blessing—and therefore a chance.

Ratification. According to Arthur Schlesinger, Jr., "The President regarded the test ban treaty as the most serious congressional issue he had thus far faced." He told others he was "determined to win if it cost him the 1964 election." As a result, Kennedy, somewhat uncharacteristically, lobbied the Senators extensively, informing them fully of the negotiation process and emerging agreements. He even went so far as to send a draft of the treaty to the Senate Foreign Relations committee two weeks prior to the completion of negotiations, and then sent a bipartisan contingent of Senators to the signing ceremony in Moscow.[69]

The foreign ministers signed the pact on August 5 in Moscow. By the time the president addressed the U.N. General Assembly on September 20, nearly 100 nations were signatories. With the 80-19 Senate ratification of the treaty on September 24, 1963, and the formal signing of the treaty in the recently refurbished White House Treaty Room on October 7, the president was both relieved and proud. As Sorensen noted, "No other single accomplishment . . . ever gave him greater satisfaction." Kennedy was heartened by the fact that a symbolic marker, if not a milestone, had been reached in his administration. He had worked tirelessly on behalf of the pact. His choice to address the nation and work behind the scenes helped secure the victory.[70]

But while Kennedy was successful in preventing further fallout with the treaty, it seemed too minute a "first step" to stop the arms race as he had hoped and argued. Neither would it, in the long run, prevent the spread of nuclear weapons to other countries. Kennedy had been bitterly disappointed that he had failed to get France and China as signatories. As he had feared, the genie remained out of the bottle. As Beschloss has observed (with the focused lens of the historian's hindsight), perhaps he should have agreed to fewer international inspection sites in December 1962 so that he could have pursued a comprehensive test ban treaty, which presumably would have had greater impact in the search for peace. Nevertheless, the treaty was an accomplishment that no other nuclear-age president could claim.[71]

CONCLUSION

John F. Kennedy's Inaugural Address successfully outlined the contours of his foreign policy—both politically and rhetorically. In his promise to "bear any burden" and "pay any price," he echoed the sounds of Cold War warriors who had come before. In counseling "never negotiate out of fear—never fear to negotiate," he charted an ambivalent "peace-through-strength" course that predicted a long, tortuous path ahead. While his foreign policy discourse often contravened his aspirations for detente, and while he seemed at times to abandon good judgment along the way, he never abandoned hope. While the defense of "freedom" would dominate his idealistic, if not nationalistic, discursive values his first two years in office, it would be trumped by "peace" in his last.

Kennedy's bungling at the Bay of Pigs engendered a public discourse that dissembled and scapegoated. It represented a rhetorical as well as political low point in the Kennedy presidency and was unworthy of any nation aspiring to greatness. The Berlin crisis seemed to be one of Kennedy's own making; however, we believe there is enough evidence to suggest that not all of the tense standoff was his creation. Kennedy's discourse on July 25, 1961, allowed him to establish himself as a leader of the free world. Only later would he exercise the magnanimity and humanity of a leader dedicated to the known world in a nuclear age.

Thus, in our view, Kennedy's continuous and sometimes ambivalent balancing act between idealism and pragmatism, what we have termed his "romantic pragmatism," tipped its delicate scales toward a dominant idealism in the June 10 address at American University. Unlike the terrifying reassurances given in the pragmatic and factual March 2 nuclear test resumption speech, which played down idealism, and the October 22 missile crisis speech, which also was factual but worked a bit harder on its idealism in an effort to create national unity behind a most threatening blockade action inviting worldwide holocaust, the address at American University concentrated its throw-weight behind a romantic vision of peaceful coexistence.[7]

Kennedy's announcement of the limited test ban treaty was neither a crowning achievement in diplomacy nor featured that way. Rather, the president suggested he had merely taken a "first step." Perhaps it was symbolic, but symbols were important. The American University address and the test ban treaty announcement would set a moral compass and encourage hopes for detente. Kennedy demonstrated he could use his bully pulpit to initiate side-tracked negotiations, finish them successfully, and lobby effectively enough to get them ratified.

During the first two years of his presidency, Kennedy's idealistic discourse on the defense of freedom sometimes seemed limitless. Whether in Cuba, Berlin, the Congo, Laos, or Vietnam, the U.S. rhetorical commitment seemed expansive and sometimes ill-advised. Kennedy's words limited his choice of options and sometimes painted him into a corner from which public extrication was difficult. His pragmatic discourse helped establish a president in command of both fact and situation. Since many of his public television addresses were concerned with foreign policy "crises," Kennedy's definition of the "facts" helped establish his presidential authority and garner public support in the United States, if not always with our allies.

The turning point was the missile crisis, which shocked all parties into more serious efforts toward peace, and, ultimately, must be credited with breaking the logjam on the test ban treaty. But, in hindsight, the price the nation paid in fear and trembling seemed hardly worth the "limited" outcome. It was only during his last year in office that Kennedy seriously seemed to entertain a rhetoric of conciliation that challenged both the political and moral imagination. At times, a more macho and bellicose president would retreat from that courageous profile, as exemplified in the "Berliner" speech. As a result, the rhetorical legacy of Kennedy's foreign policy address is mixed at best. As James N. Giglio observed, "In reality, Kennedy pursued an ambiguous course to the end."[73]

NOTES

1. Theodore C. Sorensen, *Kennedy* (New York: Harper and Row Publishers, 1965), 509.

2. "Remarks of Sen. John F. Kennedy (D.-Mass.) to Nevada State Legislature, Carson City, Nevada, February 1, 1960," Pre-Presidential Papers, 1960 Campaign, Box 1031, JFK Library.

3. Michael R. Beschloss, *The Crisis Years: Kennedy and Khrushchev 1960-1963* (New York: Edward Burlingame Books/HarperCollins, 1991), 60, 61, 65; Robert Smith Thompson, *The Missiles of October: The Declassified Story of John F. Kennedy and the Cuban Missile Crisis* (New York: Simon and Schuster, 1992), 109.

4. Thompson, *Missles*, 110-111; "State of the Union Message of President John F. Kennedy, January 30, 1961," Presidential Office Files, Annual Message to Congress on the State of the Union (As Actually Delivered), Drafts and Press Releases, Box 34, JFK Library.

5. Beschloss, *The Crisis Years*, 61, 63-64.

6. See, e.g., Sorensen, *Kennedy*, 602-633, 509-540. We find Kennedy alternately evoking a rhetoric similar to but distinct from what Philip Wander has referred to as "prophetic dualism" (moralism) and "technological realism" (pragmatism). The difference revealed in our particular analysis is that Kennedy's appeals to liberal democratic ideals imply that the United States is morally superior to the Communist system and that the Soviets are "evil." Thus, we refer to Kennedy's rhetoric of idealism as "romantic" and his definitions of fact describing the political environment as "pragmatic." We are referring to a rhetorical strategy rather than a philosophy per se. The rationale for this move follows with our definition of Kennedy's foreign policy discourse as best encompassed in the term "romantic pragmatism." We draw the term from Ernest G. Bormann, who applied this designation to Puritan discourse, which was both principled and pragmatic. For another example of Kennedy's use of idealistic and pragmatic discourse in foreign policy we refer the reader to Kennedy's public statements on Vietnam. See Philip Wander, "The Rhetoric of American Foreign Policy," *Quarterly Journal of Speech* 70 (1984): 339-361; Ernest G. Bormann, *The Force of Fantasy: Restoring the American Dream* (Carbondale: Southern Illinois University Press, 1985),

esp. pp. 18-19; 44-52; Denise M. Bostdorff and Steven R. Goldzwig, "Idealism and Pragmatism in American Foreign Policy Rhetoric: The Case of John F. Kennedy and Vietnam," *Presidential Studies Quarterly* 24 (1994): 515-530.

7. See Martin J. Medhurst, Robert L. Ivie, Philip Wander, and Robert L. Scott, *Cold War Rhetoric: Strategy, Metaphor, and Ideology* (Westport, Conn.: Greenwood Press, 1990), 11-13.

8. Medhurst et al., *Cold War*, 20-21; Sorensen, *Kennedy*, 602.

9. Scholars are divided on whether or not Kennedy substantially retreated from traditional Cold War discourse and policy. See, e.g., Thomas Brown, *JFK: History of an Image* (Bloomington: Indiana University Press, 1988), esp. p. 29.

10. Alonzo L. Hamby, *Liberalism and Its Challenges: F.D.R. to Bush* 2nd ed. (New York: Oxford University Press, 1992), 194-195; John F. Kennedy, *The Strategy of Peace*, ed. Allan Nevins (New York: Harper and Row, 1960), 6, 8-9, 199.

11. Kennedy, *The Strategy of Peace*, 37.

12. Hamby, *Liberalism*, 213.

13. See, e.g., Herbert S. Parmet, *JFK: The Presidency of John F. Kennedy* (New York: Dial Press, 1983), esp. pp. 159-160.

14. James N. Giglio, *The Presidency of John F. Kennedy* (Lawrence: University Press of Kansas, 1991), 48; Parmet, *JFK*, 158, and see pp. 158-161.

15. Beschloss, *The Crisis Years*, 99, 101-102.

16. Beschloss, *The Crisis Years*, 28-30.

17. Trumbull Higgins, *The Perfect Failure: Kennedy, Eisenhower, and the CIA at the Bay of Pigs* (New York and London: W. W. Norton, 1987), esp. pp. 53-54, 87-89.

18. Beschloss, *The Crisis Years*, 104-105, 106; Thompson, *Missiles*, 111, 113, 114.

19. Beschloss, *The Crisis Years*, 114; Harold W. Chase and Allen H. Lerman, ed. *Kennedy and the Press: The News Conferences* (New York: Thomas Y. Crowell, 1965), 59, cited hereafter as Chase and Lerman, "News Conference of," followed by the date.

20. Higgins, *The Perfect Failure*, 148; Beschloss, *The Crisis Years*, 120-121, 123. In addition to public relations and political conundrums associated with this unmitigated blunder, Kennedy was left with the immediate task of trying to free those captured in the failed episode. It would take Kennedy over eighteen months to extricate the prisoners from Cuba. He traded tractors, medical supplies, and drugs in exchange for the release of the prisoners and informed private donors who supported the effort that their gifts would be tax exempt; however, Kennedy failed to consult Congress regarding his pledge, which created even more trouble. See Lewis J. Paper, *The Promise and the Performance: The Leadership of John F. Kennedy* (New York: Crown Publishers, 1975), 178-179.

21. Beschloss, *The Crisis Years*, 127-128; Arthur M. Schlesinger, Jr., *A Thousand Days: John F. Kennedy in the White House* (Boston: Houghton Mifflin, 1965), 287-288, 291.

22. The passages quoted in this paragraph and those that follow are taken from the "Address of the President to the American Society of Newspaper Editors, Statler Hotel, Washington, D.C., April 20, 1961," Presidential Office Files, Speech Files, Box 35, JFK Library. Reprinted in the "Collected Speeches" section of this volume.

23. The points we raise about the speech to the publishers rely upon the arguments of Theodore Otto Windt, Jr., *Presidents and Protesters: Political Rhetoric in the 1960s* (Tuscaloosa and London: The University of Alabama Press, 1990), 28-35. See John F. Kennedy, "The President and the Press: Address Before the American Newspaper

Publishers Association, New York City, April 27, 1961," *Public Papers of the President 1961* (Washington, D.C.: Government Printing Office, 1962), 334-338; Chase and Lerman, "News Conference of April 21," 89.

24. See, e.g., Beschloss, *The Crisis Years*, 133. Giglio notes that after the Bay of Pigs Kennedy's Gallup rating on overall performance stood at 83 percent. Lewis Paper also reports this figure and adds that the approval rating on the Cuban action was 61 percent, with only 5 percent of Americans disapproving of the operation. For his part, Kennedy is reported to have observed: "It's just like Eisenhower. The worse I do the more popular I get." We are loath to link the rise in Kennedy's approval rating following the Bay of Pigs to his speeches and press conferences on the matter. See Giglio, *The Presidency*, 59; Paper, *The Promise*, 88; Schlesinger, *A Thousand Days*, 292.

25. Paper, *The Promise*, 88.

26. "Remarks of Sen. John F. Kennedy (D.-Mass.), Nationality Building Fund Committee Dinner, International Institute of Gary, Indiana, Thursday February 4, 1960," Pre-Presidential Papers, 1960 Campaign Files, Speeches, Statements and Sections, Foreign Affairs, Box 1030, JFK Library.

27. "Remarks of Sen. John F. Kennedy, University of Wisconsin—Milwaukee, Milwaukee, Wisconsin, March 24, 1960," Pre-Presidential Papers, 1960 Campaign Files, Speeches, Statements, and Sections, Foreign Affairs, Box 1030, JFK Library; and see Beschloss, *The Crisis Years*, 30-31.

28. Parmet, *JFK*, 210.

29. Beschloss, *The Crisis Years*, 164, 171, 173, 225; Sorensen, *Kennedy*, 585; Chase and Lerman, "News Conference of June 2, 1961: Remarks and Question and Answer Period at the Press Luncheon June 2, 1961—Paris, France," 83.

30. Beschloss, *The Crisis Years*, 223-224, 225, 231, 243; Paper, *The Promise*, p. 192; Parmet notes that the meeting in Vienna "did not so much provoke as confirm the existence of a crisis," JFK, 189.

31. "Text of the President's Report to the Nation Following his Visit to Paris, France, Vienna, Austria, and London, England from his Office in the White House, Delivered at 7 P.M. (E.D.T.), June 6, 1961 (As Actually Delivered)," Presidential Office Files, Speech Files, Box 34, JFK Library; Chase and Lerman, "News Conference of June 28," 89, "News Conference of July 19," 97. And see, e.g., Beschloss, *The Crisis Years*, 177, 258; David Burner, *John F. Kennedy and the New Generation* (Boston: Little, Brown, 1988), 73.

32. See Sorensen, *Kennedy*, 589-590. All quotations from this address are drawn from: "Text of the President's Report to the Nation on the Berlin Crisis, Delivered at 10:00 P.M. E.D.T., July 25, 1961, from his Office in the White House (As Actually Delivered)," Presidential Office Files, Speech Files, Box 35, JFK Library. Reprinted in the "Collected Speeches" section of this volume.

33. We will leave it to the reader to review section five of the speech for its alleged incongruence.

34. Memorandum to Mr. Theodore C. Sorensen from Maxwell D. Taylor, July 25, 1961, Theodore C. Sorensen Papers, Subject Files, 1961-1964, Theodore C. Sorensen Memoranda, Box 36, JFK Library.

35. Memorandum to Mr. T. C. Sorensen from W. W. Rostow, July 20, 1961, Theodore C. Sorensen Papers, Subject Files 1961-1964, Theodore C. Sorensen Memoranda, Box 36, JFK Library.

36. Memorandum to the Honorable Dean Rusk, Secretary of State from Edward R. Murrow, July 21, 1961, Theodore C. Sorensen Papers, Subject Files 1961-1964, Theodore C. Sorensen Memoranda, Box 36, JFK Library.

37. When Khrushchev heard this speech, he thought Kennedy had issued a preliminary declaration of war; see Beschloss, *The Crisis Years*, 262.

38. John Kennedy did not need a Berlin crisis as a pretext for rearmament. Two months before this address, on May 25, Kennedy delivered an address to Congress on "special needs." Pundits came to label the speech as the "second" State of the Union Address. It was here that Kennedy issued the first request for some of the items listed in this paragraph. Pledging the nation to a world leadership role in "freedom's cause," scholars have judged the speech as representative of Kennedy's attempt to remilitarize the United States. See John F. Kennedy, "Special Message to the Congress on Urgent National Needs," *Public Papers of the Presidents, 1961* (Washington, D.C.: U.S. Government Printing Office, 1962), 396-406.

39. Memorandum to McGeorge Bundy from the President, Presidential Office Files, Staff Memoranda, McGeorge Bundy, 5/61-7/61, Box 62, JFK Library; Beschloss, *The Crisis Years*, 260. Interestingly, Kennedy had publicly introduced his plans for civil defense somewhat unspectacularly two months prior to the Berlin crisis speech in his Special Message to Congress on May 25, 1961.

40. Parmet, *JFK*, 198; Beschloss, *The Crisis Years*, esp. pp. 279 and 272.

41. See Chase and Lerman, "News Conference of October 11, 1961," 122.

42. Adam Yarmolinsky blamed the press, particularly a *Life* magazine article, for "creating a brief period of near hysteria" regarding civil defense. See Adam Yarmolinsky Oral History, Interviewed by Daniel Ellsberg, JFK Library. For an excellent analysis of juxtaposition as a rhetorical stance in the July 25 speech see Kevin W. Dean, "'We Seek Peace—But We Shall Not Surrender': JFK's Use of Juxtaposition for Rhetorical Success in the Berlin Crisis," *Presidential Studies Quarterly* 21 (1991): 531-544.

43. For rhetorical studies that include discussions of the Cuban missile crisis see Wayne Brockriede and Robert L. Scott, *Moments in the Rhetoric of the Cold War* (New York: Random House, 1970), 79-117; James W. Pratt, "An Analysis of Three Crisis Speeches," *Western Journal of Speech Communication* 34 (1970): 194-203; Theodore Otto Windt, Jr., "The Presidency and Speeches on International Crises," *Speaker and Gavel*, 2 (1973): 6-14; Theodore Otto Windt, Jr., *Presidents and Protesters: Political Rhetoric in the 1960s* (Tuscaloosa: University of Alabama Press, 1990), 52-60; Denise M. Bostdorff, "The Rhetoric of Deflection: John F. Kennedy and the Cuban Missile Crisis of 1962," in Denise M. Bostdorff, *The Presidency and the Rhetoric of Foreign Policy Crisis* (Columbia: University of South Carolina, 1994), 25-55.

44. Beschloss, *The Crisis Years*, 5-6; Thompson, *Missiles*, 140, 142.

45. Beschloss, *The Crisis Years*, 371-373. The "flexible response" doctrine envisaged the use of tactical nuclear weapons in "limited wars" and the development of Special Forces (the Green Berets) for counterinsurgency efforts.

46. Chase and Lerman, "News Conference of March 7, 1962," 197; and see Beschloss, *The Crisis Years*, 384; Bostdorff, "Rhetoric of Deflection."

47. Beschloss, *The Crisis Years*, 375; Chase and Lerman, "News Conference of April 18, 1962," 230; Parmet, *JFK*, 282-284; Chase and Lerman, "News Conference of August 29, 1962," 314. Some have reported that Kennedy knew of the preparation of missile installations as early as March 1962 and preferred to keep silent on the matter in an effort

to catch the Soviets red-handed at a more propitious time. See, e.g., Thompson, *Missiles*, 213-214.

48. "Letter to the President of the Senate and the Speaker of the House Transmitting Bill Authorizing Mobilization of the Ready Reserve, September 7, 1962," *Public Papers of the Presidents, 1962* (Washington, D.C.: U.S. Government Printing Office, 1963), 665; Chase and Lerman, "News Conference of September 13, 1962," 317-318; Thompson, *Missiles*, 207. Recent scholarship has revealed evidence suggesting that the United States was indeed contemplating some form of military invasion, as Castro feared. The minimal interpretation is that Operation Mongoose was carried out with a simultaneously coordinated, Pentagon-developed contingency plan for military intervention in Cuba. This scenario, of course, suggests that both Castro and Khrushchev may have had justification in fearing an imminent conventional U.S. military invasion. See James G. Hershberg, "Before 'The Missiles of October': Did Kennedy Plan a Military Strike Against Cuba?" *Diplomatic History* 14 (1990): 163-198.

49. For an excellent description of differing historical interpretations of the missile crisis see William J. Medland, "The Cuban Missile Crisis: Evolving Historical Perspectives," *History Teacher* 23 (1990): 433-447. For interesting discussions on the crisis and the Ex Comm deliberations in particular, see, e.g., Thompson, *Missiles*, esp. pp. 187-240; Beschloss, *The Crisis Years*, esp. pp. 431-476; Sorensen, *Kennedy*, esp. pp. 678-702; Schlesinger, *A Thousand Days*, esp. pp. 801-812.

50. Thompson, *Missiles*, 265, 267; Sorensen, *Kennedy*, 701, 703.

51. All subsequent citations are taken from "Radio-TV Address of the President to the Nation from the White House, October 22, 1962 (As Actually Delivered)," Presidential Office Files, Speech Files, Radio-Television Report to the American People on the Soviet Arms Buildup in Cuba, October 22, 1962, Box 41, JFK Library. Reprinted in the "Collected Speeches" section of this volume.

52. Thompson, *Missiles*, 277-278, 272; Paper, *The Promise*, 92, 179; Memorandum from Richard E. Neustadt to Theodore Sorensen, Theodore C. Sorensen Papers, Subject Files, 1961-1964, Neustadt Memoranda, Box 36, JFK Library; Giglio, *The Presidency*, 216. Giglio describes the extent of the fear stemming from the speech, indicating that the same Gallup poll that noted 84 percent of Americans in favor of and 4 percent opposed to the blockade, also revealed that 20 percent thought World War III "inevitable"; 60 percent feared that "some shooting" would occur soon. See Giglio, *The Presidency*, 205.

53. As it turned out, both men blinked. Although unknown to the public at the time, Kennedy, in effect, would agree to respect the territorial sovereignty of Cuba and remove the missiles in Turkey in exchange for dismantlement and withdrawal of the nuclear weapons placed in Cuba. The deal was pure political horse-trading. For the president's feelings regarding impeachment, see, e.g., Beschloss, *The Crisis Years*, 448.

54. Pratt, "An Analysis," esp. p. 199. For a further discussion on the relationship between crisis, unity, and sacrifice see Murray Edelman, *Political Language: Words That Succeed and Policies That Fail* (New York: Academic Press, 1977), 44-49.

55. These and the passages that follow are taken from "State of the Union Message (As Actually Delivered)," Theodore C. Sorensen Papers, JFK Speech Files, 1962-1963, 1/14/63, Press Releases, Box 76, JFK Library.

56. Chase and Lerman, "News Conference of January 24, 1963," 369-370.

57. Chase and Lerman, "News Conference of February 21, 1963," 394, 396.

58. Chase and Lerman, "News Conference of March 21, 1963," 410; "News

Conference of April 24, 1963," 430; "News Conference of May 8, 1963," 441-442; "News Conference of May 22, 1963," 450.

59. Sorensen, *Kennedy*, 729-730; quotation, 730-731. For a different critical perspective on Kennedy's American University address see Theodore Windt, "Seeking Detente with the Superpowers: John F. Kennedy at American University," in *Essays in Presidential Rhetoric* 2nd ed., ed. Theodore Windt and Beth Ingold (Dubuque, Iowa: Kendall/Hunt Publishing, 1987), 135-148.

60. The traditional forms of public address are deliberative, forensic, and epideictic. Deliberative address focuses upon future policy decisions and is practiced wherever people formally make laws or enact policies and regulations. Forensic address, practiced in courts of law, focuses attention upon the past and tries to establish guilt or innocence by bringing public charges of accusation and defense. Epideictic address, as noted, focuses on present values and evaluates human action in moral terms like good and evil. It is often in evidence at Fourth of July celebrations, funeral orations, commencement ceremonies, or any other occasion where the ritual celebration of present communal values is in evidence. We believe epideictic address forms the baseline or foundation for the other two forms, which are often, if not always, derived from epideictic stylizations. For the original discussion see Aristotle, *On Rhetoric: A Theory of Civic Discourse*, trans. George A. Kennedy (Oxford and New York: Oxford University Press, 1991), esp. Book I, Chs. 4-15, pp. 52-118. For a discussion of overlap or hybridization of these generic categories see, e.g., Kathleen Hall Jamieson and Karlyn Kohrs Campbell, "Rhetorical Hybrids: Fusions of Generic Elements," *Quarterly Journal of Speech* 68 (1982): 146-157; A. Cheree Carlson, "John Quincy Adams' 'Amistad Address': Eloquence in a Generic Hybrid," *Western Journal of Speech Communication* 49 (1985): 14-26.

61. John F. Kennedy, "Commencement Address at American University, June 10, 1963," Presidential Office Files, Speech Files, 6/10/63-7/2/63, Box 45, JFK Library. See also "Remarks of the President at American University, Washington, D.C., June 10, 1963 (As Actually Delivered)," same citation as above. There were, of course, a few minor changes in the actual delivery of the speech. Reprinted in the "Collected Speeches" section of this volume.

62. In his theoretical treatment of the concept of entelechy, Kenneth Burke notes: "Everything that comes into existence moves toward an end." It therefore seeks "perfection." As Burke notes, the Greek "word for 'perfect' is teleios." Thus, entelechy "classifies a thing by conceiving its kind according to perfection (that is, finishedness) of which that kind is capable." Therefore, says Burke, when one maintains that "'Man is a rational animal,'" one is pointing out "that the perfection of humankind is in the order of rationality." See Kenneth Burke, *A Grammar of Motives* (Berkeley: University of California Press, 1969), 261; Kenneth Burke, *A Rhetoric of Motives* (Berkeley: University of California Press, 1969), 14.

63. Sorensen, *Kennedy*, 730.

64. Schlesinger, *A Thousand Days*, 904.

65. Chase and Lerman, "News Conference of June 24, 1963, Bonn, Germany," 455. The citations that follow are drawn from John F. Kennedy, "Remarks of the President upon Signing the Golden Book in Rudolph Wilde Plaza, Berlin, Germany, June 26, 1963," Presidential Office Files, Speech Files, 6/10/63-2/2/63, Box 45, JFK Library. The quotations also were checked against an audio recording.

66. For an excellent discussion of the limited test ban treaty from July 1963 to its eventual ratification see Beschloss, *The Crisis Years*, 618-638. For another account see Sorensen, *Kennedy*, 734-740.

67. Interestingly, when Kennedy had earlier resumed atmospheric testing, he made the argument that fallout from U.S. testing was miniscule in comparison to "natural hazards." In this address, he needed to transcend his previous argument. He appeals for self-reflection and the development of an ethic of care and responsibility.

68. The rhetorical strategies Kennedy employed helped to infuse his discourse with what Chaim Perelman would label "presence." By lending "importance and pertinency" to the arguments, these strategies "act[ed] directly on [audience] sensibilities." This allowed Kennedy to coach both imagination and reason. See Chaim Perelman and L. Olbrechts-Tyteca, The *New Rhetoric: A Treatise on Argumentation* trans. John Wilkinson and Purcell Weaver (South Bend: University of Notre Dame Press), esp. pp. 115-120; quotation, p. 116.

69. Schlesinger, *A Thousand Days*, 909-910; Paper, *The Promise*, 177-178.

70. Sorensen, *Kennedy*, 740.

71. Beschloss, *The Crisis Years*, 637.

72. While we do not treat the March 2 Nuclear Test Resumption Address in this book due to space limitations, we believe it is representative of Kennedy's pragmatic discourse. For an excellent analysis of this address see Martin J. Medhurst, "Rhetorical Portraiture in John F. Kennedy's March 2, 1962 Speech on the Resumption of Atmospheric Testing" in Martin J. Medhurst et al., *Cold War*, 51-68.

73. Giglio, *The Presidency*, 219.

5

CONCLUSION

Previous assessments of John F. Kennedy's presidency and his rhetoric have offered some dramatically different—almost bi-polar—judgments. While some friendly biographers—most notably those who worked closely with Kennedy—praise his accomplishments while discounting or minimizing his failures, less sympathetic writers are quick to state that his successes were often too little and too late. We suggest, however, that any evaluation of the legacy of John F. Kennedy must account for the fact that he never finished his term. Thus, a sense of incompleteness complicates assessment of the Kennedy presidency, as well as his public rhetoric, because, in a very real sense, each was bequeathed as a "work in progress." We contend that although Kennedy's public discourse was deficient in many ways, it did indeed—like the man himself—show a remarkable sense of evolution during his tenure in office.

CAMPAIGN DISCOURSE

Kennedy's speech to the Greater Houston Ministerial Association was an eloquent exposition concerning the American belief in the separation of church and state. In meeting his own political need to transcend the religious issue, Kennedy issued a moral plea for religious tolerance. He reprised the secular contract binding conscience to public service and proclaimed it paramount to the execution of public office, transcending all other allegiances. In doing so he reiterated eloquently the uniqueness of the American political experience and American ideals.

The Inaugural Address extended the American covenant to the world as both an image to be emulated and a model to be followed. In his attempt to make the world over into America's likeness, Kennedy reinforced the attractive ideals of freedom and self-determination. His rhetorical defenses of freedom were both bellicose and conciliatory, brandishing America's might while posturing as always ready to lie down with the lambs. In establishing his peace-through-strength theme, Kennedy both closed the campaign and opened the New Frontier with a style and a panache not seen in the White House on an inaugural day in quite some time.

By informing himself with a review of various speaking models from Lincoln to Wilson to Roosevelt, Kennedy had sought to combine an economy of words with an elegance of expression that would allow the young leader to set a tone for the new decade. In that effort, he succeeded mightily. For the inaugural expressed a politics of hope and expectation. It promised peace and prosperity, despite ever-present dangers. Its pledges of vigilance comforted both domestic and international communities and Kennedy's symbolic tenacity and resolve seemed to solidify such feelings. His youth made the promises of the new decade—including a virtuous, forward-looking foreign policy—seem all the more palpable, with fine and festive words signalling that an old order had passed away and a new political era had dawned.

Both grim and gripping, part warning and part celebration, the inaugural expressed both a dutiful vision of what was, and an exciting challenge to what could be. Most of all, the rhetoric assured both "friend and foe alike" that this president would both take and sustain control. At the time, however, it was not fully understood how much Kennedy had been shaped by Cold War thought and doctrine, nor how closely he identified his own persona and ego with America. When the new president's image suffered, so too, reasoned Kennedy, did that of America.

CIVIL RIGHTS

Kennedy's tenure in office witnessed such disparate civil rights events as the peaceful March on Washington and increasing levels of violence, intransigence and insurrection that attended the Freedom Rides, the desegregation of the University of Mississippi, and the Birmingham campaign.

Previous assessments of Kennedy's commitment to and record on civil rights have been mixed. Some are decidedly negative, pointing out that for two years Kennedy seemed to have lost his moral compass on this issue, if indeed he had ever owned such an instrument. For example, Taylor Branch judged Kennedy's civil rights record as "deficient," and observed that after his assassination his record was ascribed mythic proportions, "acquir[ing] the Lincolnesque mantle of a unifying crusader who had bled against the thorn of race. Honest biographers later found it impossible to trace an engaged personality in proportion to the honor. Because the best spirit of Kennedy was largely absent from the racial deliberations of his presidency, the issue remained an exogenous factor to the most intimate, admiring accounts of his life."[1]

However, other writers have pointed out that Kennedy's circumspection concerning civil rights was an informed—if insensitive—exercise in caution. His political judgment regarding his ability to pass a civil rights bill in 1961 and 1962 was "unassailable." Indeed, two days before his death, Kennedy's civil rights bill was languishing in the House Rules committee in the tight-fisted grasp of Virginian Howard Smith. While the president's moral compass may have been awry, his political instincts were accurately tuned to both the public and congressional pulse, and he judged precipitous action to be dead on arrival.[2]

We feel most in sympathy with a view expressed by contemporary civil rights historian Harvard Sitkoff: "Kennedy traveled in fits and starts toward a commitment to civil rights, and an identification with the movement, that he had previously resisted. Although he never fully reached that destination, he moved nearer to it than any previous American President." Acting from both personal moral imperative and political instinct, fearing increased bloodshed and violence and extremist forms of black and white activism, Kennedy conducted a rhetorical campaign that was finally worthy of his campaign promises to African Americans. For many Americans, this was a charge and a call that promised too little and came too late. But in the context of the times, it was nonetheless courageous.[3]

For the first two years of his administration, Kennedy had given little attention to civil rights, spending the majority of his focus and energy in the foreign policy arena. When he did turn his attention to domestic civil rights unrest, it was to react to violent events and issue appeals grounded in legal concerns. This is best symbolized in the president's address concerning James Meredith's admission to the University of Mississippi. Thus, for two years Kennedy's civil rights rhetoric followed rather than led public opinion on the race question. There was precious little he could point to by way of tangible political inroads; he seemed either unwilling or unable to marshal the resources of his presidency quickly enough or expansively enough to combat discrimination as he had promised. His legal arguments were a necessary part of maintaining a grip on the federal constabulary and they were directly tied to the promises he made in his oath of office. In pressing the legal rights of African Americans to vote, attend school, and enjoy the same rights to public accommodations as any other citizen, Kennedy merely stressed the need for malcontents and miscreants of whatever stripe to obey the law of the land. But sole reliance on appeal to legal principle—with its liberal tradition of the neutral application of laws—would go only so far. Much of it smacked of political expedience at the expense of true resolve. Kennedy soft-pedaled comprehensive legislation, obsessed over calculations regarding domestic politics, and expressed public concern over the international image problems civil rights unrest had created.

By 1963, however, Kennedy seemed to find his moral bearings. As the violence worsened, the president who had highlighted human rights came to realize that defending freedom abroad was made more difficult by its overt challenges at home, and his legendary facility to charm and cajole would go only so far. When one group was singled out for persecution because of race and when the unjustified violence continued, the morality of the issue became more pressing—and Kennedy fused the legal argument to a moral one. Thus, both equal justice and moral egalitarianism appear as principled, thought-provoking appeals in the June 11, 1963 address—the apex of Kennedy's rhetoric concerning civil rights. This change was underscored by the spring campaign that preceded it, which also raised the question to one of right and wrong—not merely the equal application of the laws of the United States. When the president finally grafted legal argument to moral suasion, he found a new and more powerful voice and he made the message more profound and meaningful by introducing a package of comprehensive civil rights legislation.

During his time in office, Kennedy's public rhetoric concerning civil rights evolved from pleas for law and order to a moral clarion, summoning Americans to do what was most in keeping with their self-proclaimed character. His rhetorical legacy concerning civil rights evidences a pattern of evolution that was cut tragically short in Dallas. It would be up to Lyndon Johnson to turn further civil rights expectations into reality.

FOREIGN POLICY

Evaluations of Kennedy's foreign policy discourse also evidence a wide difference of opinion. For example, Lewis Paper has argued that part of the reason for the "frustrating" nature of Kennedy's presidency was that, while he could articulate "basic values," his policies were "frozen in the past" and "unresponsive to the new realities." Indeed, Paper felt Kennedy never fulfilled the promise augured by the heady idealism of his own campaign discourse. While rhetorically defining himself as different from and more progressive than the Eisenhower administration, the actual outcome in foreign policy seemed much less distinct. Kennedy's overwhelming and intractable Cold War fear of the "Communist menace" militated against any meaningful change in traditional diplomacy, while his skepticism and caution vitiated his proclaimed idealism.[4]

Thomas G. Patterson also noted how Kennedy "remained attached to the core of Cold War thinking," "exaggerated the Communist threat to the Third World," and interpreted "most world events as tests between the East and West" with the ultimate goal of U.S. "supremacy." Thus, "Despite the rhetoric of bold, new thinking, Kennedy and his advisers never fundamentally reassessed American foreign policy assumptions. Instead, they endowed them with more vigor and less patience—inviting the shortfalls and failures that dominate the diplomatic record of John F. Kennedy." The myths associated with Camelot were woven "out of disappointment." "Actually, he had his chance, and he failed."

Frank Costigliola noted the paradox between Kennedy's foreign policy rhetoric and the policies of his administration; Kennedy "talked community, but practiced hegemony."[5]

Yet others were much less harsh. James N. Giglio observes: "In retrospect Kennedy had the misfortune of being compared to his own high expectations and lofty rhetoric and to the great achievements of Johnson's Great Society. In reality, although his presidency fell far short of both, the New Frontier did successfully embody the Roosevelt and Truman legacies. At the same time, it also offered America newer approaches." In a similar vein, Irving Bernstein notes that Kennedy's foreign policy went "from early confusion and failure to later self-confidence and success, really triumph." In October of 1963, George Kennan would write to Kennedy: "I am in full admiration, both as a historian and as a person with diplomatic experience, for the manner in which you have addressed yourself to the problems of foreign policy with which I am familiar. I don't think we have seen a better standard of statesmanship in the White House in the present century." Later, Kennan would reflect: "If he failed anywhere in his approach to foreign policy—it was in the fact that he did not do enough to try to teach the American public the basic facts about the world."[6]

We, like others, find Kennedy's speeches following the Bay of Pigs to be self-serving and unworthy of the ideals expressed in his Inaugural Address. His Berlin Crisis speech on July 25 probably did more to create a crisis than respond to one. But after Khrushchev's bluster in Vienna, Kennedy felt he had to draw a line over Berlin or risk the loss of the city and America's international prestige. As Giglio pointed out, while it is true that Kennedy's preoccupation with Berlin distracted him from important domestic matters, he "had not instigated the conflict, nor could he have ignored the Khrushchev ultimatum at Vienna. A tour de force was necessary."[7]

The Cuban Missile Crisis address was the result of a brinkmanship diplomacy intensified by Kennedy's public pledges to never allow Soviet missiles in this hemisphere. Having chosen to interpret their emplacement as an "offensive" act of aggression, Kennedy had left himself precious little political or rhetorical room for alternative definitions. This also constrained his remedial actions. Yet Kennedy showed restraint in his application of the naval blockade, which he carefully, if somewhat disingenuously, labeled a "quarantine." Having successfully negotiated the crisis—using direct communiques to Khrushchev to break through the diplomatic logjam—Kennedy probably felt himself in a better position for future negotiations with the Soviets. Having unsheathed the nuclear sword and symbolically vanquished the foe, the president could now offer the olive branch. Confrontation and conciliation may have been unequal partners in Kennedy's rhetoric, but when he chose to use either aspect of this arsenal it was always predicated upon or judged against the other.

At American University, Kennedy set the tone for detente with the Soviets. In some ways this speech reinforced diplomatic values that were precursors to later "open door" policies with the Chinese, and further inroads that helped produce glastnost and more favorable responses to the West in the Soviet Union. Kennedy's June 10 remarks stand in sharp contrast to the self-serving words used after the Bay of Pigs. At American University, Kennedy was self-reflexive rather than reactive, and struck a reformative rather than defensive posture. His attempt to make a world "safe for diversity" represented a watershed in Cold War diplomacy by pointing the way toward transcendence. By calling upon timeless principles Kennedy made timely inroads, which at the very least helped restore the vision offered in the inaugural and helped secure a final hearing on the test ban. At American University, Kennedy also transcended national interest in advocating a telos of human interest. The result was a major twentieth-century document on international diplomacy.

The Limited Nuclear Test Ban Treaty speech was interesting in that it continued the self-reflexive arguments set in motion at American University. In extending an ethic of care and responsibility for the world as his basic rationale for the test ban, Kennedy once again reinforced and magnified the human dimension of the potential ravages of massive nuclear war, and found a moral argument that transcended earlier rationalistic calls for the defense of freedom. Kennedy's pragmatism led him to fear that continued nuclear proliferation would constitute a threat to humanity for generations to come. And while the actual agreement had less teeth than Kennedy wanted, it was, as Kennedy claimed, a useful "first step." According to David Burner and Thomas R. West, "The reputation of the treaty, like the repute of Kennedy's policies on civil rights, has suffered from its being perceived by standards that came into their own as the decade progressed."[8]

Kennedy's foreign policy rhetoric reveals a president trying to demonstrate that he had the courage to protect freedom and the wisdom to keep the peace. Often, it was a rhetoric of chauvinistic nationalism that reinforced images of the political and moral superiority of American democracy. Its blessings were derived from Kennedy's ability to articulate American ideals as few presidents in this century had before. Its particular curse was the political and social inability of the nation and its president to live up to those ideals—for the idealism was out of proportion to human capacities to deliver on their sometimes grandiose promises. His militancy—cast in the peace-through-strength motif—resulted in overtures toward peace and reconciliation that were sometimes lost to the more warrior-like voice. Kennedy's discourse proved to be a precursor to the foreign policy discourse of subsequent presidencies—especially the successive rhetorics supporting the Vietnam War. In the breach between promise and performance, Lewis Paper noted that Kennedy's "ideals lingered on, with millions of people in this country and around the world grasping for the promise that remained unfulfilled." The foreign policies Kennedy implemented in a perilous hour were simultaneously idealistic and appealing—and yet somehow found wanting, short of their mark. This is partially a result of Kennedy's ambiguous rhetoric.[9]

EPILOGUE

We believe John F. Kennedy's television addresses ushered in a flowering of the rhetorical presidency. It was the immediacy with which Kennedy invaded American living rooms that made his messages all the more striking. Even though they were mostly reactionary, we believe Kennedy's crisis speeches in 1961 and 1962, in particular, reinaugurated and expanded the rhetorical influence and potential persuasive powers of the presidency. The Berlin Crisis Address and the Cuban Missile Crisis speech, for example, were worthy precursors to future presidential addresses that directly confronted the American people with crises in Vietnam, Cambodia, Panama, Grenada, and Iraq, among many others. All of these speeches justified military decisions and activities that had already been initiated and sought to dampen criticism by jingoistic, ethnocentric saber-rattling. In these endeavors, unity is procured at a cost as the drums of war drown the pleas for peace. In the early 1960s few Americans felt they had much choice. They expected the god of Mars to visit them with a vengeance, and one of the few thoughts that arrested their fears was the image of a courageous young president willing to "pay any price" and "bear any burden" in freedom's cause. The moral power of a rhetorical presidency was demonstrated in 1963 through direct national appeals on international diplomacy on June 10, civil rights on June 11, and perhaps less so, but still in evidence nonetheless, in the Test Ban Treaty speech of July 26. In each case Kennedy made a fine and eloquent use of his bully pulpit.[10]

The power of the word was something this president always respected and in fact, at times, revered. James L. Golden noted that "Kennedy's reliance on discourse, more than any other single factor, became the central element in his political leadership," and his "own words are one of his greatest legacies." His basic ebullience was one of his greatest assets. And while there was indeed a gulf between Kennedy's promise and performance, none could deny that in this president one found a consummate rhetorician-politician, a man who seemed to be coming into his own as he approached the prospect of a second term. And if, at times, Kennedy mistook America's image for his own, he was not without past and future company.[11]

If Kennedy was quick to sound the alarm, he was also slow to pull the thermonuclear trigger, and if he dragged his feet on civil rights—once committed—he marshalled a forceful eloquence to the defense of the downtrodden, using his presidential pulpit to mount an unparalleled White House campaign for the rights of African Americans. While some might fault him for not going far enough legislatively and never going too far rhetorically, he did set the stage for the Civil Rights Act of 1964 and made it possible to think about and be receptive to the Great Society. The values of Kennedy's romantic pragmatism that had been laid out in his rhetoric were valorized upon his death. Later pundits and Democratic politicians would baptize Kennedy's unique combination of idealism and pragmatism as "neo-liberal" and model their own careers after its derivative principles.[12]

Given his predispositions, rhetorical enactments, and brief history in the White House, John F. Kennedy will remain a rhetorical enigma. His grave, often humorless, public speeches on foreign policy at times misrepresented reality and seduced the public by dissembling. Indeed, instead of admitting his mistakes, Kennedy compounded them with bravado. Perhaps his most perilous legacy lay in his determination to not only stay the course but up the ante in Vietnam. While most of his discourse on this matter was recorded in press conferences, the speeches analyzed and recorded here demonstrate Kennedy's determination to contest the Communist menace whenever and wherever it reached its lengthy and multiple tentacles. But the instinct for confrontation was balanced by a vision of national comity and global human rights, each of which also was advocated powerfully and without parallel in this century. Kennedy's moral and political compass sometimes led him astray, but when he was able to find his bearings, he had few peers in eloquent, inspiring advocacy.

NOTES

1. Taylor Branch, *Parting the Waters: America in the King Years, 1954-1963* (New York: A Touchstone Book/Simon and Schuster, 1988), 918-919.

2. See Irving Bernstein, *Promises Kept: John F. Kennedy's New Frontier* (New York and Oxford: Oxford University Press, 1991), 295.

3. Harvard Sitkoff, *The Struggle for Black Equality*, 1954-1992 rev. ed. (New York: Hill and Wang, 1993), 144-145.

4. Lewis J. Paper, *The Promise and the Performance: The Leadership of John F. Kennedy* (New York: Crown Publishers, 1975), 345-346; and see, for example, 279, 352, 369. Herbert S. Parmet also noted that despite his own claims to the contrary, Kennedy never changed his basic views on foreign policy. Herbert S. Parmet, *JFK: The Presidency of John F. Kennedy* (New York: Dial Press, 1983), 193.

5. Thomas G. Patterson, "Introduction: John F. Kennedy's Quest for Victory and Global Crises" in *Kennedy's Quest for Victory: American Foreign Policy*, 1961-1963 Thomas G. Patterson ed. (New York and Oxford: Oxford University Press, 1989), 19, 22-23; Frank Costigliola, "The Pursuit of Atlantic Community: Nuclear Arms, Dollars, and Berlin" in *Kennedy's Quest For Victory*, 25.

6. James N. Giglio, *The Presidency of John F. Kennedy* (Lawrence: University Press of Kansas, 1991), 121; Bernstein, *Promises Kept*, 289; Letter to the President, Presidential Office Files, Special Correspondence, George Kennan, 10/22-10/28, 1963, Box 31, JFK Library; George Kennan Oral History. Interviewed by Louis Fischer, JFK Library.

7. Giglio, *The Presidency*, 88.

8. David Burner and Thomas R. West, *The Torch is Passed: The Kennedy Brothers and American Liberalism* (New York: Atheneum, 1984), 148.

9. Paper, *The Promise*, 380.

10. It is open to question as to whether or not Kennedy's "advancement" of the rhetorical presidency was a utilitarian "good" for political society. The legacy here, as elsewhere, appears to us to be ambivalent. For a more thorough discussion of the rhetorical presidency and its implications see Jeffrey Tulis, *The Rhetorical Presidency* (Princeton, N.J.: Princeton University Press, 1987).

11. James L. Golden, "Perspectives on the Legacy of John F. Kennedy" in *Rhetorical Studies Honoring James L. Golden,* Lawrence W. Hugenberg ed. (Dubuque, Iowa: Kendall/Hunt Publishing, 1986), 78, 80.

12. See, for example, Golden, "Perspectives," esp. pp. 90-95; Michael Weiler, "The Rhetoric of Neo-Liberalism," *Quarterly Journal of Speech* 70 (1984): 362-378.

II
COLLECTED SPEECHES

The following speech texts have been authenticated using audio recordings made available by the John F. Kennedy Library. The Public Papers of the Presidents served as a grammatical model for the text presentation of all speeches except the speech to the Greater Houston Ministerial Association.

Speech to the Greater Houston Ministerial Association

Houston, Texas, September 12, 1960

Reverend Meza, Reverend Rock, I am grateful for your generous invitation to state my views.

While the so-called religious issue is necessarily and properly the chief topic here tonight, I want to emphasize from the outset that I believe that we have far more critical issues in the 1960 campaign: the spread of Communist influence, until it now festers only 90 miles from the coast of Florida—the humiliating treatment of our President and Vice President by those who no longer respect our power—the hungry children I saw in West Virginia, the old people who cannot pay their doctors bills, the families forced to give up their farms—an America with too many slums, with too few schools, and too late to the moon and outer space.

These are the real issues which should decide this campaign. And they are not religious issues—for war and hunger and ignorance and despair know no religious barrier.

But because I am a Catholic, and no Catholic has ever been elected President, the real issues in this campaign have been obscured—perhaps deliberately, in some quarters less responsible than this. So it is apparently necessary for me to state once again—not what kind of church I believe in, for that should be important only to me—but what kind of America I believe in.

I believe in an America where the separation of church and state is absolute—where no Catholic prelate would tell the President, should he be Catholic, how to act, and no Protestant minister would tell his parishioners for whom to vote—where no church or church school is granted any public funds or political preference—and where no man is denied public office merely because his religion differs from the President who might appoint him or the people who might elect him.

I believe in an America that is officially neither Catholic, Protestant nor Jewish—where no public official either requests or accepts instructions on public policy from the Pope, the National Council of Churches or any other ecclesiastical source—where no religious body seeks to impose its will directly or indirectly upon the general populace or the public acts of its officials—and where religious liberty is so indivisible that an act against one church is treated as an act against all.

For, while this year it may be a Catholic against whom the finger of suspicion is pointed, in other years it has been, and may someday be again, a Jew—or a Quaker—or a Unitarian—or a Baptist. It was Virginia's harassment of Baptist preachers, for example, that lead to Jefferson's Statute of Religious Freedom. Today I may be the victim—but tomorrow it may be you—until the whole fabric of our harmonious society is ripped apart at a time of great national peril.

Finally, I believe in an America where religious intolerance will someday end—where all men and all churches are treated as equal—where every man has the same right to attend or not attend the church of his choice—where there is no Catholic vote, no anti-Catholic vote, no block voting of any kind—and where Catholics, Protestants and Jews, at both the lay and the pastoral levels, will refrain from those attitudes of disdain and division which have so often marred their works in the past, and promote instead the American ideal of brotherhood.

That is the kind of America in which I believe. And it represents the kind of Presidency in which I believe—a great office that must be neither humbled by making it the instrument of any religious group, nor tarnished by arbitrarily withholding it, its occupancy from the members of any one religious group. I believe in a President whose views on religion are his own private affair, neither imposed by him upon the nation, nor imposed by the nation upon him as a condition to holding that office.

I would not look with favor upon a President working to subvert the First Amendment's guarantees of religious liberty, nor would our system of checks and balances permit him to do so—and neither do I look with favor upon those who would work to subvert Article VI of the Constitution by requiring a religious test—even by indirection—for if they disagree with that safeguard, they should be openly working to repeal it.

I want a Chief Executive whose public acts are responsible to all and obligated to none—who can attend any ceremony, service or dinner his office may appropriately require of him to fulfill—and whose fulfillment of his Presidential office is not limited or conditioned by any religious oath, ritual or obligation.

This is the kind of America I believe in—and this is the kind of America I fought for in the South Pacific, and the kind my brother died for in Europe. No one suggested then that we might have a "divided loyalty," that we did "not believe in liberty" or that we belonged to a disloyal group that threatened, I quote, the "freedoms for which our forefathers died."

And in fact this is the kind of America for which our forefathers did die—when they fled here to escape religious test oaths that denied office to members of less-favored churches—when they fought for the Constitution, the Bill of

Rights, the Virginia Statute of Religious Freedom—and when they fought at the shrine I visited today, the Alamo. For side by side with Bowie and Crockett died Fuentes, and McCafferty and Bailey and Bedillio and Carey—but no one knows whether they were Catholics or not. For there was no religious test there.

I ask you tonight to follow in that tradition—to judge me on the basis of 14 years in the Congress—on my declared stands against an Ambassador to the Vatican, against unconstitutional aid to parochial schools, and against any boycott of the public schools, which I attended myself, and instead of doing this, do not judge me on the basis of these pamphlets and publications we have all seen that carefully select quotations out of context from the statements of Catholic church leaders, usually in other countries, frequently in other centuries, and rarely relevant to any situation here—and always omitting, of course, the statement of the American Bishops in 1948 which strongly endorsed church-state separation, and which more nearly reflects the views of almost every American Catholic.

I do not consider these other quotations binding upon my public acts. Why should you? But let me say, with respect to other countries, that I am wholly opposed to the state being used by any religious group, Catholic or Protestant, to compel, prohibit or prosecute the free exercise of any other religion. And that goes for any persecution at any time by anyone in any country. And I hope that you and I condemn with equal fervor those nations which deny their Presidency to Protestants and those which deny it to Catholics. And rather than cite the misdeeds of whose who differ, I would also cite the record of the Catholic church in such nations as France and Ireland—and the independence of such statesmen as DeGaulle and Adenauer.

But let me stress again that these are my views—for, contrary to common newspaper usage, I am not the Catholic candidate for President. I am the Democratic Party's candidate for President who happens also to be a Catholic. I do not speak for my church on public matters—and the church does not speak for me.

Whatever issue may come before me as President if I should be elected—on birth control, divorce, censorship, gambling, or any other subject—I will make my decision in accordance with these views, in accordance with what my conscience tells me to be in the national interest, and without regard to outside religious pressure or dictates. And no power or threat of punishment could cause me to decide otherwise.

But if the time should ever come—and I do not concede any conflict to be remotely possible—when my office would require me to either violate my conscience or violate the national interest, then I would resign the office; and I hope any other conscientious public servant would do likewise.

But I do not intend to apologize for these views to my critics of either Catholic or Protestant faith—nor do I intend to disavow either my views or my church in order to win this election. If I should lose on the real issues, I shall return to my seat in the Senate, satisfied that I had tried my best and was fairly judged. But if this election is decided on the basis that 40 million Americans lost their chance of being President on the day they were baptized, then it is the whole nation that will be the loser, in the eyes of Catholics and non-Catholics around the world, in the eyes of history, and in the eyes of our own people.

But if, on the other hand, I should win this election, then I shall devote every effort of mind and spirit to fulfilling the oath of the Presidency—practically identical, I might add, with the oath I have taken for 14 years in the Congress. For, without reservation, I can and I quote "solemnly swear that I will faithfully execute the office of President of the United States, and will to the best of my ability preserve, protect and defend the Constitution . . . so help me God."

INAUGURAL ADDRESS
WASHINGTON, D.C., JANUARY 20, 1961

Vice President Johnson, Mr. Speaker, Mr. Chief Justice, President Eisenhower, Vice President Nixon, President Truman, reverend clergy, fellow citizens: We observe today not a victory of party but a celebration of freedom—symbolizing an end as well as a beginning—signifying renewal as well as change. For I have sworn before you and Almighty God the same solemn oath our forbearers prescribed nearly a century and three quarters ago.

The world is very different now. For man holds in his mortal hands the power to abolish all forms of human poverty and all forms of human life. And yet the same revolutionary beliefs for which our forebears fought are still at issue around the globe—the belief that the rights of man come not from the generosity of the state but from the hand of God.

We dare not forget today that we are the heirs of that first revolution. Let the word go forth from this time and place, to friend and foe alike, that the torch has been passed to a new generation of Americans—born in this century, tempered by war, disciplined by a hard and bitter peace, proud of our ancient heritage—and unwilling to witness or permit the slow undoing of those human rights to which this nation has always been committed, and to which we are committed today at home and around the world.

Let every nation know, whether it wishes us well or ill, that we shall pay any price, bear any burden, meet any hardship, support any friend, oppose any foe, to assure the survival and the success of liberty.

This much we pledge—and more.

To those old allies whose cultural and spiritual origins we share, we pledge the loyalty of faithful friends. United, there is little we cannot do in a host of cooperative ventures. Divided, there is little we can do—for we dare not meet a powerful challenge at odds and split asunder.

To those new states whom we welcome to the ranks of the free, we pledge our word that one form of colonial control shall not have passed away merely to be replaced by a far more iron tyranny. We shall not always expect to find them supporting our view. But we shall always hope to find them strongly supporting their own freedom—and to remember that, in the past, those who foolishly sought power by riding the back of the tiger ended up inside.

To those people in the huts and villages of half the globe struggling to break the bonds of mass misery, we pledge our best efforts to help them help themselves, for whatever period is required—not because the communists may be doing it, not because we seek their votes, but because it is right. If a free society cannot help the many who are poor, it cannot save the few who are rich.

To our sister republics south of our border, we offer a special pledge—to convert our good words into good deeds—in a new alliance for progress—to assist free men and free governments in casting off the chains of poverty. But this peaceful revolution of hope cannot become the prey of hostile powers. Let all our neighbors know that we shall join with them to oppose aggression or subversion anywhere in the Americas. And let every other power know that this Hemisphere intends to remain the master of its own house.

To that world assembly of sovereign states, the United Nations, our last best hope in an age where the instruments of war have far outpaced the instruments of peace, we renew our pledge of support—to prevent it from becoming merely a forum for invective—to strengthen its shield of the new and the weak—and to enlarge the area in which its writ may run.

Finally, to those nations who would make themselves our adversary, we offer not a pledge but a request: that both sides begin anew the quest for peace, before the dark powers of destruction unleashed by science engulf all humanity in planned or accidental self-destruction.

We dare not tempt them with weakness. For only when our arms are sufficient beyond doubt can we be certain beyond doubt that they will never be employed.

But neither can two great and powerful groups of nations take comfort from our present course—both sides overburdened by the cost of modern weapons, both rightly alarmed by the steady spread of the deadly atom, yet both racing to alter that uncertain balance of terror that stays the hand of mankind's final war.

So let us begin anew—remembering on both sides that civility is not a sign of weakness, and sincerity is always subject to proof. Let us never negotiate out of fear. But let us never fear to negotiate.

Let both sides explore what problems unite us instead of belaboring those problems which divide us.

Let both sides, for the first time, formulate serious and precise proposals for the inspection and control of arms—and bring the absolute power to destroy other nations under the absolute control of all nations.

Let both sides seek to invoke the wonders of science instead of its terrors. Together let us explore the stars, conquer the deserts, eradicate disease, tap the ocean depths and encourage the arts and commerce.

Let both sides unite to heed in all corners of the earth the command of Isaiah—to "undo the heavy burdens . . . and let the oppressed go free."

And if a beach-head of cooperation may push back the jungle of suspicion, let both sides join in creating a new endeavor, not a new balance of power, but a new world of law, where the strong are just and the weak secure and the peace preserved.

All this will not be finished in the first one hundred days. Nor will it be finished in the first one thousand days, nor in the life of this Administration, nor even perhaps in our lifetime on this planet. But let us begin.

In your hands, my fellow citizens, more than mine, will rest the final success or failure of our course. Since this country was founded, each generation of Americans has been summoned to give testimony to its national loyalty. The graves of young Americans who answered the call to service surround the globe.

Now the trumpet summons us again—not as a call to bear arms, though arms we need—not as a call to battle, though embattled we are—but a call to bear the burden of a long twilight struggle, year in and year out, "rejoicing in hope, patient in tribulation"—a struggle against the common enemies of man: tyranny, poverty, disease and war itself.

Can we forge against these enemies a grand and global alliance, North and South, East and West, that can assure a more fruitful life for all mankind? Will you join in that historic effort?

In the long history of the world, only a few generations have been granted the role of defending freedom in its hour of maximum danger. I do not shrink from this responsibility—I welcome it. I do not believe that any of us would exchange places with any other people or any other generation. The energy, the faith, the devotion which we bring to this endeavor will light our country and all who serve it—and the glow from that fire can truly light the world.

And so, my fellow Americans: ask not what your country can do for you—ask what you can do for your country.

My fellow citizens of the world: ask not what America will do for you, but what together we can do for the freedom of man.

Finally, whether you are citizens of America or citizens of the world, ask of us here the same high standards of strength and sacrifice which we ask of you. With a good conscience our only sure reward, with history the final judge of our deeds, let us go forth to lead the land we love, asking His blessing and His help, but knowing that here on earth God's work must truly be our own.

ADDRESS BEFORE THE AMERICAN SOCIETY OF NEWSPAPER EDITORS
WASHINGTON, D.C., APRIL 20, 1961

Mr. Catledge, members of the American Society of Newspaper Editors, ladies and gentlemen: The President of a great democracy such as ours, and the editors of great newspapers such as yours, owe a common obligation to the people: an obligation to present the facts, to present them with candor, and to present them in perspective. It is with that obligation in mind that I have decided in the last 24 hours to discuss briefly at this time the recent events in Cuba.

On that unhappy island, as in so many other arenas of the contest for freedom, the news has grown worse instead of better. I have emphasized before that this was a struggle of Cuban patriots against a Cuban dictator. While we could not be expected to hide our sympathies, we made it repeatedly clear that the armed forces of this country would not intervene in any way. Any unilateral American intervention, in the absence of an external attack upon ourselves or an ally, would have been contrary to our traditions and to our international obligations. But let the record show that our restraint is not inexhaustible. Should it ever appear that the inter-American doctrine of non-interference merely conceals or excuses a policy of nonaction—if the nations of this Hemisphere should fail to meet their commitments against outside Communist penetration—then I want it clearly understood that this Government will not hesitate in meeting its primary obligations which are to the security of our Nation.

Should that time ever come, we do not intend to be lectured on "intervention" by those whose character was stamped for all time on the bloody streets of Budapest. Nor would we expect or accept the same outcome which this small band of gallant Cuban refugees must have known that they were chancing, determined as they were against heavy odds to pursue their courageous attempts to regain their Island's freedom.

But Cuba is not an island unto itself; and our concern is not ended by mere expressions of nonintervention or regret. This is not the first time in either ancient or recent history that a small band of freedom fighters has engaged the armor of totalitarianism. It is not the first time that Communist tanks have rolled over gallant men and women fighting to redeem the independence of their homeland. Nor is it by any means the final episode in the eternal struggle of liberty against tyranny, anywhere on the face of the globe, including Cuba itself.

Mr. Castro has said that these were mercenaries. According to press reports, the final message to be relayed from the refugee forces on the beach came from the rebel commander when asked if he wished to be evacuated. His answer was: "I will never leave this country." That is not the reply of a mercenary. He has gone now to join in the mountains countless other guerrilla fighters, who are equally determined that the dedication of those who gave their lives shall not be forgotten, and that Cuba must not be abandoned to the Communists. And we do not intend to abandon it either.

The Cuban people have not yet spoken their final piece. And I have no doubt that they and the Revolutionary Council, led by Dr. Cardona—and members of the families of the Revolutionary Council, I am informed by the Doctor yesterday, are involved themselves in the islands—will continue to speak up for a free and independent Cuba.

Meanwhile we will not accept Mr. Castro's attempts to blame this nation for the hatred [with] which his onetime supporters now regard his repression. But there are from this sobering episode useful lessons for us all to learn. Some may be still obscure, and await further information. Some are clear today.

First, it is clear that the forces of communism are not to be underestimated, in Cuba or anywhere else in the world. The advantages of a police state—its use of mass terror and arrests to prevent the spread of free dissent—cannot be overlooked by those who expect the fall of every fanatic tyrant. If the self-discipline of the free cannot match the iron discipline of the mailed fist—in economic, political, scientific and all the other kinds of struggles as well as the military—then the peril to freedom will continue to rise.

Secondly, it is clear that this Nation, in concert with all the free nations of this hemisphere, must take an ever closer and more realistic look at the menace of external Communist intervention and domination in Cuba. The American people are not complacent about Iron Curtain tanks and planes less than 90 miles from their shore. But a nation of Cuba's size is less a threat to our survival than it is a base for subverting the survival of other free nations throughout the hemisphere. It is not primarily our interest or our security but theirs which is now, today, in the greater peril. It is for their sake as well as our own that we must show our will.

The evidence is clear—and the hour is late. We and our Latin friends will have to face the fact that we cannot postpone any longer the real issue of survival of freedom in this hemisphere itself. On that issue, unlike perhaps some others, there can be no middle ground. Together we must build a hemisphere where freedom can flourish; and where any free nation under outside attack of any kind can be assured that all of our resources stand ready to respond to any request for assistance.

Third, and finally, it is clearer than ever that we face a relentless struggle in every corner of the globe that goes far beyond the clash of armies or even nuclear armaments. The armies are there, and in large number. The nuclear armaments are there. But they serve primarily as the shield behind which subversion, infiltration, and a host of other tactics steadily advance, picking off vulnerable areas one by one in situations which do not permit our own armed intervention.

Power is the hallmark of this offensive—power and discipline and deceit. The legitimate discontent of yearning people is exploited. The legitimate trappings of self-determination are employed. But once in power, all talk of discontent is repressed, all self-determination disappears, and the promise of a revolution of hope is betrayed, as in Cuba, into a reign of terror. Those who on instruction staged automatic "riots" in the streets of free nations over the efforts of a small group of young Cubans to regain their freedom should recall the long roll call of refugees who cannot now go back—to Hungary, to North Korea, to North Viet Nam, to East Germany, or to Poland, or to any of the other lands from which a steady stream of refugees pours forth in eloquent testimony to the cruel oppression now holding sway in their homeland.

We dare not fail to see the insidious nature of this new and deeper struggle. We dare not fail to grasp the new concepts, the new tools, the new sense of urgency we will need to combat it —whether in Cuba or South Viet Nam. And we dare not fail to realize that this struggle is taking place every day, without fanfare, in thousands of villages and markets—day and night—and in classrooms all over the globe.

The message of Cuba, of Laos, of the rising din of Communist voices in Asia and Latin America—these messages are all the same. The complacent, the self-indulgent, the soft societies are about to be swept away with the debris of history. Only the strong, only the industrious, only the determined, only the courageous, only the visionary who determine the real nature of our struggle can possibly survive.

No greater task faces this country or this administration. No other challenge is more deserving of our every effort and energy. Too long we have fixed our eyes on traditional military needs, on armies prepared to cross borders, on missiles poised for flight. Now it should be clear that this is no longer enough—that our security may be lost piece by piece, country by country, without the firing of a single missile or the crossing of a single border. We intend to profit from this lesson. We intend to reexamine and reorient our forces of all kinds—our tactics and our institutions here in this community. We intend to intensify our efforts for a struggle in many ways more difficult than war, where disappointment will often accompany us. For I am convinced that we in this country and in the free world possess the necessary resources, and the skill, and the added strength that comes from a belief in the freedom of man. And I am equally convinced that history will record the fact that this bitter struggle reached its climax in the late 1950s and the early 1960s. Let me then make clear as the President of the United States that I am determined upon our system's survival and success, regardless of the cost and regardless of the peril.

Radio and Television Report to the American People on the Berlin Crisis
Washington, D.C., July 25, 1961

Good evening: Seven weeks ago tonight I returned from Europe to report on my meeting with Premier Khrushchev and the others. His grim warnings about the future of the world, his aide-memoire on Berlin, his subsequent speeches and threats which he and his agents have launched, and the increase in the Soviet military budget that he has announced, have all prompted a series of decisions by the Administration and a series of consultations with the members of the NATO organization. In Berlin, as you recall, he intends to bring to an end, through a stroke of the pen, first our legal rights to be in West Berlin—and secondly our ability to make good on our commitment to two million people of that city. That we cannot permit.

We are clear about what must be done—and we intend to do it. I want to talk frankly with you tonight about the first steps that we shall take. These actions will require sacrifice on the part of many of our citizens. More will be required in the future. They will require, from all of us, courage and perseverance in the years to come. But if we and our allies act out of strength and unity of purpose—with calm determination and steady nerves—using restraint in our words as well as our weapons—I am hopeful that both peace and freedom will be sustained.

The immediate threat to free men is in West Berlin. But that isolated outpost is not an isolated problem. The threat is worldwide. Our effort must be equally wide and strong, and not be obsessed by any single manufactured crisis. We face a challenge in Berlin, but there is also a challenge in Southeast Asia, where the borders are less guarded, the enemy harder to find, and the dangers of communism less apparent to those who have so little. We face a challenge in our own hemisphere, and indeed wherever else the freedom of human beings is at stake.

Let me remind you that the fortunes of war and diplomacy left the free people of West Berlin in 1945, 110 miles behind the Iron Curtain.

This map makes very clear the problem that we face. The white is West Germany—the East is the area controlled by the Soviet Union, and as you can see from the chart, West Berlin is 110 miles within the area which the Soviets now dominate—which is immediately controlled by the so-called East German regime.

We are there as a result of our victory over Nazi Germany—and our basic rights to be there, deriving from that victory, include both our presence in West Berlin and the enjoyment of access across East Germany. These rights have been repeatedly confirmed and recognized in special agreements with the Soviet Union. Berlin is not a part of East Germany, but a separate territory under the control of the allied powers. Thus our rights there are clear and deep-rooted. But in addition to those rights is our commitment to sustain—and defend, if need be—the opportunity for more than two million people to determine their own future and choose their own way of life.

Thus, our presence in West Berlin, and our access thereto, cannot be ended by any act of the Soviet government. The NATO shield was long ago extended to cover West Berlin—and we have given our word that an attack upon that city will be regarded as an attack upon us all.

For West Berlin—lying exposed 110 miles inside East Germany, surrounded by Soviet troops and close to Soviet supply lines, has many roles. It is more than a showcase of liberty, a symbol, an island of freedom in a Communist sea. It is even more than a link with the Free World, a beacon of hope behind the Iron Curtain, an escape hatch for refugees.

West Berlin is all of that. But above all it has now become—as never before—the great testing place of Western courage and will, a focal point where our solemn commitments stretching back over the years since 1945, and Soviet ambitions now meet in basic confrontation.

It would be a mistake for others to look upon Berlin, because of its location, as a tempting target. The United States is there; the United Kingdom and France are there; the pledge of NATO is there—and the people of Berlin are there. It is as secure, in that sense, as the rest of us—for we cannot separate its safety from our own.

I hear it said that West Berlin is militarily untenable. And so was Bastogne. And so, in fact, was Stalingrad. Any dangerous spot is tenable if men—brave men—will make it so.

We do not want to fight—but we have fought before. And others in earlier times have made the same dangerous mistake of assuming that the West was too selfish and too soft and too divided to resist invasions of freedom in other lands. Those who threaten to unleash the forces of war on a dispute over West Berlin should recall the words of the ancient philosopher: "A man who causes fear cannot be free from fear."

We cannot and will not permit the Communists to drive us out of Berlin, either gradually or by force. The fulfillment of our pledge to that city is essential to the morale and security of Western Germany, to the unity of Western Europe, and to the faith of the entire Free World. Soviet strategy has long been aimed not merely at Berlin, but at dividing and neutralizing all of Europe, forcing us back on our own shores. We must meet our often-stated pledge to the free peoples of West Berlin—and maintain our rights and their safety, even in the face of force—in order to maintain the confidence of other free peoples in our word and our resolve. The strength of the alliance on which our security depends is dependent in turn on our willingness to meet our commitments to them.

So long as the Communists insist that they are preparing to end by themselves unilaterally our rights in West Berlin and our commitments to its people, we must be prepared to defend those rights and those commitments. We will at all times be ready to talk, if talk will help. But we must also be ready to resist with force, if force is used upon us. Either alone would fail. Together, they can serve the cause of freedom and peace.

The new preparations that we shall make to defend the peace are part of the long-term build-up in our strength which has been underway since January. They are based on our needs to meet a world-wide threat, on a basis which stretches far beyond the present Berlin crisis. Our primary purpose is neither propaganda nor provocation—but preparation.

A first need is to hasten progress toward the military goals which the North Atlantic allies have set for themselves. In Europe today nothing less will suffice. We will put even greater resources into fulfilling these goals, and we look to our allies to do the same.

The supplemental defense buildups that I asked from the Congress in March and May have already started moving us toward these and our other defense goals. They included an increase in the size of the Marine Corps, improved readiness of our reserves, expansion of our air and sea lift, and stepped-up procurement of needed weapons, ammunition, and other items. To insure a continuing invulnerable capacity to deter or destroy any aggressor, they provided for the strengthening of our missile power and for putting 50% of our B-52s and B-47s bombers on a ground alert which would send them on their way with 15 minutes warning.

These measures must be speeded up, and still others must now be taken. We must have sea and airlift capable of moving our forces quickly and in large numbers to any part of the world.

But even more importantly, we need the capability of placing in any critical area at the appropriate time a force which, combined with those of our allies, is large enough to make clear our determination and our ability to defend our rights at all costs—and to meet all levels of aggressive pressure with whatever levels of force are required. We intend to have a wider choice than humiliation or all-out nuclear action.

While it is unwise at this time either to call up or send abroad excessive number of these troops before they are needed, let me make it clear that I intend to take, as time goes on, whatever steps are necessary to make certain that such forces can be deployed at the appropriate time without lessening our ability to meet our commitments elsewhere.

Thus, in the days and months ahead, I shall not hesitate to ask the Congress for additional measures, or exercise any of the executive powers that I possess to meet this threat to peace. Everything essential to the security of freedom must be done; and if that should require more men, or more taxes, or more controls, or other new powers, I shall not hesitate to ask them. The measures proposed today will be constantly studied, and altered as necessary. But while we will not let panic shape our policy, neither will we permit timidity to direct our program.

And accordingly, I am now taking the following steps:

1. I am tomorrow requesting the Congress for the current fiscal year an additional three billion two hundred and forty-seven million dollars ($3,247,000,000) of appropriations for the Armed Forces.

2. To fill our present Army Divisions, and to make more men available for prompt deployment, I am requesting an increase in the Army's total authorized strength from eight hundred and seventy-five thousand (875,000) to approximately one (1) million men.

3. I am requesting an increase of twenty-nine thousand (29,000) and sixty-three thousand (63,000) men respectively in the active duty strength of the Navy and the Air Force.

4. To fulfill these manpower needs, I am ordering that our draft calls be doubled and tripled in the coming months; I am asking the Congress for authority to order to active duty certain ready reserve units and individual reservists, and to extend tours of duty; and, under that authority, I am planning to order to active duty a number of air transport squadrons and Air National Guard tactical air squadrons, to give us the airlift capacity and protection that we need. Other reserve forces will be called up when needed.

5. Many ships and planes once headed for retirement are to be retained or reactivated, increasing our airpower tactically and our sealift, airlift, and anti-submarine warfare capability. In addition, our strategic air power will be increased by delaying the deactivation of B-47 bombers.

6. Finally, some one point eight billion dollars ($1.8 billion)—about half of the total sum—is needed for the procurement of non-nuclear weapons, ammunition and equipment.

The details on all these requests will be presented to the Congress tomorrow. Subsequent steps will be taken to suit subsequent needs. Comparable efforts for the common defense are being discussed with our NATO allies. For their commitment and interest are as precise as our own.

And let me add that I am well aware of the fact that many American families will bear the burden of these requests. Studies or careers will be interrupted; husbands and sons will be called away; incomes in some cases will be reduced. But these are burdens which must be borne if freedom is to be defended—Americans have willingly borne them before—and they will not flinch from the task now.

We have another sober responsibility. To recognize the possibilities of nuclear war in the missile age, without our citizens knowing what they should do and where they should go if bombs begin to fall, would be a failure of responsibility. In May, I pledged a new start on Civil Defense. Last week, I assigned, on the recommendation of the Civil Defense Director, basic responsibility for this program to the Secretary of Defense, to make certain it is administered and coordinated with our continental defense efforts at the highest civilian level. Tomorrow, I am requesting of the Congress new funds for the following immediate objectives: to identify and mark space in existing structures—public and private—that could be used for fall-out shelters in case of attack; to stock those shelters with food, water, first-aid kits and other minimum essentials for our survival; to increase their capacity; to improve our air-raid warning and fall-out detection systems, including a new household warning system which is now under development; and to take other measures that will be effective at an early date to save millions of lives if needed.

In the event of an attack, the lives of those families which are not hit in a nuclear blast and fire can still be saved—if they can be warned to take shelter and if that shelter is available. We owe that kind of insurance to our families—and to our country. In contrast to our friends in Europe, the need for this kind of protection is new to our shores. But the time to start is now. In the coming months, I hope to let every citizen know what steps he can take without delay to protect his family in case of attack. I know that you will want to do no less.

The addition of two hundred seven million in Civil Defense appropriations brings our total new defense budget requests to three billion four hundred fifty-four million dollars, and a total of forty-seven billion five hundred million for the year. This is an increase in the defense budget of six billion dollars since January, and has resulted in official estimates of a budget deficit of over five billion dollars. The Secretary of the Treasury and other economic advisers assure me, however, that our economy has the capacity to bear this new request.

We are recovering strongly from this year's recession. The increase in this last quarter of our year of our total national output was greater than that for any postwar period of initial recovery. And yet, wholesale prices are actually lower than they were during the recession, and consumer prices are only 1/4 of 1 percent higher than they were last October. In fact, this last quarter was the first in eight years in which our production has increased without an increase in the overall price index. And for the first time since the Fall of 1959, our gold position has improved and the dollar is more respected abroad. These gains, it should be stressed, are being accomplished with budget deficits far smaller than those of the 1958 recession.

This improved business outlook means improved revenues; and I intend to submit to the Congress in January a budget for the next fiscal year which will be strictly in balance. Nevertheless, should an increase in taxes be needed—because of events in the next few months—to achieve that balance, or because of subsequent defense rises, those increased taxes will be requested in January.

Meanwhile, to help make certain that the current deficit is held to a safe level, we must keep down all expenditures not thoroughly justified in budget requests. The luxury of our current post-office deficit must be ended. Costs in military procurement will be closely scrutinized—and in this effort I welcome the cooperation of the Congress. The tax loopholes I have specified—on expense accounts, overseas income, dividends, interest, cooperatives and others—must be closed.

I recognize that no public revenue measure is welcomed by everyone. But I am certain that every American wants to pay his fair share, and not leave the burden of defending freedom entirely to those who bear arms. For we have mortgaged our very future on this defense—and we cannot fail to meet our responsibilities.

But I must emphasize again that the choice is not merely between resistance and retreat, between atomic holocaust and surrender. Our peace-time military posture is traditionally defensive; but our diplomatic posture need not be. Our response to the Berlin crisis will not be merely military or negative. It will be more than merely standing firm. For we do not intend to leave it to others to choose and monopolize the forum and the framework of discussion. We do not intend to abandon our duty to mankind to seek a peaceful solution.

As signers of the UN Charter, we shall always be prepared to discuss international problems with any and all nations that are willing to talk—and listen—with reason. If they have proposals—not demands—we shall hear them. If they seek genuine understanding—not concessions of our rights—we shall meet with them. We have previously indicated our readiness to remove any actual irritants in West Berlin, but the freedom of that city is not negotiable. We cannot negotiate with those who say "What's mine is mine and what's yours is negotiable." But we are willing to consider any arrangement or treaty in Germany consistent with the maintenance of peace and freedom, and with the legitimate security interests of all nations.

We recognize the Soviet Union's historical concern about their security in Central and Eastern Europe, after a series of ravaging invasions—and we believe arrangements can be worked out which will help to meet those concerns, and make it possible for both security and freedom to exist in this troubled area.

For it is not the freedom of West Berlin which is "abnormal" in Germany today, but the situation in that entire divided country. If any one doubts the legality of our rights in Berlin, we are ready to have it submitted to international adjudication. If anyone doubts the extent to which our presence is desired by the people of West Berlin, compared to East German feelings about their regime, we are ready to have that question submitted to a free vote in Berlin and, if possible, among all the German people. And let us hear at the same time from two and one-half million refugees who have fled the Communist regime in East Germany—voting for Western-type freedom with their feet.

The world is not deceived by the Communist attempt to label Berlin as a hotbed of war. There is peace in Berlin today. The source of world trouble and tension is Moscow, not Berlin. And if war begins, it will have begun in Moscow and not Berlin.

For the choice of peace or war is largely theirs, not ours. It is the Soviets who have stirred up this crisis. It is they who are trying to force a change. It is they who have opposed free elections. It is they who have rejected an all-German peace treaty, and the rulings of international law. And as Americans know from our history on our own old frontier, gun battles are caused by outlaws, and not by officers of the peace.

In short, while we are ready to defend our interests, we shall also be ready to search for peace—in quiet exploratory talks—in formal or informal meetings. We do not want military considerations to dominate the thinking of either East or West. And Mr. Khrushchev may find that his invitation to other nations to join in a meaningless treaty may lead to their inviting him to join in the community of peaceful men, in abandoning the use of force, and in respecting the sanctity of agreements.

While all of these efforts go on, we must not be diverted from our total responsibilities, from other dangers, from other tasks. If new threats in Berlin or elsewhere should cause us to weaken our program of assistance to the developing nations who are also under heavy pressure from the same source, or to halt our efforts for realistic disarmament, or to disrupt or slow down our economy, or to neglect the education of our children, then those threats will surely be the most successful and least costly maneuver in Communist history. For we can afford all these efforts, and more—but we cannot afford not to meet this challenge.

And the challenge is not to us alone. It is a challenge to every nation which asserts its sovereignty under a system of liberty. It is a challenge to all those who want a world of free choice. It is a special challenge to the Atlantic Community—the heartland of human freedom.

We in the West must move together in building military strength. We must consult one another more closely than ever before. We must together design our proposals for peace, and labor together as they are pressed at the conference table. And together we must share the burdens and the risks of this effort.

The Atlantic Community, as we know it, has been built in response to challenges: the challenge of European chaos in 1947; of the Berlin blockade in 1948, and the challenge of Communist aggression in Korea in 1950. Now, standing strong and prosperous, after an unprecedented decade of progress, the Atlantic Community will not forget either its history or the principles which gave it meaning.

The solemn vow we each of us gave to West Berlin in time of peace will not be broken in time of danger. If we do not meet our commitments to Berlin, where will we later stand? If we are not true to our word there, all that we have achieved in collective security, which relies on these words, will mean nothing. And if there is one path above all others to war, it is the path of weakness and disunity.

Today, the endangered frontier of freedom runs through divided Berlin. We want it to remain a frontier of peace. This is the hope of every citizen of the Atlantic Community; every citizen of Eastern Europe; and, I am confident, every citizen of the Soviet Union. For I cannot believe that the Russian people—who bravely suffered enormous losses in the Second World War—would now wish to see the peace upset once more in Germany. The Soviet government alone can convert Berlin's frontier of peace into a pretext of war.

The steps I have indicated tonight are aimed at avoiding that war. To sum it all up: we seek peace—but we shall not surrender. That is the central meaning of this crisis, and the meaning of this government's policy.

With your help, and the help of other free men, this crisis can be surmounted. Freedom can prevail—and peace can endure.

I would like to close with a personal word. When I ran for the Presidency of the United States, I knew that this country faced serious challenges, but I could not realize—nor could any man realize who does not bear the burdens of this office—how heavy and constant would be those burdens.

Three times in my lifetime our country and Europe have been involved in major wars. In each case serious misjudgments were made on both sides of the intentions of others, which brought about great devastation.

Now, in the thermonuclear age, any misjudgment on either side about the intentions of the other could rain more devastation in several hours than has been wrought in all the wars of human history.

Therefore I, as President and Commander-in-Chief, and all of us as Americans, are moving through serious days. I shall bear this responsibility under our Constitution for the next three and one-half years, but I am sure that we all, regardless of our occupations, will do our very best for our country, and for our cause. For all of us want to see our children grow up in a country at peace, and in a world where freedom endures.

I know that sometimes we get impatient, we wish for some immediate action that would end our perils. But I must tell you that there is no quick and easy solution. The Communists control over a billion people, and they recognize that if we should falter, their success would be imminent.

We must look to long days ahead, which if we are courageous and persevering can bring us what we all desire.

In these days and weeks I ask for your help, and your advice. I ask for your suggestions, when you think we could do better.

All of us, I know, love our country, and we shall all do our best to serve it.

In meeting my responsibilities in these coming months as President, I need your good will, and your support—and above all, your prayers.

Thank you, and goodnight.

Radio and Television Report to the American People on the Soviet Buildup in Cuba
Washington, D.C., October 22, 1962

Good evening, my fellow citizens: This Government, as promised, has maintained the closest surveillance of the Soviet military buildup on the island of Cuba. Within the past week, unmistakable evidence has established the fact that a series of offensive missile sites is now in preparation on that imprisoned island. The purpose of these bases can be none other than to provide a nuclear strike capability against the Western Hemisphere.

Upon receiving the first preliminary hard information of this nature last Tuesday morning at 9:00 A.M., I directed that our surveillance be stepped up. And having now confirmed and completed our evaluation of the evidence and our decision on a course of action, this Government feels obliged to report this new crisis to you in fullest detail.

The characteristics of these new missile sites indicate two distinct types of installations. Several of them include medium range ballistic missiles, capable of carrying a nuclear warhead for a distance of more than 1,000 nautical miles. Each of these missiles, in short, is capable of striking Washington, D.C., the Panama Canal, Cape Canaveral, Mexico City, or any other city in the southeastern part of the United States, in Central America, or in the Caribbean area.

Additional sites not yet completed appear to be designed for intermediate range ballistic missiles—capable of traveling more than twice as far—and thus capable of striking most of the major cities in the Western Hemisphere, ranging as far north as Hudson Bay, Canada, and as far south as Lima, Peru. In addition, jet bombers, capable of carrying nuclear weapons, are now being uncrated and assembled in Cuba, while the necessary air bases are being prepared.

This urgent transformation of Cuba into an important strategic base—by the presence of these large, long-range, and clearly offensive weapons of sudden mass destruction—constitutes an explicit threat to the peace and security of all the Americas, in flagrant and deliberate defiance of the Rio Pact of 1947, the traditions of this Nation and hemisphere, the joint resolution of the 87th Congress, the Charter of the United Nations, and my own public warnings to the Soviets on September 4 and 13. This action also contradicts the repeated assurances of Soviet spokesmen, both publicly and privately delivered, that the arms buildup in Cuba would retain its original defensive character, and that the Soviet Union had no need or desire to station strategic missiles on the territory of any other nation.

The size of this undertaking makes clear that it has been planned for some months. Yet only last month, after I had made clear the distinction between any introduction of ground-to-ground missiles and the existence of defensive antiaircraft missiles, the Soviet Government publicly stated on September 11 that, and I quote, "the armaments and military equipment sent to Cuba are designed exclusively for defensive purposes," unquote, that there is, and I quote the Soviet Government, "there is no need for the Soviet Government to shift its weapons . . . for a retaliatory blow to any other country, for instance Cuba," unquote, and that, and I quote their government, "The Soviet Union has [such] powerful rockets to carry these nuclear warheads that there is no need to search for sites for them beyond the boundaries of the Soviet Union." Unquote. That statement was false.

Only last Thursday, as evidence of this rapid offensive buildup was already in my hand, Soviet Foreign Minister Gromyko told me in my office that he was instructed to make it clear once again, as he said his government had already done, that Soviet assistance to Cuba, and I quote, "pursued solely the purpose of contributing to the defense capabilities of Cuba," unquote. That, and I quote him, "training by Soviet specialists of Cuban nationals in handling defensive armaments was by no means offensive," and that "if it were otherwise," Mr. Gromyko went on, "the Soviet Government would never become involved in rendering such assistance." Unquote. That statement also was false.

Neither the United States of America nor the world community of nations can tolerate deliberate deception and offensive threats on the part of any nation, large or small. We no longer live in a world where only the actual firing of weapons represents a sufficient challenge to a nation's security to constitute maximum peril. Nuclear weapons are so destructive and ballistic missiles are so swift, that any substantially increased possibility of their use or any sudden change in their deployment may well be regarded as a definite threat to peace.

For many years, both the Soviet Union and the United States, recognizing this fact, have deployed strategic nuclear weapons with great care, never upsetting the precarious status quo which insured that these weapons would not be used in the absence of some vital challenge. Our own strategic missiles have never been transferred to the territory of any other nation, under a cloak of secrecy and deception; and our history—unlike that of the Soviets since the end of World War II—demonstrates that we have no desire to dominate or conquer any other nation or impose our system upon its people. Nevertheless, American citizens have become adjusted to living daily on the bull's-eye of Soviet missiles located inside the U.S.S.R. or in submarines.

In that sense, missiles in Cuba add to an already clear and present danger—although it should be noted the nations of Latin America have never previously been subjected to a potential nuclear threat.

But this secret, swift extraordinary buildup of Communist missiles—in an area well known to have a special and historical relationship to the United States and the nations of the Western Hemisphere, in violation of Soviet assurances, and in defiance of American and hemispheric policy—this sudden, clandestine decision to station strategic weapons for the first time outside of Soviet soil—is a deliberately provocative and unjustified change in the status quo which cannot be accepted by this country, if our courage and our commitments are ever to be trusted again by either friend or foe.

The 1930s taught us a clear lesson; aggressive conduct, if allowed to go unchecked and unchallenged, ultimately leads to war. This nation is opposed to war. We are also true to our word. Our unswerving objective, therefore, must be to prevent the use of these missiles against this or any other country, and to secure their withdrawal or elimination from the Western Hemisphere.

Our policy has been one of patience and restraint, as befits a peaceful and powerful nation, which leads a worldwide alliance. We have been determined not to be diverted from our central concerns by mere irritants and fanatics. But now further action is required—and it is under way; and these actions may only be the beginning. We will not prematurely or unnecessarily risk the costs of worldwide nuclear war in which even the fruits of victory would be ashes in our mouth—but neither will we shrink from that risk at any time it must be faced.

Acting, therefore, in the defense of our own security and of the entire Western Hemisphere, and under the authority entrusted to me by the Constitution as endorsed by the resolution of the Congress, I have directed that the following initial steps be taken immediately:

First: To halt this offensive buildup, a strict quarantine on all offensive military equipment under shipment to Cuba is being initiated. All ships of any kind bound for Cuba from whatever nation or port will, if found to contain cargoes of offensive weapons, be turned back. This quarantine will be extended, if needed, to other types of cargo and carriers. We are not at this time, however, denying the necessities of life as the Soviets attempted to do in their Berlin blockade of 1948.

Second: I have directed the continued and increased close surveillance of Cuba and its military buildup. The foreign ministers of the OAS, in their communique of October 6, rejected secrecy on such matters in this hemisphere. Should these offensive military preparations continue, thus increasing the threat to the hemisphere, further action will be justified. I have directed the Armed Forces to prepare for any eventualities; and I trust that in the interest of both the Cuban people and the Soviet technicians at the sites, the hazards to all concerned of continuing this threat will be recognized.

Third: It shall be the policy of this Nation to regard any nuclear missile launched from Cuba against any nation in the Western Hemisphere as an attack by the Soviet Union on the United States, requiring a full retaliatory response upon the Soviet Union.

Fourth: As a necessary military precaution, I have reinforced our base at Guantanamo, evacuated today the dependents of our personnel there, and ordered additional military units to be on a standby alert basis.

Fifth: We are calling tonight for an immediate meeting of the Organization of Consultation under the Organization of American States, to consider this threat to hemispheric security and to invoke Articles 6 and 8 of the Rio Treaty in support of all necessary action. The United Nations Charter allows for regional security arrangements—and the nations of this hemisphere decided long ago against the military presence of outside powers. Our other allies around the world have also been alerted.

Sixth: Under the Charter of the United Nations, we are asking tonight that an emergency meeting of the Security Council be convoked without delay to take action against this latest Soviet threat to world peace. Our resolution will call for the prompt dismantling and withdrawal of all offensive weapons in Cuba, under the supervision of U.N. observers, before the quarantine can be lifted.

Seventh, and finally: I call upon Chairman Khrushchev to halt and eliminate this clandestine, reckless and provocative threat to world peace and to stable relations between our two nations. I call upon him further to abandon this course of world domination, and to join in an historic effort to end the perilous arms race and to transform the history of man. He has an opportunity now to move the world back from the abyss of destruction—by returning to his government's own words that it had no need to station missiles outside its own territory, and withdrawing these weapons from Cuba—by refraining from any action which will widen or deepen the present crisis—and then by participating in a search for peaceful and permanent solutions.

This Nation is prepared to present its case against the Soviet threat to peace, and our own proposals for a peaceful world, at any time and in any forum—in the OAS, in the United Nations, or in any other meeting that could be useful—without limiting our freedom of action. We have in the past made strenuous efforts to limit the spread of nuclear weapons. We have proposed the elimination of all arms and military bases in a fair and effective disarmament treaty. We are prepared to discuss new proposals for the removal of tensions on both sides—including the possibilities of a genuinely independent Cuba, free to determine its own destiny. We have no wish to war with the Soviet Union—for we are a peaceful people who desire to live in peace with all other people.

But it is difficult to settle or even discuss these problems in an atmosphere of intimidation. That is why this latest Soviet threat—or any other threat which is made either independently or in response to our actions this week—must and will be met with determination. Any hostile move anywhere in the world against the safety and freedom of peoples to whom we are committed—including in particular the brave people of West Berlin—will be met by whatever action is needed.

Finally, I want to say a few words to the captive people of Cuba, to whom this speech is being directly carried by special radio facilities. I speak to you as a friend, as one who knows of your deep attachment to your fatherland, as one who shares your aspirations for liberty and justice for all. And I have watched and the American people have watched with deep sorrow how your nationalist revolution was betrayed—and how your fatherland fell under foreign domination. Now your leaders are no longer Cuban leaders inspired by Cuban ideals. They are puppets and agents of an international conspiracy which has turned Cuba against your friends and neighbors in the Americas—and turned it into the first Latin American country to become a target for nuclear war—the first Latin American country to have these weapons on its soil.

These new weapons are not in your interest. They contribute nothing to your peace and well-being. They can only undermine it. But this country has no wish to cause you to suffer or to impose any system upon you. We know that your lives and land are being used as pawns by those who deny your freedom.

Many times in the past, the Cuban people have risen to throw out tyrants who destroyed their liberty. And I have no doubt that most Cubans today look forward to the time when they will be truly free—free from foreign domination, free to choose their own leaders, free to select their own system, free to own their own land, free to speak and write and worship without fear or degradation. And then shall Cuba be welcomed back to the society of free nations and to the associations of this Hemisphere.

My fellow citizens: let no one doubt that this is a difficult and dangerous effort on which we have set out. No one can foresee precisely what course it will take or what costs or casualties will be incurred. Many months of sacrifice and self-discipline lie ahead—months in which both our patience and our will will be tested—months in which many threats and denunciations will keep us aware of our dangers. But the greatest danger of all would be to do nothing.

The path we have chosen for the present is full of hazards, as all paths are—but it is the one most consistent with our character and courage as a nation and our commitments around the world. The cost of freedom is always high—but Americans have always paid it. And one path we shall never choose, and that is the path of surrender or submission.

Our goal is not the victory of might, but the vindication of right—not peace at the expense of freedom, but both peace and freedom, here in this hemisphere, and, we hope, around the world. God willing, that goal will be achieved.

Thank you, and good night.

Radio and Television Report to the American People on Civil Rights
Washington, D.C., June 11, 1963

Good evening, my fellow citizens: This afternoon, following a series of threats and defiant statements, the presence of Alabama National Guardsmen was required on the University of Alabama campus to carry out the final and unequivocal order of the United States District Court of the Northern District of Alabama. That order called for the admission of two clearly qualified young Alabama residents who happened to have been born Negro.

That they were admitted peacefully on the campus is due in good measure to the conduct of the students of the University of Alabama, who met their responsibilities in a constructive way.

I hope that every American, regardless of where he lives, will stop and examine his conscience about this and other related incidents. This Nation was founded by men of many nations and backgrounds. It was founded on the principle that all men are created equal, and that the rights of every man are diminished when the rights of one man are threatened.

Today we are committed to a worldwide struggle to promote and protect the rights of all who wish to be free. And when Americans are sent to Viet-Nam or West Berlin, we do not ask for whites only. It ought to be possible, therefore, for American students of any color to attend any public institution they select without having to be backed up by troops.

It ought to be possible for American consumers of any color to receive equal service in places of public accommodation, such as hotels and restaurants and theaters and retail stores, without being forced to resort to demonstrations in the street, and it ought to possible for American citizens of any color to register and to vote in a free election without interference or fear of reprisal.

It ought to be possible, in short, for every American to enjoy the privileges of being American without regard to his race or his color. In short, every American ought to have the right to be treated as he would wish to be treated, as one would wish his children to be treated. But this is not the case.

The Negro baby born in America today, regardless of the section of the state in which he is born, has about one-half as much chance of completing high school as a white baby born in the same place on the same day, one-third as much chance of completing college, one-third as much chance of becoming a professional man, twice as much chance of becoming unemployed, about one-seventh as much chance of earning $10,000 a year, a life expectancy which is seven years shorter, and the prospects of earning only half as much.

This is not a sectional issue. Difficulties over segregation and discrimination exist in every city, in every State of the Union, producing in many cities a rising tide of discontent that threatens the public safety. Nor is this a partisan issue. In a time of domestic crisis, men of good will and generosity should be able to unite regardless of party or politics. This is not even a legal or legislative issue alone. It is better to settle these matters in the courts than on the streets, and new laws are needed at every level. But law alone cannot make men see right.

We are confronted primarily with a moral issue. It is as old as the scriptures and is as clear as the American Constitution.

The heart of the question is whether all Americans are to be afforded equal rights and equal opportunities, whether we are going to treat our fellow Americans as we want to be treated. If an American, because his skin is dark, cannot eat lunch in a restaurant open to the public, if he cannot send his children to the best public school available, if he cannot vote for the public officials who represent him, if, in short, he cannot enjoy the full and free life which all of us want, then who among us would be content to have the color of his skin changed and stand in his place? Who among us would then be content with the counsels of patience and delay?

One hundred years of delay have passed since President Lincoln freed the slaves, yet their heirs, their grandsons, are not fully free. They are not yet freed from the bonds of injustice. They are not yet freed from social and economic oppression, and this Nation, for all its hopes and all its boasts, will not be fully free until all its citizens are free.

We preach freedom around the world, and we mean it, and we cherish our freedom here at home. But are we to say to the world, and much more importantly, to each other, that this is a land of the free, except for the Negroes; that we have no second-class citizens, except Negroes; that we have no class or cast[e] systems, no ghettoes, no master race, except with respect to Negroes?

Now the time has come for this Nation to fulfill its promise. The events in Birmingham and elsewhere have so increased the cries for equality that no city or State or legislative body can prudently choose to ignore them.

The fires of frustration and discord are burning in every city, North and South, where legal remedies are not at hand. Redress is sought in the streets, in demonstrations, parades and protests which create tensions and threaten violence and threaten lives.

We face, therefore, a moral crisis as a country and a people. It cannot be met by repressive police action. It cannot be left to increased demonstrations in the streets. It cannot be quieted by token moves or talk. It is a time to act in the Congress, in your State and local legislative body and, above all, in all of our daily lives.

It is not enough to pin the blame on others, to say this is a problem of one section of the country or another, or deplore the facts that we face. A great change is at hand, and our task, our obligation, is to make that revolution, that change, peaceful and constructive for all.

Those who do nothing are inviting shame as well as violence. Those who act boldly are recognizing right as well as reality.

Next week I shall ask the Congress of the United States to act, to make a commitment it has not fully made in this century to the proposition that race has no place in American life or law. The Federal judiciary has upheld that proposition in a series of forthright cases. The executive branch has adopted that proposition in the conduct of its affairs, including the employment of Federal personnel, the use of Federal facilities, and the sale of federally financed housing.

But there are other necessary measures which only the Congress can provide, and they must be provided at this session. The old code of equity law under which we live commands for every wrong a remedy, but in too many communities, in too many parts of the country, wrongs are inflicted on Negro citizens and there are no remedies at law. Unless the Congress acts, their only remedy is the street.

I am, therefore, asking the Congress to enact legislation giving all Americans the right to be served in facilities which are open to the public—hotels, restaurants, theaters, retail stores and similar establishments.

This seems to me to be an elementary right. Its denial is an arbitrary indignity that no American in 1963 should have to endure, but many do.

I have recently met with scores of business leaders urging them to take voluntary action to end this discrimination and I have been encouraged by their response, and in the last two weeks over 75 cities have seen progress made in desegregating these kinds of facilities. But many are unwilling to act alone, and for this reason, nationwide legislation is needed if we are to move this problem from the streets to the courts.

I am also asking Congress to authorize the Federal Government to participate more fully in lawsuits designed to end segregation in public education. We have succeeded in persuading many districts to desegregate voluntarily. Dozens have admitted Negroes without violence. Today a Negro is attending a State-supported institution in every one of our 50 States, but the pace is very slow.

Too many Negro children entering segregated grade schools at the time of the Supreme Court's decision nine years ago will enter segregated high schools this fall, having suffered a loss which can never be restored. The lack of an adequate education denies the Negro a chance to get a decent job.

The orderly implementation of the Supreme Court decision, therefore, cannot be left solely to those who may not have the economic resources to carry the legal action or who may be subject to harassment.

Other features will be also requested, including greater protection for the right to vote. But legislation, I repeat, cannot solve this problem alone. It must be solved in the homes of every American in every community across our country.

In this respect, I want to pay tribute to those citizens North and South who have been working in their communities to make life better for all. They are acting not out of a sense of legal duty but out of a sense of human decency.

Like our soldiers and sailors in all parts of the world they are meeting freedom's challenge on the firing line, and I salute them for their honor and their courage.

My fellow Americans, this is a problem which faces us all—in every city of the North as well as the South. Today there are Negroes unemployed, two or three times as many compared to whites, inadequate education, moving into the large cities, unable to find work, young people particularly out of work without hope, denied equal rights, denied the opportunity to eat at a restaurant or a lunch counter or go to a movie theater, denied the right to a decent education, denied almost today the right to attend a State university even though qualified. It seems to me that these are matters which concern us all, not merely Presidents or Congressmen or Governors, but every citizen of the United States.

This is one country. It has become one country because all of us and all the people who came here had an equal chance to develop their talents.

We cannot say to ten percent of the population that you can't have that right; that your children can't have the chance to develop whatever talents they have; that the only way that they are going to get their rights is to go into the street and demonstrate. I think we owe them and we ourselves a better country than that.

Therefore, I am asking for your help in making it easier for us to move ahead and to provide the kind of equality of treatment which we would want ourselves; to give a chance for every child to be educated to the limit of his talents.

As I have said before, not every child has an equal talent or equal ability or an equal motivation, but they should have the equal right to develop their talent and their ability and their motivation to make something of themselves.

We have a right to expect that the Negro community will be responsible, will uphold the law, but they have a right to expect that the law will be fair, that the Constitution will be color blind, as Justice Harlan said at the turn of the century.

This is what we are talking about and this is a matter which concerns this country and what it stands for, and in meeting it I ask the support of all of our citizens.

Thank you very much.

Commencement Address at American University
Washington, D.C., June 10, 1963

President Anderson, members of the faculty, board of trustees, distinguished guests, my old colleague, Senator Bob Byrd, who has earned his degree through many years of attending night law school, while I am earning mine in the next 30 minutes, distinguished guests, ladies and gentlemen:

It is with great pride that I participate in this ceremony of the American University, sponsored by the Methodist Church, founded by Bishop John Fletcher Hurst, and first opened by President Woodrow Wilson in 1914. This is a young and growing university, but it has already fulfilled Bishop Hurst's enlightened hope for the study of history and public affairs in a city devoted to the making of history and to the conduct of the public's business. By sponsoring this institution of higher learning for all who wish to learn, whatever their color or their creed, the Methodists of this area and the Nation deserve the Nation's thanks, and I commend all those who are today graduating.

Professor Woodrow Wilson once said that every man sent out from a university should be a man of his nation as well as a man of his time, and I am confident that the men and women who carry the honor of graduating from this institution will continue to give from their lives, from their talents, a high measure of public service and public support.

"There are few earthly things more beautiful than a University," wrote John Masefield, in his tribute to the English Universities—and his words are equally true today. He did not refer to towers or the campuses. He admired the splendid beauty of a University because it was, he said, "a place where those who hate ignorance may strive to know, where those who perceive truth may strive to make others see."

I have, therefore, chosen this time and place to discuss a topic on which ignorance too often abounds and the truth too rarely perceived—and that is the most important topic on earth: peace.

What kind of a peace do I mean, and what kind of a peace do we seek? Not a Pax Americana enforced on the world by American weapons of war. Not the peace of the grave or the security of the slave. I am talking about genuine peace—the kind of peace that makes life on earth worth living—the kind that enables men and nations to grow and to hope and build a better life for their children—not merely peace for Americans but peace for all men and women—not merely peace in our time but peace in all time.

I speak of peace because of the new face of war. Total war makes no sense in an age where great powers can maintain large and relatively invulnerable nuclear forces and refuse to surrender without resort to those forces. It makes no sense in an age where a single nuclear weapon contains almost ten times the explosive force delivered by all of the allied air forces in the Second World War. It makes no sense in an age when the deadly poisons produced by a nuclear exchange would be carried by wind and water and soil and seed to the far corners of the globe and to generations yet unborn.

Today, the expenditure of billions of dollars every year on weapons acquired for the purpose of making sure we never need them is essential to keeping the peace. But surely the acquisition of such idle stockpiles—which can only destroy and never create—is not the only, much less the most efficient, means of assuring peace.

I speak of peace, therefore, as the necessary rational end of rational men. I realize the pursuit of peace is not as dramatic as the pursuit of war—and frequently the words of the pursuers fall on deaf ears. But we have no more urgent task.

Some say that it is useless to speak of peace or world law or world disarmament—and that it will be useless until the leaders of the Soviet Union adopt a more enlightened attitude. I hope they do. I believe we can help them do it. But I also believe that we must re-examine our own attitude—as individuals and as a Nation—for our attitude is as essential as theirs. And every graduate of this school, every thoughtful citizen who despairs of war and wishes to bring peace, should begin by looking inward—by examining his own attitude towards the possibilities of peace, towards the Soviet Union, towards the course of the Cold War and towards freedom and peace here at home.

First: Examine our attitude towards peace itself. Too many of us think it is impossible. Too many think it is unreal. But that is a dangerous, defeatist belief. It leads to the conclusion that war is inevitable—that mankind is doomed—that we are gripped by forces we cannot control.

We need not accept that view. Our problems are manmade—therefore, they can be solved by man. And man can be as big as he wants. No problem of human destiny is beyond human beings. Man's reason and spirit have often solved the seemingly unsolvable—and we believe they can do it again.

I am not referring to the absolute, infinite concept of universal peace and good will of which some fantasies and fanatics dream. I do not deny the value of hopes and dreams but we merely invite discouragement and incredulity by making that our only and immediate goal.

Let us focus instead on a more practical, more attainable peace—based not on a sudden revolution in human nature but on a gradual evolution in human institutions—on a series of concrete actions and effective agreements which are in the interest of all concerned. There is no single, simple key to this peace—no grand or magic formula to be adopted by one or two powers. Genuine peace must be the product of many nations, the sum of many acts. It must be dynamic, not static, changing to meet the challenge of each new generation. For peace is a process—a way of solving problems.

With such a peace, there will still be quarrels and conflicting interests, as there are within families and nations. World peace, like community peace, does not require that each man love his neighbor—it requires only that they live together in mutual tolerance, submitting their disputes to a just and peaceful settlement. And history teaches us that enmities between nations, as between individuals, do not last forever. However fixed our likes and dislikes may seem, the tide of time and events will often bring surprising changes in the relations between nations and neighbors.

So let us persevere. Peace need not be impracticable—and war need not be inevitable. By defining our goal more clearly—by making it seem more manageable and less remote—we can help all people to see it, to draw hope from it, and to move irresistibly towards it.

And second: Let us re-examine our attitude towards the Soviet Union. It is discouraging to think that their leaders may actually believe what their propagandists write. It is discouraging to read a recent authoritative Soviet text on military strategy and find, on page after page, wholly baseless and incredible claims—such as the allegation that American imperialist circles are preparing to unleash different types of war, that there is a very real threat of a preventive war being unleashed by American imperialists against the Soviet Union, and that the political aims, and I quote "of the American imperialists are to enslave economically and politically the European and other capitalist countries . . . and to achieve world domination . . . by means of aggressive war." Unquote.

Truly, as it was written long ago: "The wicked flee when no man pursueth." Yet it is sad to read these Soviet statements—to realize the extent of the gulf between us. But it is also a warning—a warning to the American people not to fall into the same trap as the Soviets, not to see only a distorted and desperate view of the other side, not to see conflict as inevitable, accommodation as impossible and communication as nothing more than an exchange of threats.

No government or social system is so evil that its people must be considered as lacking in virtue. As Americans, we find communism profoundly repugnant as a negation of personal freedom and dignity. But we can still hail the Russian people for their many achievements—in science and space, in economic and industrial growth, in culture and acts of courage.

Among the many traits the peoples of our two countries have in common, none is stronger than our mutual abhorrence of war. Almost unique, among the major world powers, we have never been at war with each other. And no nation in the history of battle ever suffered more than the Soviet Union in the Second World War. At least 20 million lost their lives. Countless millions of homes and families were burned or sacked. A third of the nation's territory, including two thirds of its industrial base, was turned into a wasteland—a loss equivalent to the destruction of this country east of Chicago.

Today, should total war ever break out again—no matter how—our two countries will be the primary targets. It is an ironic but accurate fact that the two strongest powers are the two in the most danger of devastation. All we have built, all we have worked for, would be destroyed in the first 24 hours. And even in the Cold War, which brings burdens and dangers to so many countries, including this Nation's closest allies—our two countries bear the heaviest burdens. For we are both devoting massive sums of money to weapons that could be better devoted to combat ignorance, poverty and disease. We are both caught up in a vicious and dangerous cycle with suspicion on one side breeding suspicion on the other, and new weapons begetting counter-weapons.

In short, both the United States and its allies, and the Soviet Union and its allies, have a mutually deep interest in a just and genuine peace and in halting the arms race. Agreements to this end are in the interests of the Soviet Union as well as ours—and even the most hostile nations can be relied upon to accept and keep those treaty obligations, and only those treaty obligations, which are in their own interest.

So, let us not be blind to our differences—but let us also direct attention to our common interests and the means by which those differences can be resolved. And if we cannot end now our differences, at least we can help make the world safe for diversity. For, in the final analysis, our most basic common link is that we all inhabit this small planet. We all breathe the same air. We all cherish our children's futures. And we are all mortal.

Third: Let us re-examine our attitude towards the Cold War, remembering we are not engaged in a debate, seeking to pile up debating points. We are not here distributing blame or pointing the finger of judgment. We must deal with the world as it is, and not as it might have been had the history of the last eighteen years been different.

We must, therefore, persevere in the search for peace in the hope that constructive changes within the Communist block might bring within reach solutions which now seem beyond us. We must conduct our affairs in such a way that it becomes in the Communists' interest to agree on a genuine peace. And above all, while defending our own vital interests, nuclear powers must avert those confrontations which bring an adversary to a choice of either a humiliating retreat or a nuclear war. To adopt that kind of course in the nuclear age would be evidence only of the bankruptcy of our policy—or of a collective death-wish for the world.

American University Address   185

To secure these ends, America's weapons are nonprovocative, carefully controlled, designed to deter and capable of selective use. Our military forces are committed to peace and disciplined in self-restraint. Our diplomats are instructed to avoid unnecessary irritants and purely rhetorical hostility.

For we can seek a relaxation of tensions without relaxing our guard. And, for our part, we do not need to use threats to prove we are resolute. We do not need to jam foreign broadcasts out of fear our faith will be eroded. We are unwilling to impose our system on any unwilling people—but we are willing and able to engage in peaceful competition with any people on earth.

Meanwhile, we seek to strengthen the United Nations, to help solve its financial problems, to make it a more effective instrument for peace, to develop it into a genuine world security system—a system capable of resolving disputes on the basis of law, of insuring the security of the large and the small, and of creating conditions under which arms can finally be abolished.

At the same time we seek to keep peace inside the non-communist world, where many nations, all of them our friends, are divided over issues which weaken western unity, which invite communist intervention or which threaten to erupt into war. Our efforts in West New Guinea, in the Congo, in the Middle East and the Indian subcontinent, have been persistent and patient despite criticism from both sides. We have also tried to set an example for others—by seeking to adjust small but significant differences with our own closest neighbors in Mexico and Canada.

Speaking of other nations, I wish to make one point clear. We are bound to many nations by alliances. These alliances exist because our concern and theirs substantially overlap. Our commitment to defend Western Europe and West Berlin, for example, stands undiminished because of the identity of our vital interests. The United States will make no deal with the Soviet Union at the expense of other nations and other peoples, not merely because they are our partners, but also because their interests and ours converge.

Our interests converge, however, not only in defending the frontiers of freedom, but in pursuing the paths of peace. It is our hope—and the purpose of Allied policy—to convince the Soviet Union that she, too, should let each nation choose its own future, so long as that choice does not interfere with the choices of others. The communist drive to impose their political and economic system on others is the primary cause of world tension today. For there can be no doubt that, if all nations could refrain from interfering in the self-determination of others, the peace would be much more assured.

This will require a new effort to achieve world law—a new context for world discussions. It will require increased understanding between the Soviets and ourselves. And increased understanding will require increased contact and communication. One step in this direction is the proposed arrangement for a direct line between Moscow and Washington, to avoid on each side the dangerous delays, misunderstandings, and misreadings of other's actions which might occur at a time of crisis.

We have also been talking in Geneva about our first-step measures of arm controls, designed to limit the intensity of the arms race and reduce the risks of accidental war. Our primary long-range interest in Geneva, however, is general and complete disarmament—designed to take place by stages, permitting parallel political developments to build the new institutions of peace which would take the place of arms. The pursuit of disarmament has been an effort of this Government since the 1920s. It has been urgently sought by the past three administrations. And however dim the prospects are today, we intend to continue this effort—to continue it in order that all countries, including our own, can better grasp what the problems and the possibilities of disarmament are.

The only major area of these negotiations where the end is in sight—yet where a fresh start is badly needed—is in a treaty to outlaw nuclear tests. The conclusion of such a treaty—so near and yet so far—would check the spiraling arms race in one of its most dangerous areas. It would place the nuclear powers in a position to deal more effectively with one of the greatest hazards which man faces in 1963, the further spread of nuclear arms. It would increase our security—it would decrease the prospects of war. Surely this goal is sufficiently important to require our steady pursuit, yielding neither to the temptation to give up the whole effort nor the temptation to give up our insistence on vital and responsible safeguards.

I am taking this opportunity, therefore, to announce two important decisions in this regard.

First: Chairman Khrushchev, Prime Minister Macmillan and I have agreed that high-level discussions will shortly begin in Moscow looking towards early agreement on a comprehensive test ban treaty. Our hopes must be tempered with the caution of history—but with our hopes go the hopes of all mankind.

Second: To make clear our good faith and solemn convictions on the matter, I now declare that the United States does not propose to conduct nuclear tests in the atmosphere so long as other states do not do so. We will not be the first to resume. Such a declaration is no substitute for a formal binding treaty—but I hope it will help us achieve one. Nor would such a treaty be a substitute for disarmament—but I hope it will help us achieve it.

Finally, my fellow Americans, let us examine our attitude towards peace and freedom here at home. The quality and spirit of our own society must justify and support our efforts abroad. We must show it in the dedication of our own lives—as many of you who are graduating today will have an opportunity to do—by serving without pay in the Peace Corps abroad or in the proposed National Service Corps here at home.

But wherever we are, we must all, in our daily lives, live up to the age-old faith that peace and freedom walk together. In too many of our cities today, the peace is not secure because freedom is incomplete.

It is the responsibility of the Executive Branch at all levels of government—local, state and national—to provide and protect that freedom for all of our citizens by all means within our authority. It is the responsibility of the Legislative Branch at all levels, wherever the authority is not now adequate, to make it adequate. And it is the responsibility of all citizens in all sections of this country to respect the rights of others and respect the law of the land.

All this is not unrelated to world peace. "When a man's way please[s] the Lord," the Scriptures tell us, "he maketh even his enemies to be at peace with him." And is not peace, in the last analysis, basically a matter of human rights—the right to live out our lives without fear of devastation—the right to breathe air as nature provided it—the right of future generations to a healthy existence?

While we proceed to safeguard our national interests, let us also safeguard human interests. And the elimination of war and arms is clearly in the interest of both. No treaty, however much it may be to the advantage of all, however tightly it may be worded, can provide absolute security against the risks of deception and evasion. But it can—if it is sufficiently effective in its enforcement and it is sufficiently in the interests of its signers—offer far more security and far fewer risks than an unabated, uncontrolled, unpredictable arms race.

The United States, as the world knows, will never start a war. We do not want a war. We do not now expect a war. This generation of Americans has already had enough—more than enough—of war and hate and oppression. We shall be prepared if others wish it. We shall be alert to try to stop it. But we shall also do our part to build a world of peace where the weak are safe and the strong are just. We are not helpless before that task or hopeless of its success. Confident and unafraid, we must labor on—not towards a strategy of annihilation but towards a strategy of peace.

Radio and Television Address to the American People on the Nuclear Test Ban Treaty
Washington, D.C., July 26, 1963

Good evening, my fellow citizens: I speak to you tonight in a spirit of hope. Eighteen years ago the advent of nuclear weapons changed the course of the world as well as the war. Since that time, all mankind has been struggling to escape from the darkening prospect of mass destruction on earth. In an age when both sides have come to possess enough nuclear power to destroy the human race several times over, the world of communism and the world of free choice have been caught up in a vicious circle of conflicting ideology and interest. Each increase of tension has produced an increase of arms; each increase of arms has produced an increase of tension.

In these years, the United States and the Soviet Union have frequently communicated suspicion and warnings to each other, but very rarely hope. Our representatives have met at the summit and at the brink; they have met in Washington and in Moscow; in Geneva and at the United Nations. But too often these meetings have produced only darkness, discord, or disillusion.

Yesterday a shaft of light cut into the darkness. Negotiations were concluded in Moscow on a treaty to ban all nuclear tests in the atmosphere, in outer space, and under water. For the first time, an agreement has been reached on bringing the forces of nuclear destruction under international control—a goal first sought in 1946 when Bernard Baruch presented a comprehensive control plan to the United Nations.

That plan, and many subsequent disarmament plans, large and small, have all been blocked by those opposed to international inspection. A ban on nuclear tests, however, requires on-the-spot inspection only for underground tests. This Nation now possesses a variety of techniques to detect the nuclear tests of other nations which are conducted in the air or under water, for such tests produce unmistakable signs which our modern instruments can pick up.

The treaty initialed yesterday, therefore, is a limited treaty which permits continued underground testing and prohibits only those tests that we ourselves can police. It requires no control posts, no on-site inspection, no international body.

We should also understand that it has other limits as well. Any nation which signs the treaty will have an opportunity to withdraw if it finds that extraordinary events related to the subject matter of the treaty have jeopardized its supreme interests; and no nation's right of self-defense will in any way be impaired. Nor does this treaty mean an end to the threat of nuclear war. It will not reduce nuclear stockpiles; it will not halt the production of nuclear weapons; it will not restrict their use in time of war.

Nevertheless, this limited treaty will radically reduce the nuclear testing which would otherwise be conducted on both sides; it will prohibit the United States, the United Kingdom, the Soviet Union, and all others who sign it, from engaging in atmospheric tests which have so alarmed mankind; and it offers to all the world a welcome sign of hope.

For this is not a unilateral moratorium, but a specific and solemn legal obligation. While it will not prevent this Nation from testing underground, or from being ready to conduct atmospheric tests if the acts of others so require, it gives us a concrete opportunity to extend its coverage to other nations and later to other forms of nuclear tests.

This treaty is in part the product of Western patience and vigilance. We have made clear—most recently in Berlin and Cuba—our deep resolve to protect our security and our freedom against any form of aggression. We have also made clear our steadfast determination to limit the arms race. In three administrations, our soldiers and diplomats have worked together to this end, always supported by Great Britain. Prime Minister Macmillan joined with President Eisenhower in proposing a limited test ban in 1959, and again with me in 1961 and 1962.

But the achievement of this goal is not a victory for one side—it is a victory for mankind. It reflects no concessions either to or by the Soviet Union. It reflects simply our common recognition of the dangers in further testing.

This treaty is not the millennium. It will not resolve all conflicts, or cause the Communists to forego their ambitions, or eliminate the dangers of war. It will not reduce our need for arms or allies or programs of assistance to others. But it is an important first step—a step towards peace—a step towards reason—a step away from war.

Here is what this step can mean to you and to your children and your neighbors:

First, this treaty can be a step towards reduced world tension and broader areas of agreement. The Moscow talks have reached no agreement on any other subject, nor is this treaty conditioned on any other matter. Under-Secretary Harriman made it clear that any non-aggression arrangements across the division in Europe would require full consultation with our allies and full attention to their interests. He also made clear our strong preference for a more comprehensive treaty banning all tests everywhere, and our ultimate hope for general and complete disarmament. The Soviet Government however, is still unwilling to accept the inspection such goals require.

No one can predict with certainty, therefore, what further agreements, if any, can be built on the foundations of this one. They could include controls on preparations for surprise attack, or on numbers and type of armaments. There could be further limitations on the spread of nuclear weapons. The important point is that efforts to seek new agreements will go forward.

But the difficulty of predicting the next step is no reason to be reluctant about this step. Nuclear test ban negotiations have long been a symbol of East-West disagreement. If this treaty can also be a symbol—if it can symbolize the end of one era and the beginning of another—if both sides can by this treaty gain confidence and experience in peaceful collaboration—then this short and simple treaty may well become an historic mark in man's age-old pursuit of peace.

Western policies have long been designed to persuade the Soviet Union to renounce aggression, direct or indirect, so that their people and all people may live and let live in peace. The unlimited testing of new weapons of war cannot lead towards that end—but this treaty, if it can be followed by further progress, can clearly move in that direction.

I do not say that a world without aggression or threats of war would be an easy world. It will bring new problems, new challenges from the Communists, new dangers of relaxing our vigilance or of mistaking their intent.

But those dangers pale in comparison to those of the spiraling arms race and a collision course toward war. Since the beginning of history, war has been mankind's constant companion. It has been the rule, not the exception. Even a nation so young and as peace-loving as our own has fought through eight wars. And three times in the last two years and a half I have been required to report to you as President that this nation and the Soviet Union stood on the verge of direct military confrontation—in Laos, in Berlin and in Cuba.

A war today or tomorrow, if it led to nuclear war, would not be like any war in history. A full-scale nuclear exchange, lasting less than 60 minutes, with the weapons now in existence, could wipe out more than 300 million Americans, Europeans and Russians, as well as untold millions elsewhere. And the survivors, as Chairman Khrushchev warned the Communist Chinese, "the survivors would envy the dead," For they would inherit a world so devastated by explosion and poison and fire that today we cannot even conceive of its horrors. So let us try to turn the world away from war. Let us make the most of this opportunity, and every opportunity, to reduce tension, to slow down the perilous nuclear arms race, and to check the world's slide toward final annihilation.

Second, this treaty can be a step towards freeing the world from the fears and dangers of radioactive fallout. Our own atmospheric tests last year were conducted under conditions which restricted such fallout to an absolute minimum. But over the years the number and the yield of weapons tested have rapidly increased and so have the radioactive hazards from such testing. Continued unrestricted testing by the nuclear powers, joined in time by other nations which may be less adept in limiting pollution, will increasingly contaminate the air that all of us must breathe.

Even then, the number of children and grandchildren with cancer in their bones, with leukemia in their blood, or with poison in their lungs might seem statistically small to some, in comparison with natural health hazards. But this is not a natural health hazard—and it is not a statistical issue. The loss of even one human life, or the malformation of even one baby—who may be born long after all of us have gone—should be of concern to us all. Our children and grandchildren are not merely statistics towards which we can be indifferent.

Nor does this affect the nuclear powers alone. These tests befoul the air of all men and all nations, the committed and the uncommitted alike, without their knowledge and without their consent. That is why the continuation of atmospheric testing causes so many countries to regard all nuclear powers as equally evil; and we can hope that its prevention will enable those countries to see the world more clearly, while enabling all the world to breathe more easily.

Third, this treaty can be a step towards preventing the spread of nuclear weapons to nations not now possessing them. During the next several years, in addition to the four current nuclear powers, a small but significant number of nations will have the intellectual, physical, and financial resources to produce both nuclear weapons and the means of delivering them. In time it is estimated, many other nations will have either this capacity or other ways of obtaining nuclear warheads, even as missiles can be commercially purchased today.

I ask you to stop and think for a moment what it would mean to have nuclear weapons in so many hands, in the hands of countries large and small, stable and unstable, responsible and irresponsible, scattered throughout the world. There would be no rest for anyone then, no stability, no real security, and no chance of effective disarmament. There would be only the increased chance of accidental war, and an increased necessity for the great powers to involve themselves in what otherwise would be local conflicts.

If only one thermonuclear bomb were to be dropped on any American, Russian, or any other city, whether it was launched by accident or design, by a madman or by an enemy, by a large nation or by a small, from any corner of the world, that one bomb could release more destructive power on the inhabitants of that one helpless city than all the bombs dropped in the Second World War.

Neither the United States nor the Soviet Union nor the United Kingdom nor France can look forward to that day with equanimity. We have a great obligation, all four nuclear powers have a great obligation, to use whatever time remains to prevent the spread of nuclear weapons, to persuade other countries not to test, transfer, acquire, possess, or produce such weapons.

This treaty can be the opening wedge in that campaign. It provides that none of the parties will assist other nations to test in the forbidden environments. It opens the door for further agreements on the control of nuclear weapons, and it is open for all nations to sign, for it is in the interest of all nations, and already we have heard from a number of countries who wish to join with us promptly.

Fourth and finally, this treaty can limit the nuclear arms race in ways which, on balance, will strengthen our Nation's security far more than the continuation of unrestricted testing. For in today's world, a nation's security does not always increase as its arms increase, when its adversary is doing the same, and unlimited competition in the testing and development of new types of destructive nuclear weapons will not make the world safer for either side. Under this limited treaty, on the other hand, the testing of other nations could never be sufficient to offset the ability of our strategic forces to deter or survive a nuclear attack and to penetrate and destroy an aggressor's homeland.

We have, and under this treaty we will continue to have, the nuclear strength that we need. It is true that the Soviets have tested nuclear weapons of a yield higher than that which we thought to be necessary, but the hundred megaton bomb of which they spoke two years ago does not and will not change the balance of strategic power. The United States has chosen, deliberately, to concentrate on more mobile and more efficient weapons, with lower but entirely sufficient yield, and our security is, therefore, not impaired by the treaty I am discussing.

It is also true, as Mr. Khrushchev would agree, that nations cannot afford in these matters to rely simply on the good faith of their adversaries. We have not, therefore, overlooked the risk of secret violations. There is at present a possibility that deep in outer space, that hundreds and thousands and millions of miles away from the earth illegal tests might go undetected. But we already have the capability to construct a system of observation that would make such tests almost impossible to conceal, and we can decide at any time whether such a system is needed in the light of the limited risk to us and the limited reward to others of violations attempted at that range. For any tests which might be conducted so far out in space, which cannot be conducted more easily and efficiently and legally underground, would necessarily be of such a magnitude that they would be extremely difficult to conceal. We can also employ new devices to check on the testing of smaller weapons in the lower atmosphere. Any violation, moreover, involves, along with the risk of detection, the end of the treaty and the worldwide consequences for the violator.

Secret violations are possible and secret preparations for a sudden withdrawal are possible, and, thus, our own vigilance and strength must be maintained, as we remain ready to withdraw and to resume all forms of testing, if we must. But it would be a mistake to assume that this treaty will be quickly broken. The gains of illegal testing are obviously slight compared to their costs, and the hazard of discovery, and the nations which have initialed and will sign this treaty prefer it, in my judgment, to unrestricted testing as a matter of their own self-interest, for these nations, too, and all nations, have a stake in limiting the arms race, in holding the spread of nuclear weapons, and in breathing air that is not radioactive. While it may be theoretically possible to demonstrate the risks inherent in any treaty, and such risks in this treaty are small, the far greater risks to our security are the risks of unrestricted testing, the risk of a nuclear arms race, the risks of new nuclear powers, nuclear pollution, and nuclear war.

This limited test ban, in our most careful judgment, is safer by far for the United States than an unlimited nuclear arms race. For all these reasons, I am hopeful that this Nation will promptly approve the limited test ban treaty. There will, of course, be debate in the country and in the Senate. The Constitution wisely requires the advice and consent of the Senate to all treaties, and that consultation has already begun. All this is as it should be. A document which may mark an historic and constructive opportunity for the world deserves an historic and constructive debate.

It is my hope that all of you will take part in that debate, for this treaty is for all of us. It is particularly for our children and our grandchildren, and they have no lobby here in Washington. This debate will involve military, scientific, and political experts, but it must be not left to them alone. The right and the responsibility are yours.

If we are to open new doorways to peace, if we are to seize this rare opportunity for progress, if we are to be as bold and farsighted in our control of weapons as we have been in their invention, then let us now show all the world on this side of the wall and the other that a strong America also stands for peace.

There is no cause for complacency. We have learned in times past that the spirit of one moment or place can be gone in the next. We have been disappointed more than once, and we have no illusions now that there are shortcuts on the road to peace. At many points around the globe the Communists are continuing their efforts to exploit weakness and poverty. Their concentration of nuclear and conventional arms must still be deterred.

The familiar contest between choice and coercion, the familiar places of danger and conflict, are all still there, in Cuba, in Southeast Asia, in Berlin, and all around the globe, still requiring all the strength and the vigilance that we can muster. Nothing could more greatly damage our cause than if we and our allies were to believe that peace has already been achieved, and that our strength and unity were no longer required.

But now, for the first time in many years, the path of peace may be open. No one can be certain what the future will bring. No one can say whether the time has come for an easing of the struggle. But history and our own conscience will judge us harsher if we do not now make every effort to test our hopes by action, and this is the place to begin. According to the ancient Chinese proverb, "A journey of a thousand miles must begin with a single step."

My fellow Americans, let us take that first step. Let us, if we can, step back from the shadows of war and seek out the way of peace. And if that journey is a thousand miles, or even more, let history record that we, in this land, at this time, took the first step.

Thank you, and good night.

Selected Chronology of Major Presidential Speeches and Remarks

1961

Inaugural Address, January 20
Annual Message to the Congress on the State of the Union, January 30
Address at a White House Reception for Members of Congress and for the Diplomatic Corps of the Latin American Republics, March 13
Remarks at the Protocolary Session of the Council of the Organization of American States, April 14
Address Before the American Society of Newspaper Editors, April 20
Address Before the American Newspaper Publishers Association, New York City, April 27
Address in Chicago at a Dinner of the Democratic Party of Cook County, April 28
Address at the 39th Annual Convention of the National Association of Broadcasters, May 8
Address Before the Canadian Parliament in Ottawa, May 17
Special Message to Congress on Urgent National Needs, May 25
Radio and Television Report to the American People on Returning from Europe, June 6
Radio and Television Report to the American People on the Berlin Crisis, July 25
Address in New York City Before the General Assembly of the United Nations, September 25
Address at the University of North Carolina upon Receiving an Honorary Degree, October 12
Address in Seattle at the University of Washington's 100th Anniversary Program, November 16
Address in Los Angeles at a Dinner of the Democratic Party of California, November 18

196 *"In a Perilous Hour"*

Address in New York City to the National Association of Manufacturers, December 6
Address in Miami at the Opening of the AFL-CIO Convention, December 7
Address at a Dinner at the San Carlos Palace in Bogotá, December 17

1962

Annual Message to the Congress on the State of the Union, January 11
Radio and Television Address to the American People: "Nuclear Testing and Disarmament," March 2
Address on the First Anniversary of the Alliance for Progress, March 13
Address Before the U.S. Chamber of Commerce on its 50th Anniversary, April 30
Address in New Orleans at the Opening of the New Dockside Terminal, May 4
Address Before the Conference on Trade Policy, May 17
Remarks to Members of the White House Conference on National Economic Issues, May 21
Remarks to the White House Conference on Conservation, May 25
Remarks at West Point to the Graduating Class of the U.S. Military Academy, June 6
Commencement Address at Yale University, June 11
Remarks at a Meeting with the Headquarters Staff of the Peace Corps, June 14
Address at Independence Hall, Philadelphia, July 4
Radio and Television Report to the American People on the State of the National Economy, August 13
Address at Rice University in Houston on the Nation's Space Effort, September 12
Remarks to the Board of Governors of the World Bank and the International Monetary Fund, September 20
Remarks to the White House Conference on Narcotic and Drug Abuse, September 27
Remarks at the Wheeling Stadium, Wheeling, West Virginia, September 27
Radio and Television Report to the Nation on the Situation at the University of Mississippi, September 30
Remarks at a Democratic Rally in Detroit, October 6
Remarks at Fitzgerald Field House, University of Pittsburgh, October 12
Radio and Television Report to the American People on the Soviet Arms Buildup in Cuba, October 22
Radio and Television Remarks on the Dismantling of Soviet Missile Bases in Cuba, November 2
Address and Question and Answer Period at the Economic Club of New York, December 14

Selected Chronology 197

Remarks in Miami at the Presentation of the Flag of the Cuban
  Invasion Brigade, December 29

1963

Annual Message to the Congress on the State of the Union, January 14
Remarks and Question and Answer Period Before the American
  Society of Newspaper Editors, April 19
Address and Question and Answer Period at the 20th Anniversary Meeting of the
  Committee for Economic Development, May 9
Remarks in Nashville at the 90th Anniversary Convocation of Vanderbilt
  University, May 18
Remarks at Muscle Shoals, Alabama, at the 30th Anniversary Celebration of the
  Tennesee Valley Authority, May 18
Remarks at Colorado Springs to the Graduating Class of the U.S. Air Force
  Academy, June 5
Commencement Address at San Diego State College, June 6
Address in Honolulu Before the United States Conference of Mayors, June 9
Commencement Address at American University in Washington, June 10
Radio and Television Report to the American People on Civil Rights, June 11
Address in the Assembly Hall at the Paulskirche in Frankfurt, June 25
Remarks in the Rudolph Wilde Platz, Berlin, June 26
Address at the Free University of Berlin, June 26
Remarks in Naples at NATO Headquarters, July 2
Radio and Television Message to the American People After Returning From
  Europe, July 5
Radio and Television Statement Following Action to Postpone the Nationwide
  Railroad Strike, July 10
Radio and Television Address to the American People on the Nuclear Test Ban
  Treaty, July 26
Remarks at the National Conference of the Business Committee for Tax
  Reduction in 1963, September 10
Address Before the White House Conference on Exports, September 17
Radio and Television Address to the Nation on the Test Ban Treaty and Tax
  Reduction Bill, September 18
Address Before the 18th General Assembly of the United Nations, September 20
Address at the Pinchot Institute for Conservation Studies, Milford, Pennsylvania,
  September 24
Address at the University of North Dakota, September 25
Address at the University of Wyoming, September 25
Address in Salt Lake City at the Mormon Tabernacle, September 26

198 "In a Perilous Hour"

Address at the Meeting of the International Monetary Fund, September 30
Remarks at the Arkansas State Fairgrounds in Little Rock, October 3
Remarks at the Signing of the Nuclear Test Ban Treaty, October 7
Address at the University of Maine, October 19
Address at the Anniversary Convocation of the National Academy of Sciences, October 22
Remarks at Amherst College Upon Receiving an Honorary Degree, October 26
Remarks in Philadelphia at a Dinner Sponsored by the Democratic County Executive Committee, October 30
Remarks at the Dinner of the Protestant Council of the City of New York, November 8
Remarks in New York City at the AFL-CIO Convention, November 15
Address and Question and Answer Period in Tampa Before the Florida Chamber of Commerce, November 18
Address in Miami Before the Inter-American Press Association, November 18
Remarks at the Breakfast of the Fort Worth Chamber of Commerce, November 22
Remarks Prepared for Delivery at the Trade Mart in Dallas, November 22
Remarks Prepared for Delivery to the Texas Democratic State Committee in the Municipal Auditorium in Austin, November 22

Selected Bibliography

ARCHIVAL MATERIALS FROM JFK LIBRARY

Oral Histories

Donald F. Barnes Oral History. Interviewed by John Plank.
Senator William Benton Oral History. Interviewed by Newton Minow.
Frederick G. Dutton Oral History. Interviewed by Charles T. Morrissey.
George Kennan Oral History. Interviewed by Louis Fischer.
Joseph Kraft Oral History. Interviewed by John Stewart.
Edward P. Morgan Oral History. Interviewed by William McHugh.
Kenneth O'Donnell Oral History. Interview One, with Paige E. Mulhollan. (Reference copy from LBJ Library collection).
Adam Yarmolinsky Oral History. Interviewed by Daniel Ellsberg.

Speech Texts and Related Documents

Pre-Presidential Addresses and Papers

"Presidential Candidacy Statement of Senator John F. Kennedy (D.-Mass.), January 2, 1960." Theodore C. Sorensen Papers, Campaign Files, 1959-1960, Box 21.
"Remarks of Sen. John F. Kennedy (D.-Mass.) to Nevada State Legislature, February 1, 1960." Pre-Presidential Papers, 1960 Campaign, Box 1031.
"Remarks of Sen. John F. Kennedy (D.-Mass.) Nationality Building Fund Committee Dinner, Carson City, Nevada, February 4, 1960." Pre-Presidential Papers, 1960 Campaign, Box 1031
"Remarks of Senator John F. Kennedy (D.-Mass.), Reception, Jewish Community Center, Milwaukee, Wisconsin, Wednesday Evening, March 23,

1960." Pre-Presidential Papers, 1960 Campaign Files, Speeches, Statements and Sections, March 19, 1960–March 31, 1960, Box 1028.

"Remarks of Sen. John F. Kennedy, University of Wisconsin—Milwaukee, Milwaukee, Wisconsin, March 24, 1960." Pre-Presidential Papers, 1960 Campaign Files, Speeches, Statements, and Sections, Foreign Affairs, Box 1030.

"Remarks of Sen. John F. Kennedy, NAACP Rally, Sunday, June 10, 1960, Los Angeles, California." Pre-Presidential Papers, 1960 Campaign Files, Speeches Statements and Sections, Civil Rights-Job Discrimination File, NAACP Rally, Box 1028.

"Remarks of Sen. John F. Kennedy Accepting the Democratic Presidential Nomination, Democratic National Convention, July 15, 1960." JFK Pre-Presidential Papers, 1960 Campaign Files, General, The New Frontier Acceptance Speech, Box 1032.

"Speech to Greater Houston Ministerial Association, September 12, 1960, Delivery Copy." JFK Pre-Presidential Papers, Senate Files, Speech Files, Rice Hotel, Houston Texas, September 12, 1960, Box 911.

"Remarks of Senator John F. Kennedy, Question and Answer Period, Ministerial Association of Greater Houston, September 12, 1960." JFK Pre-Presidential Papers, Senate Files, Speech Files, Greater Houston Ministerial Association, Rice Hotel. Houston, Texas, September 12, 1960, Box 911.

"Remarks of Sen. John F. Kennedy (D.-Mass.) International Institute of Gary, Indiana," Undated. Pre-Presidential Papers, 1960 Campaign Files, Speeches, Statements and Sections, Foreign Affairs, Box 1030.

"Remarks of Senator John F. Kennedy (Dem.-Mass.) Luncheon in Honor of the African Diplomatic Corp," Undated. Pre-Presidential Papers, Press Secretary Subject File, Box 1044.

"The Presidency in 1960." Undated. Address by the Hon. John F. Kennedy, rpt. of *Congressional Record*. Pre-Presidential Papers, 1960 Campaign Files, Speeches, Statements, and Sections, The Presidency, Box 1031.

"'We Must Climb to the Mountaintop.'" Undated. Pre-Presidential Papers, 1960 Campaign Files, General Speeches, Statements, and Sections, Box 1032.

Presidential Addresses and Papers

"The Inaugural Address of President John F. Kennedy—As Actually Delivered, January 20, 1961." Theodore C. Sorensen Papers, JFK Speech Files, Inaugural Address File, Box 62.

"State of the Union Message of President John F. Kennedy, January 30, 1961." Presidential Office Files, Annual Message to Congress on the State of the Union (As Actually Delivered). Drafts and Press Releases, Box 34.

"State of the Union Message of President John F. Kennedy." Presidential Office Files, Speech Files, Annual Message to Congress on the State of the Union, Drafts and Press Releases, January 30, 1961, Box 34.

"Address of the President to the American Society of Newspaper Editors. Statler Hotel, Washington D.C., April 20, 1961." Presidential Office Files, Speech Files, Box 35.

"Text of the President's Report to the Nation Following his Visit to Paris, France, Vienna, Austria, and London, England from his Office in the White House Delivered at 7 P.M. (E.D.T.), June 6, 1961 (As Actually Delivered)." Presidential Office Files, Speech Files, Box 34.

"Text of the President's Report to the Nation on the Berlin Crisis, Delivered at 10:00 P.M. (E.D.T.), July 25, 1961, from his office in the White House (As Actually Delivered)." Presidential Office Files, Speech Files, Box 35.

"Radio-TV Address of the President to the Nation from the White House, October 22, 1962 (As Actually Delivered)." Presidential Office Files, Speech Files, Radio-Television Report to the American People on the Soviet Arms Buildup in Cuba, October 22, 1962, Box 41.

"Commencement Address at American University, June 10, 1963." Presidential Office Files, Speech Files, June 10, 1963-July 2, 1963, Box 45.

"Remarks of the President at American University, Washington D.C., June 10, 1963 (As Actually Delivered)." Theodore C. Sorensen Papers, JFK Speech Files, 1962-1963.

"Radio and Television Report to the American People on Civil Rights, June 11, 1963." Presidential Office Files, Speech Files, Box 45.

"State of the Union Message (As Actually Delivered) January 14, 1963." Presidential Office Files, Press Releases, Box 76.

"Remarks of the President Upon Signing the Golden Book in Rudolph Wilde Plaza, Berlin, Germany, June 26, 1963." Presidential Office Files, Speech Files, Box 45.

Memoranda and Printed Materials

"Addendum to Excerpts from Speeches by Senator John F. Kennedy August 31, 1960." Pre-Presidential Papers, 1960 Campaign Files, Speeches, Statements and Sections, Foreign Affairs, Addendum and Excerpts, Box 1030.

"Administration Accomplishments in Civil Rights." Theodore C. Sorensen Papers, Subject Files, 1961-1964, Civil Rights, Box 30.

Bloc Wire For Suggestions from Theodore C. Sorensen, December 23, 1960. Theodore C. Sorensen Papers, JFK Speech Files 1961-1963, Box 62, Inaugural Address, January 20, 1961, Memoranda, Speech Material Correspondence December 10, 1960-April 23, 1961, Box 62.

"Conducting Political Campaigns Using the Media." Untitled Report. Theodore C. Sorensen Papers, Campaign Files, 1959-1960, Box 22.

"From Attorney General." Printed Material, Undated. Theodore C. Sorensen Papers, JFK Speech Files, 1961-1963, Box 73.

Memorandum for Speech Writers, Copies to TV Writers, Draft No. 1, July 23

1960. Theodore C. Sorensen Papers, Campaign Files, 1959-1960, Speechwriters, Box 26.

Memorandum from Archibald Cox to Senator John F. Kennedy, August 31, 1960. Theodore C. Sorensen Papers, Campaign Files, 1959-1960, U-2 Incident, Box 26.

Memorandum from Edward R. Murrow to Dean Rusk, July 21, 1961. Theodore C. Sorensen Papers, Subject Files 1961-1964, Theodore C. Sorensen Memoranda, Box 36.

Memorandum from Richard E. Neustadt to Theodore Sorensen. Theodore C. Sorensen Papers, Subject Files, 1961-1964, Neustadt Memoranda, Box 36.

Memorandum from the President to McGeorge Bundy. Presidential Office Files, Staff Memoranda, McGeorge Bundy, May 1961-June 1961, Box 62.

Memorandum from from W. W. Rostow to Theodore Sorensen, July 20, 1961. Theodore C. Sorensen Papers, Subject Files 1961-1964, Theodore C. Sorensen Memoranda, Box 36.

Memorandum From Maxwell D. Taylor to Theodore Sorensen, July 25, 1961. Theodore C. Sorensen Papers, Subject Files, 1961-1964, Theodore C. Sorensen Memoranda, Box 36.

Memorandum From USIA to the President. Presidential Office Files, Civil Rights Mississippi, October 1, 1961—November 1, 1962, Box 98.

Memorandum on the Religious Issue from Theodore C. Sorensen, Campaign Materials, August 15, 1960. Theodore C. Sorensen Papers, Campaign Files 1959-1960, Box 25.

Undated, Untitled, Unsigned Memorandum, United States Senate Letterhead, Theodore C. Sorensen Papers, JFK Speech Files, Inaugural Address, Box 62.

Letters

Letter from Douglas Dillon to Theodore Sorensen, December 29, 1960. Theodore C. Sorensen Papers, JFK Speech Files, Inaugural Address, Box 62.

Letter from George Kennan to the President. Presidential Office Files, Special Correspondence, George Kennan October 22—October 28, 1963, Box 31.

Letter from Sen. John F. Kennedy to Professor Loren Reid, December 3, 1959. Theodore C. Sorensen Papers, Campaign Files, 1959-1960, Speeches, Box 25.

Letter from Allen Nevins to Theodore Sorensen, December 29, 1960. Theodore C. Sorensen Papers, JFK Speech Files, Inaugural Address, Box 62.

Letter from Adlai E. Stevenson to Theodore C. Sorensen c/o Hon. John F. Kennedy (re: Inaugural Address). Theodore C. Sorensen Papers, JFK Speech Files, Box 62.

PRIMARY SPEECH, PRESS CONFERENCE, ORAL HISTORY, AND MEMORANDA MATERIALS

Claflin, Edward B., ed. *JFK Wants to Know: Memos from the President's Office, 1961–1963*. New York: William Morrow, 1991.
Kennedy, John F. *A Compendium of Speeches Statements and Remarks Delivered During His Service in the Congress of the United States*. Washington, D.C.: U. S. Government Printing Office, 1964.
Kennedy, John F. *The Joint Appearances of Senator John F. Kennedy and Vice President Richard M. Nixon: Presidential Campaign of 1960*. Washington, D.C.: U. S. Government Printing Office, 1961.
Kennedy, John F. *Kennedy and the Press: The News Conferences*. Edited and Annotated by Harold W. Chase and Allen H. Lerman. New York: Thomas Y. Crowell, 1965.
Kennedy, John F. *Public Papers of the Presidents of the United States: John F. Kennedy, 1961*. Washington, D.C.: U.S. Government Printing Office, 1962.
Kennedy, John F. *Public Papers of the Presidents of the United States: John F. Kennedy, 1962*. Washington, D.C.: U. S. Government Printing Office, 1963.
Kennedy, John F. *Public Papers of the Presidents of the United States: John F. Kennedy, 1963*. Washington, D. C.: U. S. Government Printing Office, 1964.
Kennedy, John F. *The Speeches of John F. Kennedy: Presidential Campaign of 1960*. Washington, D.C.: U. S. Government Printing Office, 1961.
Strober, Gerald S. and Deborah H. Strober eds., *Let Us Begin Anew: An Oral History of the Kennedy Presidency*. New York: HarperCollins, 1993.

BOOKS BY JOHN F. KENNEDY

Kennedy, John F. *A Nation of Immigrants*. New York: Harper and Row, 1964.
Kennedy, John F. *As We Remember Joe*. Privately Printed, 1945.
Kennedy, John F. *Profiles in Courage*. New York: Harper and Row, 1956.
Kennedy, John F. *The Strategy of Peace*. Edited by Allen Nevins. New York: Harper and Row, 1960.
Kennedy, John F. *To Turn the Tide*. Edited by John W. Gardner. New York: Harper and Brothers, 1962.
Kennedy, John F. *Why England Slept*. New York: Wilfred Funk, 1940.

BOOKS

Allison, Graham T. *Essence of Decision: Explaining the Cuban Missile Crisis*. Boston: Little Brown, 1971.

Aristotle. *On Rhetoric: A Theory of Civic Discourse.* Translated by George A. Kennedy. Oxford and New York: Oxford University Press, 1991.

Ashmore, Harry S. *Hearts and Minds: The Anatomy of Racism from Roosevelt to Reagan.* New York: McGraw Hill, 1982.

Barber, James David. *Presidential Character: Predicting Performance in The White House.* 3rd ed. Englewood Cliffs, N.J: Prentice-Hall, 1985.

Barrett, Patricia. *Religious Liberty and the American Presidency: A Study in Church-State Relations.* New York: Herder and Herder, 1963.

Bernstein, Irving. *Promises Kept: John F. Kennedy's New Frontier.* New York and Oxford: Oxford University Press, 1991.

Berry, Joseph P. *John F. Kennedy and the Media: The First Television President.* Lanham, Md.: University Press of America, 1987.

Beschloss, Michael R. *The Crisis Years: Kennedy and Khrushchev, 1960-1963.* New York: Edward Burlingame/HarperCollins, 1991.

Blum, James M. *Years of Discord: American Politics and Society, 1961-1974.* New York: W.W. Norton, 1991.

Booth, Wayne C. Booth. *Modern Dogma and the Rhetoric of Assent.* Chicago and London: University of Chicago Press, 1974.

Bormann, Ernest G. *The Force of Fantasy: Restoring the American Dream.* Carbondale: Southern Illinois University Press, 1985.

Bostdorff, Denise M. *The Presidency and the Rhetoric of Foreign Policy Crisis.* Columbia: University of South Carolina Press, 1994.

Branch, Taylor. *Parting the Waters: America in the King Years, 1954-1963.* New York: Touchstone/Simon and Schuster, 1989.

Brauer, Carl M. *John F. Kennedy and the Second Reconstruction.* New York: Columbia University Press, 1977.

Brockriede, Wayne, and Robert L. Scott. *Moments in the Rhetoric of the Cold War.* New York: Random House, 1970.

Brown, Thomas. *JFK: History of an Image.* Bloomington: Indiana University Press, 1988.

Burke, Kenneth. *A Grammar of Motives.* Berkeley: University of California Press, 1969.

Burke, Kenneth. *A Rhetoric of Motives.* Berkeley: University of California Press, 1969.

Burner, David. *John F. Kennedy and the New Generation.* Boston: Little, Brown, 1988.

Burner, David, and Thomas R. West. *The Torch is Passed: The Kennedy Brothers and American Liberalism.* New York: Atheneum, 1984.

Burns, James MacGregor. *John Kennedy: A Political Profile.* New York: Harcourt, Brace, Jovanovich, 1960.

Campbell, Karlyn Kohrs, and Kathleen Hall Jamieson. *Deeds Done in Words: Presidential Rhetoric and the Genres of Governance.* Chicago and London: University of Chicago Press, 1990.

Chase, Harold W., and Allen H. Lerman, eds. *Kennedy and the Press: The News Conferences.* New York: Thomas Y. Crowell, 1965.
Donald, Aida DiPace, ed. *John F. Kennedy and the New Frontier.* New York: Hill and Wang, 1966.
Dulce, Berton, and Edward J. Richter. *Religion and the Presidency: A Recurring American Problem.* New York: MacMillan, 1962.
Dworkin, Ronald M. *A Matter of Principle.* Cambridge, Mass.: Harvard University Press, 1985.
Dworkin, Ronald M. *Taking Rights Seriously.* Cambridge, Mass.: Harvard University Press, 1977.
Edelman, Murray. *Constructing the Political Spectacle.* Chicago: University of Chicago Press, 1988.
Edelman, Murray. *Political Language: Words That Succeed and Policies That Fail.* New York: Academic Press, 1977.
Edelman, Murray. *The Symbolic Uses of Politics.* Urbana: University of Illinois Press, 1964.
Fairlie, Henry. *The Kennedy Promise: The Politics of Expectation.* Garden City, N.Y.: Doubleday, 1973.
Firestone, Bernard. *The Quest For Nuclear Stability: John F. Kennedy and the Soviet Union.* Westport, Conn.: Greenwood Press, 1982.
Fuchs, Lawrence H. *John F. Kennedy and American Catholicism.* New York: Meredith Press, 1967.
Galloway, John. *The Kennedys and Vietnam.* New York: Facts on File, 1971.
Gardner, Gerald. *The Mocking of the President: A History of Campaign Humor From Ike to Bush.* New York: Harper and Row, 1989.
Giglio, James N. *The Presidency of John F. Kennedy.* Lawrence: The University Press of Kansas, 1991.
Goodwin, Richard N. *Remembering America: A Voice from the 60s.* Boston and Toronto: Little, Brown, 1988.
Graber, Doris A. *Verbal Behavior and Politics.* Urbana: University of Illinois Press, 1976.
Halberstam, David. *The Best and the Brightest.* New York: Random House, 1972.
Halberstam, David. *The Powers That Be.* New York: Dell Publishing, 1979.
Hamby, Alonzo L. *Liberalism and Its Challenges: F.D.R. to Bush.* 2nd ed. New York: Oxford University Press, 1992.
Hart, Roderick P. *The Sound of Leadership: Presidential Communication in the Modern Age.* Chicago: University of Chicago Press, 1987.
Higgins, Trumbull. *The Perfect Failure: Kennedy, Eisenhower, and the CIA at the Bay of Pigs.* New York and London: W. W. Norton, 1987.
Jamieson, Kathleen Hall. *Dirty Politics: Deception, Distraction and Democracy.* New York: Oxford University Press, 1992.
Jamieson, Kathleen Hall. *Eloquence in an Electronic Age: The Transformation*

of Political Speechmaking. New York and Oxford: Oxford University Press, 1988.

Jamieson, Kathleen Hall. *Packaging the Presidency: A History and Criticism of Presidential Campaign Advertising*. New York and Oxford: Oxford University Press, 1984.

Kahin, George Mc T. *Intervention: How America Became Involved in Vietnam*. New York: Alfred A. Knopf, 1986.

Kennedy, Robert F. *In His Own Words: The Unpublished Recollections of the Kennedy Years*. Edited by Edward O. Guthman and James Shulman. New York: Bantam Books, 1988.

King, Martin Luther, Jr. *Why We Can't Wait*. New York: Signet Books, 1963/1964.

Kraus, Sidney. *The Great Debates: Background, Perspective, Effects*. Gloucester, Mass.: P. Smith, 1968.

Manchester, William. *The Glory and the Dream: A Narrative History of America, 1932-1972*. Boston: Little Brown, 1973/1974.

Matusow, Alan J. *The Unraveling of America: A History of Liberalism in the 1960s*. New York: Harper and Row, 1984.

Medhurst, Martin J., Robert L. Ivie, Philip Wander, and Robert L. Scott. *Cold War Rhetoric: Strategy, Metaphor, and Ideology*. Westport, Conn.: Greenwood Press, 1990.

Navasky, Victor S. *Kennedy Justice*. New York: Atheneum, 1971.

Newman, John M. *JFK and Vietnam*. New York: Warner Books, 1992.

O'Donnell, Kenneth P., David F. Powers, and Joe McCarthy. *"Johnny We Hardly Knew Ye": Memories of John Fitzgerald Kennedy*. Boston: Little Brown and Company, 1970.

Paper, Lewis J. *The Promise and the Performance: The Leadership of John F. Kennedy*. New York: Crown Publishers, 1975.

Parmet, Herbert S. *Jack: The Struggles of John F. Kennedy*. New York: Dial Press, 1980.

Parmet, Herbert S. *JFK: The Presidency of John F. Kennedy*. New York: Dial Press, 1983.

Perelman, Chaim, and L. Olbrechts-Tyteca. *The New Rhetoric: A Treatise on Argumentation*. Translated by John Wilkinson and Purcell Weaver. South Bend, Ind.: University of Notre Dame Press, 1971.

Reeves, Richard. *President Kennedy: Profile of Power*. New York: Simon and Schuster, 1993.

Reeves, Thomas C. *A Question of Character: A Life of John F. Kennedy*. New York: Free Press, 1991.

Rust, William J. *Kennedy in Vietnam*. New York: Charles Scribner's Sons, 1985.

Salinger, Pierre. *With Kennedy*. Garden City, NY: Doubleday and Company, 1966.

Schlesinger, Arthur M., Jr. *Robert Kennedy and His Times*. Boston: Houghton Mifflin, 1978.

Schlesinger, Arthur M., Jr. *A Thousand Days: John F. Kennedy in the White House*. Boston: Houghton Mifflin, 1965.

Sidey, Hugh. *John F. Kennedy, President*. New York: Atheneum, 1964.

Sitkoff, Harvard. *The Struggle for Black Equality, 1954-1980*. New York: Hill and Wang, 1981.

Sitkoff, Harvard. *The Struggle for Black Equality, 1954-1992*. Rev. Ed. New York: Hill and Wang, 1993.

Sobel, Lawrence A., ed. *Civil Rights: 1960-1966*. New York: Facts on File, 1967.

Sorensen, Theodore C. *Kennedy*. New York: Harper and Row, 1965.

Sorensen, Theodore C. *The Kennedy Legacy*. New York: Macmillan, 1969.

Sorensen, Theodore C. ed. *"Let the Word Go Forth": The Speeches, Statements, and Writings of John F. Kennedy, 1947-1963*. New York: Bantam/ Doubleday/Dell Publishing, 1988.

Stern, Mark. *Calculating Visions: Kennedy, Johnson, and Civil Rights*. New Brunswick, N.J.: Rutgers University Press, 1992.

Thompson, Robert Smith. *The Missiles of October: The Declassified Story of John F. Kennedy and the Cuban Missile Crisis*. New York: Simon and Schuster, 1992.

Tulis, Jeffrey. *The Rhetorical Presidency*. Princeton, N.J.: Princeton University Press, 1987.

Turner, James H., Richard Singleton, and David Musick. *Oppression: A Socio-History of Black-White Relations in America*. Chicago: Nelson-Hall, 1984.

Walton, Richard J. *Cold War and Counter-Revolution: The Foreign Policy of John F. Kennedy*. New York: Viking Press, 1972.

Watson, Mary Ann. *The Expanding Vista: American Television in the Kennedy Years*. New York: Oxford University Press, 1990.

Weisbrot, Robert. *Freedom Bound: A History of America's Civil Rights Movement*. New York: Plume/Penguin Books, 1991.

White, Theodore H. *The Making of the President, 1960*. New York: Atheneum, 1962.

Wilkins, Roy. *Standing Fast: The Autobiography of Roy Wilkins*. With Tom Matthews. New York: Viking, 1982.

Windt, Theodore Otto, Jr. *Presidents and Protesters: Political Rhetoric in the 1960s*. Tuscaloosa and London: The University of Alabama Press, 1990.

Zarefsky, David. *President Johnson's War on Poverty: Rhetoric and History*. Tuscaloosa: University of Alabama Press, 1986.

Zelizer, Barbie. *Covering the Body: The Kennedy Assassination, The Media, and the Shaping of Collective Memory*. Chicago: University of Chicago Press, 1992.

BOOK CHAPTERS

Beschloss, Michael R. "John Kennedy: A Political Profile Revisited." In *Essays in Honor of James MacGregor Burns*, edited by Michael R. Beschloss and Thomas E. Cronin, 66-74. Englewood Cliffs, NJ: Prentice Hall, 1989.

Campbell, Karlyn Kohrs, and Kathleen Hall Jamieson. "Form and Genre in Rhetorical Criticism: An Introduction." In *Form and Genre: Shaping Rhetorical Action*, edited by Karlyn Kohrs Campbell and Kathleen Hall Jamieson, 9-32. Falls Church, VA: Speech Communication Association, 1978.

Corbett, Edward P. J. "Analysis of the Style of John F. Kennedy's Inaugural Address." In *Essays in Presidential Rhetoric*, 3rd ed., edited by Theodore Windt and Beth Ingold, 61-70. Dubuque, Iowa: Kendall/Hunt Publishing, 1992.

Costigliola, Frank. "The Pursuit of Atlantic Community: Nuclear Arms, Dollars, and Berlin." In *Kennedy's Quest for Victory: American Foreign Policy, 1961-1963*, edited by Thomas G. Patterson, 24-56. New York and Oxford: Oxford University Press, 1989.

Golden, James L. "Perspectives on the Legacy of John F. Kennedy." In *Rhetorical Studies Honoring James L. Golden*, edited by Lawrence W. Hugenberg, 69-95. Dubuque, Iowa: Kendall/Hunt Publishing, 1986.

Henry, David. "Senator John F. Kennedy Encounters the Religious Question: 'I am Not the Catholic Candidate for President.'" In *Oratorical Encounters: Selected Studies and Sources of Twentieth-Century Political Accusations and Apologies*, edited by Halford Ross Ryan, 153-173. New York: Greenwood Press, 1988.

Patterson, Thomas G. "Introduction: John F. Kennedy's Quest for Victory and Global Crises." In *Kennedy's Quest for Victory: American Foreign Policy, 1961-1963*, edited by Thomas G. Patterson, 3-23. New York and Oxford: Oxford University Press, 1989.

Stelzner, Hermann G. "John F. Kennedy at Houston, Texas, September 12, 1960." In *Rhetoric and Communication: Studies in the University of Illinois Tradition*, edited by Jane Blankenship and Hermann G. Stelzner, 223-235. Urbana: University of Illinois Press, 1976.

Windt, Theodore. "The President and Speeches on International Crisis: Repeating the Rhetorical Past." In *Essays in Presidential Rhetoric*, 3rd ed., edited by Theodore Windt and Beth Ingold, 91-100. Dubuque, Iowa: Kendall/Hunt Publishing, 1992.

Windt, Theodore. "Presidential Rhetoric: Definition of a Discipline of Study." In *Essays in Presidential Rhetoric*, 3rd ed., edited by Theodore Windt and Beth Ingold, xvii-xlv. Dubuque, Iowa: Kendall/Hunt Publishing, 1992.

Windt, Theodore. "Presidential Rhetoric: An Update, 1992." In *Essays in Presidential Rhetoric*, 3rd ed., edited by Theodore Windt and Beth Ingold, xlvi-lix. Dubuque, Iowa: Kendall/Hunt Publishing, 1992.

Windt, Jr., Theodore Otto. "John Fitzgerald Kennedy: (1917-1963), Thirty-Fifth President of the United States." In *American Orators of the Twentieth Century: Critical Studies and Sources*, edited by Bernard K. Duffy and Halford R. Ryan, 245-253. New York: Greenwood Press, 1987.

Windt, Theodore. "Seeking Detente with the Superpowers: John F. Kennedy at American University." In *Essays in Presidential Rhetoric*, 2nd ed., edited by Theodore Windt and Beth Ingold, 135-148. Dubuque, Iowa: Kendall/Hunt Publishing Company, 1987.

Windt, Jr., Theodore Otto. "President John F. Kennedy's Inaugural Address, 1961." In *The Inaugural Addresses of Twentieth Century American Presidents*, edited by Halford Ryan, 181-193. Westport, Conn.: Praeger, 1993.

Windt, Jr., Theodore Otto. "The Public Presidency: A Psychological Inquiry into John F. Kennedy." *In Politics and Psychology: Contemporary Psychodynamic Perspectives*, edited by Joan Offerman-Zuckerberg, 83-98. New York and London: Plenum Press, 1991.

SCHOLARLY ARTICLES AND REVIEWS

Ball, Moya Ann. "A Case Study of the Kennedy Administration Decision Making Concerning the Diem Coup of November, 1963." *Western Journal of Speech Communication* 54 (1990): 557-574.

Barrett, Harold. "John F. Kennedy Before the Greater Houston Ministerial Association." *Central States Speech Journal* 15 (1964): 259-266.

Barrow, Lionel C., Jr. "Factors Related to Attention in the First Kennedy-Nixon Debate." *Journal of Broadcasting* 5 (1961): 229-238.

Beck, Kent M. "The Kennedy Image: Politics, Camelot, and Vietnam." *Wisconsin Magazine of History* 58 (1964): 45-55.

Berthold, Carol A. "Kenneth Burke's Cluster-Agon Method: Its Development and an Application." *Central States Speech Journal* 27 (1976): 302-309.

Berquist, Goodwin F. "The Kennedy-Humphrey Debate." *Communication Quarterly* 8 (1960): 2-3.

Bostdorff, Denise M., and Steven R. Goldzwig. "Idealism and Pragmatism in American Foreign Policy Rhetoric: The Case of John F. Kennedy and Vietnam." *Presidential Studies Quarterly* 24 (1994): 515-530.

Bostrom, Robert N. "'I Give You a Man'—Kennedy's Speech for Adlai Stevenson." *Speech Monographs* 35 (1968): 129-136.

Carlson, A. Cheree. "John Quincy Adams' 'Amistad Address': Eloquence in a Generic Hybrid." *Western Journal of Speech Communication* 49 (1985): 14-26.

Ceaser, James W., Glen E. Thurow, Jeffery Tulis, and Joseph M. Bessette. "The Rise of the Rhetorical Presidency." *Presidential Studies Quarterly* 11 (1981): 158-171.

Cherwitz, Richard A. and Kenneth S. Zagacki. "Consummatory Versus

Justificatory Crisis Rhetoric." *Western Journal of Speech Communication* 50 (1986): 307-324.
Conley, Thomas M. "Ancient Rhetoric and Modern Genre Criticism." *Communication Quarterly*, 27 (1979): 47-53.
Dean, Kevin W. "'We Seek Peace—But We Shall Not Surrender': JFK's Use of Juxtaposition for Rhetorical Success in the Berlin Crisis." *Presidential Studies Quarterly* 21 (1991): 531-544.
Depoe, Stephen P. "Space and the 1960 Presidential Campaign: Kennedy, Nixon, and Public Time." *Western Journal of Speech Communication* 55 (1991): 215-233.
Einhorn, Lois J. "The Ghosts Talk: Personal Interviews with Three Former Speechwriters." *Communication Quarterly* 36 (1988): 94-108.
Etzioni, Amitai. "The Kennedy Experiment." *Western Political Quarterly* 20/2 (1967): 361-380.
Fisher, Walter R. "Reaffirmation and Subversion of the American Dream." *Quarterly Journal of Speech* 59 (1973): 160-167.
Freeley, Austin J. "The Presidential Debates and the Speech Profession." *Quarterly Journal of Speech* 48 (1961): 60-64.
Gilbert, Robert. "John F. Kennedy and Civil Rights for Black Americans." *Presidential Studies Quarterly* 12 (1982): 386-399.
Godden, Richard, and Richard Maidment. "Anger, Language, and Politics: John F. Kennedy and The Steel Crisis." *Presidential Studies Quarterly* 10 (1980): 317-331.
Golden, James L. "John F. Kennedy and the 'Ghosts.'" *Quarterly Journal of Speech* 52 (1966): 348-357.
Goldman, Sheldon. "Characteristics of Eisenhower and Kennedy Appointees to the Lower Federal Courts." *The Western Political Quarterly* 18 (1965): 755-762.
Goldzwig, Steven R., and George N. Dionisopoulos. "John F. Kennedy's Civil Rights Discourse: From 'Principled Bystander' to Public Advocate." *Communication Monographs* 56 (1989): 179-198.
Griffin, Leland M. "When Dreams Collide: Rhetorical Trajectories in the Assassination of President Kennedy." *Quarterly Journal of Speech* 70 (1984): 111-131.
Gustainis, Justin. "John F. Kennedy and the Green Berets: The Rhetorical Use of the Hero Myth." *Communication Studies* 40 (1989): 41-53.
Hahn, Dan F. "Ask Not What a Youngster Can Do For You: Kennedy's Inaugural Address." *Presidential Studies Quarterly* 12 (1982): 610-614.
Harding, H. F. "John F. Kennedy: Campaigner." *Quarterly Journal of Speech* 46 (1960): 362-364.
Hartley, Anthony. "John Kennedy's Foreign Policy." *Foreign Policy* 4 (1971): 77-87.
Hershberg, James G. "Before the 'Missiles of October': Did Kennedy Plan a Military Strike Against Cuba?" *Diplomatic History* 14 (1990): 163-198.
Highlander, John P., and Lloyd I. Watkins. "A Closer Look at the Great Debates." *Western Speech* 26 (1962): 39-48.

Hutchison, Earl R. "Kennedy and the Press: The First Six Months." *Journalism Quarterly* 38 (1961): 453-459.

Jamieson, Kathleen Hall, and Karlyn Kohrs Campbell. "Rhetorical Hybrids: Fusions of Generic Elements." *Quarterly Journal of Speech* 68 (1982): 146-157.

Kane, Peter E. "Evaluating the Great Debates." *Western Speech* 30 (1966): 89-96.

Kaufer, David S. "The Ironist and Hypocrite as Presidential Symbols: A Nixon-Kennedy Analog." *Communication Quarterly* 27 (1979): 20-26.

Kenny, Edward B. "Another Look at Kennedy's Inaugural Address." *Today's Speech* 13 (1965): 17-19.

Kerr, Henry P. "John F. Kennedy." *Quarterly Journal of Speech* 46 (1960): 241-242.

McClerren, Beryl F. "Southern Baptists and the Religious Issue During the Presidential Campaign of 1928 and 1960." *Central States Speech Journal* 18 (1967): 104-112.

Medland, William J. "The Cuban Missile Crisis: Evolving Historical Perspectives." *History Teacher* 23 (1990): 433-447.

Murphy, John M. "Comic Strategies and the American Covenant." *Communication Studies* 40 (1989): 266-279.

Murphy, John M. "Domesticating Dissent: The Kennedys and the Freedom Rides." *Communication Monographs* 59 (1992): 61-78.

Nelson, Anna Kasten. "President Kennedy's National Security Policy." *Reviews in American History* 19 (1991): 1-14.

Neustadt, Richard E. "Kennedy in the Presidency: A Premature Appraisal." *Political Science Quarterly* 79 (1964): 321-334.

Osborne, Leonard L. "Rhetorical Patterns in President Kennedy's Major Speeches." *Presidential Studies Quarterly* 10 (1980): 332-335.

Ostman, Ronald E. "Relation of Questions and Answers in Kennedy's Press Conferences." *Journalism Quarterly* 58 (1981): 575-581.

Parmet, Herbert S. "The Kennedy Myth and American Politics." *The History Teacher* 24 (1990): 31-35.

Patterson, Thomas G. "Bearing the Burden: A Critical Look at JFK's Foreign Policy." *Virginia Quarterly Review* 54 (1978): 193-212.

Patterson, Thomas G., and William J. Brophy. "October Missiles and November Elections: The Cuban Missile Crisis and American Politics, 1962." *Journal of American History* 73 (1986): 87-119.

Pollard, James E. "The Kennedy Administration and the Press." *Journalism Quarterly* 41 (1964): 3-14.

Powell, James G. "Reactions to John F. Kennedy's Acting Skills During the 1960 Campaign." *Western Speech* 32 (1968): 59-68.

Pratt, James W. "An Analysis of Three Crisis Speeches." *Western Speech* 34 (1970): 194-203.

Riemer, Neal. "Kennedy's Grand Democratic Design." *Review of Politics* 27 (1965): 3-16.

Samovar, Larry A. "Ambiguity and Unequivocation in the Kennedy-Nixon Television Debates." *Quarterly Journal of Speech* 48 (1962): 277-279.

Samovar, Larry A. "Ambiguity and Unequivocation in the Kennedy-Nixon Television Debates: A Rhetorical Analysis." *Western Speech*, 29 (1965): 211-218.

Sharp, Jr., Harry. "Live From Washington: The Telecasting of President Kennedy's News Conferences." *Journal of Broadcasting* 13 (1968/1969): 23-32.

Spragens, William C. "Kennedy Era Speech Writing, Public Relations, and Public Opinion." *Presidential Studies Quarterly* 14 (1984): 78-86.

Stelzner, Hermann G. "Humphrey and Kennedy Court West Virginia, May 3, 1960." *Southern Speech Communication Journal* 37 (1971): 21-33.

Stewart, Charles S. "Catholic and Jewish Pulpit Reaction to the Kennedy Assassination." *Western Speech* 31 (1967): 131-139.

Stewart, Charles S. "The Pulpit in Time of Crisis 1865 and 1963." *Speech Monographs* 32 (1965): 427-434.

Thompson, Dennis L. "The Kennedy Court: Left and Right of Center." *Western Political Quarterly* 26 (1970): 263-279.

Vancil, David L. and Sue D. Pendell. "The Myth of Viewer-Listener Disagreement in the First Kennedy-Nixon Debate." *Central States Speech Journal* 38 (1987): 16-27.

Wagner, Gerhard A. "JFK and the Offshore Islands." *Communication Quarterly* 15 (1967): 27-29.

Wander, Philip. "The Rhetoric of American Foreign Policy." *Quarterly Journal of Speech* 70 (1984): 339-361.

Watson, Mary Ann. "How Kennedy Invented Political Television." *Television Quarterly* 25 (1991): 61-71.

Weiler, Michael. "The Rhetoric of Neo-Liberalism," *Quarterly Journal of Speech* 70 (1984): 362-378.

Williams, Robert J. and David A. Kershaw, "Kennedy and Congress: The Struggle for The New Frontier." *Political Studies* 27 (1979): 390-404.

Windt, Theodore Otto, Jr. "The President and Speeches on International Crisis: Repeating the Rhetorical Past." *Speaker and Gavel* 2 (1973): 6-14.

Wolfarth, Donald L. "John F. Kennedy in the Tradition of Inaugural Speeches." *Quarterly Journal of Speech* 47 (1961): 124-132.

NEWSPAPER ARTICLES

Albright, Robert C. "Kennedy Affirms Stand on Religion to Texas Pastors, Senator Pledges Separation of Church and State." *Washington Post*, September 13, 1960, A16.

Baker, Russell. "Nixon Endorses Kennedy Pledge." *New York Times*, September 14, 1960, A1, A26.
Braestrup, Peter. "Protestant Group Applauds Kennedy for Houston Speech." *New York Times*, September 14, 1960, A33.
Carroll, Wallace. "A Time of Change Facing Kennedy." *New York Times*, January 21, 1961, A9.
Childs, Marquis. "Kennedy's View of Church Issue." *Washington Post*, September 14, 1960, A20.
Davis, Lawrence E. "How Kennedy Is Being Received: The Texas and California Tours, Religious Issue Debated." *New York Times*, September 14, 1960, A1, A32.
Duscha, Julius. "Jackson Asks for Help in Tracing Source of Anti-Catholic Material." *Washington Post*, September 15, 1960, A2.
"Enough Said." *Washington Post*, September 14, 1960, A20.
Grutzner, Charles. "Poling Praises Kennedy's Stand on Religious Issue." *New York Times*, September 14, 1960, A34.
Krock, Arthur. "Inaugural Contrast: Kennedy Dramatizes the Change but the Basic Aspirations Remain." *New York Times*, January 22, 1961, 11E.
Lawrence, W. H. "Kennedy Assures Texas Ministers of Independence." *New York Times*, September 13, 1960, A1, A22.
Morris, John D. "Kennedy Pledges Firm Presidency." *New York Times*, January 15, 1960, A1.
"Protestant Groups' Statements." *New York Times*, September 8, 1960, 25.
Reston, James. "Dallas: Economic and Religious Coalition in Texas." Editorial. *New York Times*, September 14, 1960, A42.
Reston, James. "Washington: President Kennedy's Inaugural—Speech on Policy." Editorial. *New York Times*, January 22, 1961, E10.
Spivak, Alvin. "Kennedy Asks Faith Talk End." *Washington Post*, September 12, 1960, A2.
"What Presidents Think About." Editorial. *New York Times*, January 22, 1961, E10.

MAGAZINE ARTICLES

"A New Leader." *Time*, November 16, 1960, 3.
"A Size-Up of Kennedy: An Interview With His Biographer James MacGregor Burns." *U.S. News & World Report*, November 28, 1960, 72-76.
"As Kennedy Takes Over." Photo Caption. *U.S. News & World Report*, January 23, 1961, 37.
Boorstin, Daniel J. "Our Only American Ritual." *U.S. News & World Report*, January 30, 1989, 35.
"Campaign '60: 43 Days Before Election Day." *Newsweek*, September 26, 1960, 41-42.

Clark, Blair. "Book in the News: *The Strategy of Peace*." *Saturday Review*, May 28, 1960, 19.
"Dawn of the New Congress." *Newsweek*, January 9, 1961, 19-20.
"Democrats: Candidate in Orbit." *Time*, November 7, 1960, 26.
"Democrats: The Reverberating Issue." *Time*, July 18, 1960, 10.
Donaghy, Patrick. "The New Frontier." Interview. *Catholic World*, November, 1960, 80-86.
"If the 'New Idea' Men Have Their Way." *Newsweek*, January 23, 1961, 38-40.
Lindley, Ernest K. "The Switch." *Newsweek*, January 23, 1961, 32.
"Man of the New Frontier." *Time*, November 16, 1960, 5-7.
"Mr. Kennedy Today: The Change in Him." *Newsweek*, January 23, 1961, 16-20.
"Operation Rooney." *Time*, January 6, 1961, 15.
"Political Notes: Fight Talk." *Time*, January 25, 1960, 20.
"Politics: The Catholic Issue." *Time*, April 18, 1960, 16.
"Ring in the New." *Time*, January 6, 1961, 13-16.
"Rooney's Rule." *Newsweek*, January 9, 1961, 24-25.
Smith, Beverly. "Campaigning with Kennedy." *Saturday Evening Post*, October 29, 1960, 80.
"Sticky Issue." *Newsweek*, October 31, 1960, 21.
"Test of Religion." *Time*, September 26, 1960, 21.
"The Campaign: The Power of Negative Thinking." *Time*, September 19, 1960, 21.
"The Issue That Just Won't Die." *Newsweek*, September 12, 1960, 61.
"The Kennedy Story." *U.S. News & World Report*, November 21, 1960, 46-55.
"The Kennedy Strategy: Clues to the Next 4 Years." *U.S. News & World Report*, December 19, 1960, 38-41.
"The Tilt Toward Kennedy." *Newsweek*, April 18, 1960, 14.
"Washington: Handle with Care." *Newsweek*, January 2, 1961, 13-14.
"What Kennedy Will Do as President." *U.S. News & World Report*, November 21, 1960, 40-45.
White, William S. "High Style in White House Politics." *Harpers*, January 1961, 99-102.

INDEX

Adenauer, Konrad, 42
Alsop, Stewart, 109
American Society of Newspaper Editors, 15, 28, 97
American Society of Newspaper Editors Address, 97-101
American University, 15, 72, 80, 119-121, 124-131, 143-44
American University Address, 119-125

Barber, James David, 4
Barnes, Donald F., 8
Barnett, Ross, 64-65, 72
Batista, Fulgencio, 95-96
Bay of Pigs, 15, 61, 95-98, 100-1, 109, 117, 131, 133 n.20, 134 n.34, 143-44
Bell, Nelson, 25
Berlin, 72, 102
Berlin crisis, 15, 92, 101-108, 110-117, 126, 131, 135 n.38, 143, 145
Berlin Crisis Message, 101-9
Bernstein, Irving, 143
Beschloss, Michael, 92, 103, 107, 130
Bissell, Richard, 96
Bowles, Chester, 39

Branch, Taylor, 140
Brauer, Carl M., 74
Bundy, McGeorge, 96, 107
Burner, David, 47, 144
Burns, James MacGregor, 55

Castro, Fidel, 95-99, 101, 109-111, 114-15
China, 39, 91, 118, 130
Christian Herald, 25
Christianity Today, 25
Citizens for Religious Freedom, 25, 33
Civil Rights Act of 1964, 145
Civil Rights Commission, 60, 63, 69, 75, 89
Clark, Blair, 14
Commonweal, 28
Congo, 38-39, 131
CORE (Congress of Racial Equality), 61, 66
Connor, Eugene "Bull," 70
Costigliola, Frank, 143
Cox, Archibald, 36
Cuba, 38-39, 45, 92, 95-102, 109-116, 131
Cuban missile crisis, 15, 109-111, 113-117, 120, 143, 145

Cuban Missile Crisis Address, 111-117
Cushing, Richard Cardinal, 43

de Gaulle, Charles, 42, 102
Defense, Department of, 125
Dillon, Douglas, 39-40
Dobrynin, Anatoly F., 111
Du Bois, W.E.B., 58
Dulles, Allen, 96-97
Dutton, Frederick G., 8, 39
Dworkin, Ronald, 79

East Germany, 99, 102-3, 105, 108
Eastland, James O., 59, 60
Edelman, Murray, 6, 47
Eisenhower, Dwight D., 4, 14, 38, 42-43, 57, 96; administration, 35, 118; and 1956 election 8; and 1960 election, 24; and civil rights, 55; and Cuba, 96-97; and foreign policy, 5, 95, 142
Emancipation Proclamation, 67, 76, 86 n.45
Equal Employment Opportunity Commission, 60-61, 83.20
Evers, Medgar, 68

Farmer, James, 61
Federal Security Agency, 9
Feldman, Myer, 39
Fleming, Robert, 111
Formosa Strait, 14
Frankfurter, Felix, 9
Freedom Rides, 61-63, 68, 140
Frost, Robert, 43

Gagarin, Yuri, 83-84 n.23, 109
Galbraith, John Kenneth, 39, 41
Germany, 39, 102-3, 107, 126
Giglio, James N., 96, 132, 143
Goldberg, Arthur, 39
Goodwin, Richard N., 9-10, 39

Graber, Doris A., 6
Great Britain, 119, 127
Great Society, 143, 145
Greater Houston Ministerial Association, 21, 27-28, 30, 33, 139
Greater Houston Ministerial Association Address, 28-33
Gromyko, Andrei, 111, 113

Halberstam, David, 27, 33
Hamby, Alonzo L., 8, 74, 95
Harriman, Averell, 126
Harvard University Law School, 9
Hitler, Adolph, 95
Holmes, Oliver Wendell, 40
House Judiciary Committee, 59
House Rules Committee, 59, 141
Houston Chronicle, 27
Humphrey, Hubert, 23, 119
Hungary, 44, 97-99

ICC (Interstate Commerce Commission), 84 n.29
Inaugural Address, 42-48
Izvestia, 111, 125

Jamieson, Kathleen Hall, 34, 40
Jefferson, Thomas, 30, 43, 118
Justice, Department of, 57, 59, 61, 81

Kefauver, Estes, 8
Kennan, George, 143
Kennedy, John F., and Bay of Pigs, 96-97, 101, 109; and Berlin crisis, 102-3, 108-9, 143; and civil rights, 15, 55-67, 69-77, 80-81, 140-142; and Cuban missile crisis, 96, 110-11, 116-17, 143; and domestic issues, 15, 38, 41, 46; and foreign affairs, 16, 38, 42, 44-45, 56,

59, 61, 80, 91-95, 101-2, 118, 142-44; and military affairs, 92-95, 97, 99, 103, 107, 117; and on-site inspection treaty, 118-19; and religious question, 21-23, 25-29, 33, 49-50, 139; and rhetorical presidency, 145; and speech-writing process, 9-13, 19, 35, 40-42, 104, 120; and test ban treaty, 119, 124, 126, 130, 144; and Vienna Conference, 103; as historical figure, 3, 42; as public speaker, 8, 12-14, 27-28, 32, 34, 43, 120, 140; early political career, 7, 8; evaluation of, 47-48, 57-58, 63-64, 68, 71, 74-82, 92, 98-103, 108-9, 114-116, 118, 120, 124-25, 127-132, 139-144, 146; presidential candidacy of, 14, 21, 23, 26-27, 33, 35-37, 55-59, 91, 94, 96, 102; presidential rhetoric of, 14-16, 58, 62, 64, 68, 72, 81, 93, 95, 102, 108, 116, 120, 131-132, 139, 141-145; public image of, 34-37, 55, 59, 81, 116-117, 140; public writings of, 35; study of, 3-5, 15-16, 139-40, 142-43
Kennedy, Robert, 60-62, 66-67, 72, 75, 81
Khrushchev, Nikita, 25, 47, 61, 80, 91-92, 125; and Berlin, 103-4, 108, 143; and Cuba, 109-10, 114, 118, 143; and national liberation speech, 42, 91; and test ban treaty, 118, 127
King, Martin Luther, Jr., 62, 64, 68, 70, 75, 78
Kraft, Joseph, 39-40

Lansdale, Edward, 109
Laos, 39, 102, 109, 131

Lebanon, 14
Library of Congress, 7
Life, 35
Lincoln, Abraham, 41, 67, 73, 76, 78, 82, 140
Lippmann, Walter, 41
Little Rock crisis, 57, 61, 66
Lloyd, David, 39
Look, 21, 28
Louisville Courier-Journal, 74

Mao Tse-tung, 42
March on Washington, 68-69, 77, 78, 140
Masefield, John, 121
Matusow, Allen J., 48
McNamara, Robert, 91
Meredith, James, 55, 64-66, 141
Meza, Herbert, 28
McKinley, William, 16 n.1
Milwaukee Journal, 74
Mississippi National Guard, 64
Morgan, Edward, 8
Murrow, Edward R., 105, 108

NAACP (National Association for the Advancement of Colored People), 57
National Association of Evangelicals, 25
National Council of Churches, 30
NATO (North Atlantic Treaty Organization), 38
Nebraska Law School, University of, 9
Neibuhr, Reinhold, 26
Neustadt, Richard E., 115
Nevins, Allen, 39-40
New York Times, 25, 33, 47
New York Times Magazine, 9
Nixon, Richard M., 43, 57, 96; and 1960 election, 24, 27, 34, 37; and Cuba, 96

Index

O'Donnell, Kenneth, 27
OAS (Organization of American States), 38, 114
Ockenga, Harold J., 25
Operation Mongoose, 109, 136 n.48
Operation Zapata, 97

Paper, Lewis J., 101, 142, 144
Parmet, Herbert S., 74, 96, 102
Patterson, John, 62
Patterson, Thomas G., 142
Pauling, Linus, 115
Peace Corp, 38
Peale, Norman Vincent, 25-26, 33
Pike, James, 26
Poling, Daniel, 25, 32-33
Powers, Dave, 28
Pritchett, Laurie, 66
Profiles in Courage, 13
Protestants and Other Americans United, 24

Reeves, Thomas C., 47
Reid, Loren, 14
Reston, James, 47
Rhetorical presidency, 5, 17 n.6, 34, 145
Rio Pact of 1947, 112
Roosevelt, Franklin D., 111, 125, 140, 143
Roosevelt, Theodore, 16 n1, 42, 116
Rostow, W.W., 105
Rusk, Dean, 39, 105, 108, 111
Russell, Bertrand, 115

Salinger, Pierre, 13, 111
San Diego State University, 71
Saturday Review, 14
Schlesinger, Arthur, Jr., 9-10, 40, 75, 98, 130
SCLC (Southern Christian Leadership Conference), 66

Seigenthaler, John, 62
Senate Foreign Relations Committee, 94, 130
Simulatics Corporation, 27, 33
Sitkoff, Harvard, 141
Smith, Howard, 59-60, 141
Sorensen, Theodore, 9-10, 12, 14, 22, 23, 56, 74, 91-93, 130; and American University Address, 120, 124; and Berlin crisis, 104-5; and Cuban missile crisis, 115; and Inaugural Address, 39-42, 45; as presidential speech writer, 8-13, 28, 35, 72, 97
Soviet Union, 5, 15, 67, 93, 101, 107, 111-114, 118, 122, 127, 144
Sputnik, 51 n.31
St. Louis Post-Dispatch, 74
State, Department of, 8, 10, 99, 102, 105, 107, 111
State of the Union Message, 40, 59, 64, 91-92, 117-118
Stevenson, Adlai, 8, 39, 44, 45
Strategy of Peace, The, 5, 14, 94-96, 119
SNCC (Student Nonviolent Coordinating Committee), 66

Taiwan, 39
Taylor, Maxwell D., 104
Telos, 121-122, 144
Test Ban Treaty Address, 126-29, 144
Thompson, Robert S., 91
Time, 33, 38
Treasury, Department of, 40
Truman, Harry S., 10, 43, 95, 143
Turkey, 113
Turner, Dr. Robert, 10

U Thant, 115

United Nations (UN), 44, 114, 125; Charter, 112; General Assembly, 111, 130; Security Council, 114
USIA (United States Information Agency), 105
University of Mississippi, 15, 55, 64-65, 140-141

Vanderbilt University, 70-71
Vietnam, 72, 99, 100, 131, 144-146
Voter Education Project, 63

Wallace, George, 68-72, 74, 78, 88 n.60

Walton, William, 43
Warren, Earl, 43
Weisbrot, Robert, 61, 70
West, Thomas R., 47, 144
White Citizens Council of New Orleans, 85 n.34
Why England Slept, 13
Windt, Theodore, 6
Wofford, Harris, 56, 58-59
Wright, Bishop John, 50 n.19

Yarmolinsky, Adam, 135 n.42

Zarefsky, David, 6

Great American Orators

Anna Howard Shaw: Suffrage Orator and Social Reformer
Wil A. Linkugel and Martha Solomon

William Jennings Bryan: Orator of Small-Town America
Donald K. Springen

Robert M. La Follette, Sr.: The Voice of Conscience
Carl R. Burgchardt

Ronald Reagan: The Great Communicator
Kurt Ritter and David Henry

Clarence Darrow: The Creation of an American Myth
Richard J. Jensen

"Do Everything" Reform: The Oratory of Frances E. Willard
Richard W. Leeman

Abraham Lincoln the Orator: Penetrating the Lincoln Legend
Lois J. Einhorn

Mark Twain: Protagonist for the Popular Culture
Marlene Boyd Vallin

Delightful Conviction: Jonathan Edwards and the Rhetoric of Conversion
Stephen R. Yarbrough and John C. Adams

Harry S. Truman: Presidential Rhetoric
Halford R. Ryan

Dwight D. Eisenhower: Strategic Communicator
Martin J. Medhurst

Ralph Waldo Emerson: Preacher and Lecturer
Lloyd Rohler

ABOUT THE AUTHORS

Steven R. Goldzwig is an Associate Professor of Communication Studies at Marquette University. His research areas include rhetorical criticism, political and legal communication, ethics, and public address. His research has been published in *The Quarterly Journal of Speech, Communication Monographs, Western Journal of Communication, Communication Studies, The Southern Communication Journal,* and *The Journal of Communication and Religion.*

George N. Dionisopoulos is an Associate Professor in the School of Communication at San Diego State University. His research areas include rhetorical criticism, political communication, and public address. His research has been published in *The Quarterly Journal of Speech, Communication Monographs, Western Journal of Communication, Communication Studies,* and *The Southern Communication Journal.*